TITANIC

Women and Children First

'Isn't that an iceberg on the horizon, Captain?'
'Yes, Madam.'
'What if we get in a collision with it?'
'The iceberg, Madam, will move right along as though nothing had happened.'

Carl Sandburg, *The People, Yes*, 1936

TITANIC

Women and Children First

JUDITH B. GELLER

Foreword by John P. Eaton

*Poignant accounts of those caught up in
the world's worst maritime disaster*

W·W·NORTON

NEW YORK · LONDON

To Samantha, my inspiration; Lois, my cheerleader;
and to Arnie, my own personal patron of the arts without whom
this book would never have come to life.

Original edition published in Great Britain
by Patrick Stephens Limited, an imprint of Haynes Publishing,
Sparkford, Nr. Yeovil, Somerset BA22 7JJ

Designed & Typeset by
G&M, Raunds, Northamptonshire
Printed in France

The pre-decimalisation sterling/dollar equivalents given in the book
are based on the 1912 exchange rate of £1 to $5.

Old coins: a shilling (s) is equivalent to one-twentieth of £1, or 12p;
a penny (d) is equivalent of one-hundredth of £1

ISBN 0-393-04666-4

W.W. Norton & Company, Inc.,
500 Fifth Avenue, New York, NY 10110

http://www.wwnorton.com

W.W. Norton & Company, Ltd,
10 Coptic Street, London WC1A 1PU

1 2 3 4 5 6 7 8 9 0

CONTENTS

The Daily Mirror

THE MORNING JOURNAL WITH THE SECOND LARGEST NET SALE.

No. 2,650.   MONDAY, APRIL 22, 1912   One Halfpenny.

MRS. ELEANOR SMITH, WIFE OF THE TITANIC'S COMMANDER, WHOSE HUSBAND
WENT DOWN WITH HIS VESSEL SHOUTING "BE BRITISH."

Mrs Eleanor Smith, widow of the Titanic's *Captain Smith, with her daughter, sends a message of understanding: 'To my poor fellow sufferers, My heart overflows with grief for you all, and is laden with sorrow that you are weighed down with this terrible burden that has been thrust upon us. May God be with you and comfort us all. Yours in deep sympathy. (Signed) Eleanor Smith. April 18 1912.'* (The British Library)

FOREWORD

by John P. Eaton

ON 26 FEBRUARY 1852, while on a trooping voyage to supply reinforcements to the army fighting the Eighth Kaffir War in South Africa, the British transport *Birkenhead* struck an uncharted rock off Danger Point, in False Bay, about 50 miles east of Cape Town.

Aboard at the time were 638 persons, including troops, 21 women, 34 infants and children – troops' dependents – and ship's crew.

The ship's captain immediately ordered the boats to be lowered. But the vessel struck the rock a second time, causing an inrush of water that hastened the sinking. Under the command of Colonel Alexander Seton of the 74th Highlanders, the senior officer aboard, the troops paraded on deck, holding fast in their formation as the ship continued to settle. Col Seton quickly assigned squads to help man the pumps and see to the loading of women and children into the boats. Eventually three boats crowded with people were successfully launched. The remaining troops lined up on deck in military formation. With the boats away they stood fast under the commands of their officers, and with their officers at their head they went down in perfect order.

Though near to land, the survivors were under attack by sharks. Only 68 came ashore on floating wreckage. Clinging overnight to the wreck's masts and spars, another 40 men were rescued by a schooner that arrived the next day. The drowned numbered 445, while the 193 saved included all the women and children.

By command of Queen Victoria, a mural tablet and brass plates bearing the names of the lost were placed in the colonnade of London's Chelsea Hospital 'to record heroic constancy and unbroken discipline'.

On 11 April 1912 the American-owned, British-operated White Star liner *Titanic*, on her maiden voyage, departed from the Irish port of Queenstown. Aboard, as can be best determined, were 2,228 passengers and crew. Of these 1,697 were men (12 years of age and older) and 528 were women and children.

Four days later, the world's largest man-made moving object, the world's newest and most luxurious ocean liner, sank ignominiously to the sea's bottom two hours and 40 minutes after striking the submerged spur of a medium-sized iceberg.

It is estimated that of the 1,523 lost on that cruel night, 158 were women and children, fewer than 10 per cent of all aboard. As the contemporary poet Richard Beamish wrote in the 1912 book *The Sinking of the Titanic*:

'"And most who drowned were men." 'Tis good to hear
Those strong fair words. They tell of manhood tried,
Of those who saw the weak ones safe, then died ...'

Just as aboard *Birkenhead*, 60 years earlier, what of the women? What of their bravery? What of the women survivors, many with infants and children, who had just seen their husbands and sons drown, who had to carry on in spite of the loss of loved ones? There are few stories of women's acts of bravery aboard *Titanic*: of Ida Straus's refusal to part from her dear husband; of Edith Corse Evans's surrender of her lifeboat seat to an older woman; of Molly Brown's determination to row. There may be more, but they pass unrecorded. Women and Children Last.

What of the women who remained aboard the doomed liner, lost in the confusion, seeking help, perhaps shepherding large broods of offspring, searching for an open deck, then vainly for a lifeboat seat? What of the women and – perhaps, were the truth known – children who performed uncounted acts of courage and sacrifice on that cold, dark April morning in mid-ocean?

Most if not all of the world's monuments to heroism aboard the sinking *Titanic* are dedicated to men: the several musicians' memorials; Harvard's Widener Library; memorials to journalist William Thomas Stead, to Captain Edward John Smith, to Thomas Andrews.

Even the monument whose origins might have inspired a remembrance of *Titanic*'s heroic women, the Women's Titanic Memorial, at Washington, DC, is dedicated to 'The Brave Men Who Perished in the Wreck of the *Titanic*. They Gave Their Lives That Women and Children Might be Saved. Erected by the Women of America.' But among the world's *Titanic* memorials this one is unique. It was designed and made by a woman, Gertrude Vanderbilt Whitney, and constructed with contributions from more than 25,000 American women all over the world.

Thus, by participating in their monument's creation, American women celebrated the heroism of their men and also recognised the role of the women in the disaster. Along the Potomac River's quiet bank is their recognition: a large statue of a draped figure, arms spread, poised as for flight upward to the heavens. Here are commemorated unknown and unknowable acts of gallantry and constancy.

Women and Children Last? Perhaps. But only because of the failure of History's timely recognition.

In the pages of this book the reader can finally encounter the acts of valour and courage, the quiet lives, the fruitful lives, the unknown lives of *Titanic*'s women and children who gave up so much, who sacrificed all, but who gained immortality.

April 1998

PREFACE

IN 1993 I STOOD on the deck of the French research vessel *Nadir*, positioned in the North Atlantic over the exact coordinates of the *Titanic* tragedy. Staring deep into the shadowy sea, I thought of the command Captain Smith uttered with steely determination as he gave the order to rouse the passengers and begin the evacuation: 'Women and children first.' Smith knew that his magnificent, 'unsinkable' *Titanic* was equipped with every luxury man could imagine – except sufficient lifeboats. At best only half of the passengers could be saved from a death of agonising proportions. I imagined the suffering of that woeful night. Suspended still in the air around me were the heart-wrenching goodbyes, the hasty prayers, the final screams for help as exposure to the frigid sea took the breath of life from one passenger after another.

Two and a half miles below the deck of the *Nadir*, on the seabed, a three-man titanium submersible named *Nautile* was searching for the only tangible remains of those lost souls, their watches, hair-brushes, reading glasses and tea-cups. These remnants of another era would now be exposed to the light of day for the first time since Captain Smith gave his painful order.

Later that day, when *Nautile* returned to the surface and the day's retrieved artefacts were being catalogued and stabilised by the conservators, I noticed a layer of mud remaining in the submarine's collection box. Its velvety surface invited touching. With the permission of the conservation team, I reached into the alluvial mixture ground smooth by the incessant rushing of undersea currents. It felt cool and mysterious, a substance reminiscent of a fine facial scrub, and I couldn't resist smearing a dab on my face as if I were cruising on a nautical spa instead of a high-tech research vessel.

Shaping my hands in the form of a scoop, I was instructed to dig further in the dove-grey mixture, letting it slip and slide through my fingers to search for any small piece of *Titanic* fragments possibly missed when the more dazzling pieces had been lifted to safety. As the last bit of sea-bed oozed away, two tiny treasures revealed themselves – a woman's faceted jet bead in my left hand and a child's marble in my right.

These minuscule remembrances, remarkably plucked from the vast ocean floor, spoke to me as none of the larger artefacts had. How astonishing that in 83 years they had not been carried away with the drifting sands. Questions rushed through my mind. What woman and child had last touched these small bits of a life? Had they survived? Was the woman married? Did the child kiss a father goodbye, never to see him again? Had the owners been mother and son? Mother and daughter? What had become of them? So many questions generated by objects no larger than a green garden pea.

I have now researched the lives of *Titanic*'s women and children for five years in period newspapers, books and documents – consulting with historians, speaking with relatives of survivors and, wherever possible, to the survivors themselves. I know that except for those celebrity few, most were just ordinary people. Were it not for their journey on the *Titanic* they would have lived lives of quiet anonymity, known only to their relatives, neighbours and friends. The fortunate who were rescued survived the sinking, yes, but none totally survived the trauma. The more resilient gave thanks for their survival by helping others. For those who could not recover, it was a big enough job just to get through each day. Through all their lives runs the common thread of a reluctance to discuss 15 April 1912, but the darker consequences of alcoholism, multiple marriages and depression also occur.

We will never know the exact identity of the lady whose necklace contained the jet bead or of the child who last played with the marble. But

no matter – they have become symbolic to me of every woman and child who made that maiden voyage into the world's collective consciousness and who suffered dreadfully for having done so.

Titanic: Women and Children First is my way of honouring them all by honouring those who appear in these pages.

Judith B. Geller
Atlanta, Georgia

All artefacts are shown courtesy of RMS Titanic Inc.

PART ONE

FIRST CLASS
ALL THE WAY

THE ROYAL MAIL steamship *Titanic* was built in that period of history called the Edwardian Era in Britain, La Belle Époque in France and the Gilded Age in America. Western society, driven by the Industrial Revolution, was distinctly divided into the haves and the have-nots, with the rising middle class in between. *Titanic* was the steam and steel embodiment of that time.

At the tip of this split-level society were the super-rich. On their decks the air was fresher, the cabins more spacious, the furnishings more elegant, the meals more sumptuous. And here, at sea as on land, these privileged few had no necessity to mingle with their 'below stairs' neighbours.

First Class carried more than 300 passengers as it headed into history. It was a gathering of kindred spirits whose coming together gave this maiden voyage the aura of a stellar social event. Frequent transatlantic passengers comfortable the world over, *Titanic*'s First Class voyagers were the early-20th-century predecessors of our modern-day 'jet set'. Not only did many among them have businesses and residences on two continents, but they also appeared in Paris and London for the season,

took the cure in Baden-Baden, scaled the Pyramids, trekked the jungles of Indonesia, and shot big game in Africa.

The First Class passenger list presented a smattering of the wealthy from Britain and the Continent, among them a Countess, and a Lord and Lady. But the majority striding those polished teak decks were American industrial barons and their families, financial giants with names like Astor, Guggenheim, Straus and Widener. Collectively they were worth over half a billion dollars. Their steel mills and railroads, coal mines and banks fuelled this unprecedented era of economic growth and with it the introduction of automobiles, wireless, cinema, skyscrapers, suspension bridges and aeroplanes. This same technology had built *Titanic*, advertised as the 'Largest and Finest Steamer in the World'.

And that it was. It had the elite ambience and white-gloved service of a world-class hotel. Its public rooms were adorned with glass domes, gold-burnished carvings, rare woods, silken fabrics and works of art to rival the finest stately homes of Europe. There were curved staircases for grand entrances, cosy reading corners, a barber shop, masculine dens for wheeling and dealing, a Turkish bath and swimming bath, one of the first aboard a ship, and a squash court and gymnasium for keeping trim and fit. The latter amenity was a must considering the richness of the meals provided in the Grand Dining Saloon and the À la Carte Restaurant. Just think of all that filet mignon, lobster, double cream, pastry, wine and port, rounded off by an after-dinner cigar, which fortunately were in abundance on the ship.

Among the 350 First Class staterooms were parlour suites, two with private promenades costing ten times more than an ordinary worker made in a year, and private cabins that far exceeded the average hotel room in size and appointments. The rooms were fitted out in a dizzying display of interior design: Adam, Regency, Empire, Italian Renaissance, Louis XV and XVI. In *Titanic*'s First Class, portholes became full windows and beds were commodious bedsteads, rather than the usual narrow fixed berths. Hot and cold running water, private baths with lavatory, individually controlled electric heaters, and stewards and stewardesses at the ready added to the comfort.

Chroniclers of the era have been known to take to task the women lounging in these rooms for the artificiality of their lives, but an emerging number of them were involved in much more than the luxury that surrounded them. True, it was still a man's world in 1912, but for the First Class woman passenger wealth

had begun to have its liberating effect. Among their ranks were authors, art patrons, explorers, philanthropists and business women. Well-educated and often multi-lingual, their travels had exposed them to books by James and London, plays by Shaw and Ibsen; the theories of Freud, Lenin's politics, the dances of Duncan; the music of Puccini and Berlin; and the paintings of Monet and fellow shipboard traveller Millet. Their sons and daughters were being reared (albeit with nannies) with the same advantages and groomed to become the leaders of the next generation.

Commenting on the loss of life soon after the disaster, Henry Moy Fot, special agent for the Chinese Merchants Association of America, said:

'It is the duty of sailors when a Chinese vessel goes down to save men first, children next and women last. This is on the theory that men are most valuable to the state, that adoptive parents can be found for the children, and that women without husbands are destitute.'

However, when the American-owned *Titanic* flying the British flag met with disaster, that rule of the sea was reversed. The surviving women and children of First Class, while not left destitute like so many of their counterparts in the other classes, were no longer isolated by their wealth. That night the egalitarian Atlantic took their husbands, fathers, sons and brothers as well.

Bess Daniels Allison (25)
Helen Loraine Allison (2)
Hudson Trevor Allison (11
  months)
Nurse Alice Cleaver

'Mrs Allison refused to leave her husband's side: nurse saved the child.'
Newspaper account, 1912

NOT ENTIRELY TRUE, but that was Nurse Cleaver's tale and she was sticking to it. You see, Nurse Cleaver had a past. In fact, she was not a nurse at all; she was Alice Mary Cleaver from Tottenham, North London, England, convicted child murderer, running from her past.

Obviously Bess knew nothing of this when the nurse she had brought to England quit and she hired Alice to care for Loraine and Trevor. Today it would seem natural to assume that since Bess was travelling with a cook, a maid and a chauffeur there would be adults aplenty to look after the children. But the style in which the Allisons lived dictated that a child nurse should also be a part of the entourage.

Forms of transport provided the beginning, middle and, tragically, the end of the relationship between Bess and her husband Hudson. They had met while travelling on a train between Montreal and Winnipeg in 1907 and were married in December of that same year in Bess's home town of Milwaukee, Wisconsin. By 1912 Hudson Allison was a very successful young man and Bess must have felt lucky indeed and proud of his achievements. His was not a wealth bestowed by birth, but achieved the old-fashioned way – he earned it. His meteoric climb had taken him from farmer's son to top insurance salesman, finally at the age of 30 becoming a stockbroker and partner in the Montreal firm of Johnson, McConnell & Allison.

Accustomed to gracious living, the wealthy young couple had several residences, the primary one in Montreal, another in Chesterville, Ontario, Hudson's birthplace, where they raised thoroughbred horses, and a third in West Hampstead, London.

In December 1911 the Allison family went to England on a combined business and pleasure trip. Bess made the rounds of the antique and fabric establishments buying for their various residences, while Hud, as he was known to his friends, had meetings with the British Canadian Lumber Association on whose board he served. Being very devout Methodists, they also managed to have Trevor baptised at the church in Epworth, Lincolnshire, where John Wesley, Methodism's founder, had been born and preached.

It had been a wonderful trip until their nursemaid left, and it was then that Alice Mary

Trevor and Loraine Allison. (Courtesy of Ella Deeks)

Cleaver entered the Allisons' lives, hired for her supposed skills rather than her good looks; she was a most unattractive lady, so unattractive, in fact, that after the disaster some newspapers enhanced her photos to make her more appealing.

Miss Cleaver had been convicted of killing her new-born son by throwing him from a train in January 1909. Vehemently denying her guilt, Alice swore at her trial that the child had been given for adoption to a Mrs Gray of Tottenham. But the truth prevailed and she was found guilty and given a prison sentence. Ultimately she was pardoned by a forward-thinking judge, well before the term postpartum depression entered the lexicon, who attributed her act to the depression of having given birth out of wedlock, then being deserted by the father.

Alice brought her instability of character and inexperience in childcare into the bosom of the Allison family. She was nervous but convinced that she could manage given enough time; it was a golden opportunity not to be wasted.

There are many versions of what happened on the night of the sinking – all of them Alice's. The Allisons had booked two cabins, C26 and C22. Alice was in one with Trevor and the maid, Sarah Daniels, while Bess and Hudson were in the other with little Loraine. When disaster struck Alice grabbed the sleeping baby, wrapped him in his fur pram blanket and rushed on deck. She claimed to have brushed by Mr Allison, who was returning from an investigation of why the engines had stopped, but in his haste he had not acknowledged her. She also did not call out to him, let it be said. In this version Alice swore that she wanted to go back for her employers once she reached the

This gold pill box and heavy gold bracelet are items a wealthy young couple might have carried with them on the Titanic.

deck, but the crew would not allow it, forcing her into a lifeboat instead.

In version two Alice claimed she was left with Bess Allison and the two children when Mr Allison went to investigate. She helped Bess, incapacitated by fear, to dress, poured her a calming brandy, then grabbed Trevor, saying that she would see to his safety, and made for the lifeboats – all presumably with Bess's approval. However it happened, Alice was determined to give a positive slant to her involvement.

Bess and Hudson had no idea what had happened to their son. Taking Loraine they searched the ship in desperation as the bow sank lower and lower and their chances of survival became slimmer and slimmer. Major Arthur Peuchen, a fellow Canadian, saw the Allisons at least twice during those last hours. Early on they discussed the seriousness of the accident and Mrs Allison commented that she had been advised to leave the ship, but would not until she found Trevor. Near the end Peuchen saw them again, this time standing in the vicinity of the lifeboats. He watched as a seaman beckoned toddler Loraine to safety. Afraid of being parted from another child, Bess and Hud called her back to their side, thus condemning her, along with themselves, to a certain death.

(Peuchen himself was asked by Second Officer Lightoller to man a lifeboat. He left £60,000/$300,000 in money, jewellery and securities in a box in his cabin and took three oranges and a good-luck pin instead.)

Winnie Troutt, a Second Class passenger, remembers Mrs Allison standing on deck screaming, with some justification as Loraine was the only First Class child and Bess one of only four First Class women to perish (the others being Ann Isham, Edith Evans and Ida Straus). Perhaps in the end the Allisons wanted to leave, but time got away from them and the boats were gone. Perhaps … perhaps …

When the rescue ship *Carpathia* reached New York, Alice, hugging Trevor tightly, gave her name to the press as 'Jane' and proceeded immediately to the area assigned to waiting relatives. At the pier were George and Percy Allison, Hud's brothers, who had no idea what Alice looked like and feared that she might just wander off taking Trevor with her. Little did they know that this was exceedingly unlikely, as Alice was very much enjoying her position as the rescuer of the Allison heir.

Alice and the two other Allison servants who managed to escape, Sarah Daniels and Mildred Brown, accompanied Trevor and his uncles back to Montreal, Alice heralded a heroine by the press. However, it did not take long for the family to discover the truth and to blame Cleaver for the loss of Hudson, Bess and Loraine, deeming her rush to the lifeboat a

Alice Mary Cleaver holding baby Trevor Allison in New York after rescuing him from the Titanic. (Author's collection)

selfish act of cowardice. Cleaver and the Allisons parted company, but not for ever.

In the autumn of 1940 a most bizarre story appeared in the *Philadelphia Inquirer* under the title 'Alien Told She Escaped From the Titanic'. Not a space alien – although stranger stories have been written in *Titanic*'s name – but a Mrs Laurence Kramer, a British citizen, who was attempting to convince the Alien Registration Board in Detroit, Michigan, that she was indeed Loraine Allison, long presumed dead.

Mrs Kramer stated that for 28 years she had believed that she was the daughter of English parents from whom she had requested her birth certificate, a requirement for legal permission to live in Michigan with her American husband. In his reply, her supposed father had written:

Bess and Hudson Allison. (Alan Hustak/Michael Findlay collection)

'I was standing on the deck after putting my wife and child in a lifeboat, and a man came running up to me and pressed you into my arms and begged me to take care of you. I think you were about three or four then. He told me he was going to get his wife and your baby brother. As he left he said his name was H. J. Allison and your name was Lorraine and that you were from Pennsylvania.'

'Lorraine' Allison Kramer maintained that Master Allison from the ship's passenger list must have been her brother 'Travers', but she was unaware of his whereabouts.

However, besides the misspellings of their names and the mistake in the real Loraine's birthplace, the story was full of holes. Do we have here the hovering hand of Alice Cleaver? By 1940 Cleaver would certainly have known that there was cash to be had, as Trevor, who had inherited all of the family money, had died in 1929 from ptomaine poisoning at the age of 18. His fortune was in the hands of George and Lillian Allison, the aunt and uncle who had raised him. If Lorraine Kramer could be accepted by the family, she would inherit the money, and if Alice Cleaver were involved, her percentage would give her back something of what she had lost. Eventually, however, the whole sordid scheme fell apart and 'Lorraine Kramer' disappeared.

Stories of Alice Cleaver, however, kept cropping up. She was spotted in England at a British Historical Society event, contacted Walter Lord when he wrote *A Night To Remember*, got married to a Mr Williams, did not get married, stayed in Canada, dying in 1984, and moved back to England, dying there also in 1984.

People who knew the Mrs Williams in England described her as a sweet old lady who kept to herself, suffered from extremely painful arthritis, had two daughters and was well looked after. She spoke to them only rarely of her *Titanic* experiences, but when she did the story went as follows:

She had been contacted by a Harley Street doctor to work for the Allisons because Trevor was recovering from a bout of pneumonia and needed special attention. During one of her free hours on the *Titanic* she had been shown around by an officer and remembered that the ship was far from finished. During their tour her escort had showed her a Marconigram indicating icebergs in the vicinity. On the night in question she had begged the Allisons to leave their suite and save themselves, but when they would not do so she had grabbed Trevor and headed for the lifeboats. She could never understand why the Allison family had blamed her for the death of Bess, Hudson and Loraine.

The real truth? We may never know.

Hudson Joshua Creighton Allison
9 December 1881–15 April 1912

Bess Waldo Daniels Allison
14 November 1886–15 April 1912

Helen Loraine Allison
5 June 1909–15 April 1912

Hudson Trevor Allison
7 May 1911–7 August 1929

Alice Mary Cleaver Williams
Fate uncertain

Lucy, Lady Duff Gordon (48)

'Fancy strawberries in April, and in mid-ocean. The whole thing is positively uncanny. Why, you would think you were at the Ritz.'
Lucy, Lady Duff Gordon

YOU HAVE TO LOVE this woman! Red haired and peppery, she knew her own mind, made her own living and blazed her own trail. However, in her 1932 autobiography, *Discretions and Indiscretions*, 'Lucile' (her public persona) expressed a wistful desire to be other than she was:

'I do not think that, on the whole, it is good for a woman to have temperament. It is much better for her to be a vegetable, and certainly much safer, but I never had the choice … I have always had too much imagination and splashed the blank canvas of my life with such brilliant colours that there had to be a good bas-relief of black to make them stand out.'

Born to an aesthetic British bridge-builder and a Canadian beauty of charm and practicality, Lucile was christened Lucy Christiana. The family was living in England when Lucy and her younger sister, Eleanor Glyn (a well-known novelist in England during the early 20th century) were born. Unfortunately, their adored father died young and their mother was forced to return with them to her parents' farm in Canada.

Lucy grew up a tomboy roaming the fields and 'riding everything in sight' with the neighbourhood boys. Her grandmother, a French expatriate, attempted to counteract this barbarism by instilling manners and the love of fashion in her rambunctious grandchild. All of this – artistic talent, charm, practicality, love of fashion – formed the personality that produced Lucile the couturier.

Like her father she was a bridge-builder, but while his were of steel, hers were of cloth, guiding the women of her era into the demands of the 20th century by easing their manner of dress.

It is strange that Lucile's name is not as well known in the turn-of-the-century pantheon of couturiers as Poiret, Panquin, Worth or Lanvin. She was certainly as successful and collected her own number of firsts: she was the first to use mannequins in the presentation of her collections, the first to do away with the constrictions of the corset, the first to introduce slits in skirts for ease of movement (thinking the fashion for hobble skirts ridiculous), and she coined the word 'chic',

A silver jewellery box with an inscription that looks very much like the monogram 'DG'. Maybe it held this lovely diamond ring.

Lucy, Lady Duff Gordon. (Author's collection)

without which we would be speechless when speaking of fashion today.

She herself was the epitome of chic and quite tiny, although her pictures show a woman of great size, such was her commanding demeanour. She socialised with and dressed the avant-garde and fashionable of the day, from Margot Asquith, wife of the British Prime Minister, to Lillie Langtry, mistress of Edward, Prince of Wales, Isadora Duncan, and Sarah Bernhardt.

Madame Lucile had fashion houses in Paris, London, New York and Chicago and was always ready with good fashion sense: 'One never grows tired of a simple gown, and neither do one's friends. Such a gown is always in fashion, and, with a smart hat and neat shoes, one is always becomingly dressed. And for the career girl, wear black by all means.'

She took her own advice when she and Sir Cosmo, her second husband, testified before the British Court of Enquiry into the *Titanic* disaster on 20 May (they had travelled as Mr and Mrs Morgan, occupying two cabins, his A16, hers A20). They had been forced to speak to clear their names, the popular press having made much of the 'money boat', which had left with the Duff Gordons and few other passengers aboard, and vilifying Sir Cosmo, who was saved when many women were not.

But Lucile also made it a stellar day for fashion. All eyes followed as Madame walked to the stand in a black dress with a significant white lace jabot, set off by a black veiled hat perched on her flaming hair. The gallery was packed with her supporters, every bit as elegant as their mentor.

Sir Cosmo was no slouch himself. He was attired in a black frock coat and striped trousers, with his hair slicked back and his moustache groomed to perfection. The hall was also bulging with *his* supporters: Prince Leopold of Battenburg, Prince Albert of Schleswig-Holstein, Count Benckendorff, the Russian Ambassador and Lord Clarendon to name but a few.

The matter that had prompted the Duff Gordons to be called was the allegation that Sir Cosmo had bribed the seamen in his lifeboat – George Symons, Charles Hendrickson, Robert Pusey, Albert Horswill, Samuel Collins, Thomas Shea, and James Taylor – with £5 not to return for survivors for fear of being swamped. Though Symons had taken responsibility for the conduct in the boat, Sir Cosmo was blamed by innuendo; his opponents called him a coward, saying that if he had raised his voice the boat would have returned to help the struggling – which may or may not have been true. With regard to the money, Sir Cosmo testified that it had been offered not as a bribe, but as a donation when he heard that the seamen's wages had stopped as of the sinking and they could not afford to replace their kits – in his opinion proper conduct for a well-to-do gentleman.

To make good loss of kit, a cheque for £5, inaccurately made out to J. Horswell not Albert Horswill, was signed by Sir Cosmo Duff Gordon. (Author's collection)

Another issue was why the Duff Gordon boat had left with so few aboard (12 in a boat capable of carrying 40), and why Sir Cosmo had been in it in the first place. Lady Duff Gordon testified that her husband was encouraged to board by the officer loading the craft and that two American men had followed suit when no ladies were found to fill the vacant seats. Their attorney pointed out that theirs was not the only boat that had left under-loaded, and it was not the only one that did not return to the scene, but this had precious little impact on the British public, whom Lucile believed were looking for a scapegoat.

With no legal grounds to attack Sir Cosmo, the attorneys for the unions and the Third Class passengers had every intention of putting him on the moral rack. But the testimony of their witnesses was not well thought out and they did not present the united front against the aristocracy for which the press was baying. Even so, it was a trying experience for the Duff Gordons and their appearance did not totally resurrect their good name. The scandal never disappeared, and Sir Cosmo kept a low profile for the rest of his life.

Lucile, however, continued to appear in public with her head held high. She reported on fashion from the capitals of Europe for *Harper's Bazaar* in a column called 'The Last Word of Fashions', she wrote for the *Daily Sketch* and the Hearst papers, designed costumes for the Ziegfeld Follies, and automobile interiors for a precursor of the Chrysler Motor Company. Her fashion house thrived until 1924 when she ran foul of import laws and faulty business practices. In all fairness, she was more creative than businesslike and had left the day-to-day management to others, but this apparent mismanagement eventually caused Maison Lucile to close.

In 1931 Sir Cosmo died and it was then that she sat down to write *Discretions and Indiscretions*. She had always promised him that

Pages from Harper's Bazaar *showing Lady Duff Gordon's column 'The Last Word of Fashions'.* (Author's collection)

one day she would set the *Titanic* record straight, and she attempted to do so in her book; in fact, she confused it. At the hearings she had testified that her lifeboat had been too far away to have heard any screams for help, which would have prompted their return. But she wrote: 'For a few seconds she [*Titanic*] stayed motionless while the agonised cries from her decks grew in intensity, and then, with one awful downward rush she plunged to her grave through fathoms of water, and the air was rent with those awful shrieks.' Had there been grounds for the allegations after all? If so, why admit it so long after the fact?

She called Sir Cosmo 'the great love of my life'. She had married him after the failure of her first marriage when she was engaged in dressmaking to support herself and her child, Esmé. He became an investor in her business and together they had built Maison Lucile. Members of his social circle had frowned upon his marrying a common dressmaker, and Lucile was never presented at court as should have been her due as Lady Duff Gordon. This bothered Sir Cosmo more than it did Lucy Christiana. She knew who she was and revelled in it. At the end of her memoir she wrote:

'... I do regret the passing of so much of the romance which made the world a very pleasant place in the past. It is possible to look upon realities too much, so that you lose the power of make-believe, and I think that perhaps it is a mistake which we are all making today.'

Lucy Christiana Sutherland Wallace Duff Gordon
1863–21 April 1935

Sir Cosmo Duff Gordon
22 July 1862–20 April 1931

Madeleine Force Astor (19)

'People do not die immediately for us, but remain bathed in a sort of aura of life ... It is as though they were travelling abroad.'
Proust

POOR MADELEINE ASTOR. Perhaps using 'poor' and 'Astor' in the same breath might seem like an oxymoron, but money did not provide an easy life for Ms Madeleine. In 1910 18-year-old schoolgirl Madeleine Force had met John Jacob Astor IV in Bar Harbor, Maine. After making her formal debut into society the

next year, she and John Jacob had begun to keep company. No one thought much of it, because 'Jack', as he was referred to by those who knew him well, was considered a playboy, favouring sweet young things. After all, the poor chap was entitled, having been just granted a divorce.

But they were forced to take notice when Madeleine and Jack announced their engagement in the late summer of 1911. Undoubtedly the Colonel, a title he had earned in the Spanish American War and of which he was particularly fond, was taken by her slender, blonde attractiveness, refreshing uncertainty and passionate nature; especially since his first wife, Ava, had been a domineering, imperious

Madeleine Talmadge Force in 1911, just prior to her marriage to John Jacob Astor IV. (Museum of the City of New York)

woman who often spoke down to him, if she spoke at all. Madeleine was the breath of fresh air that 47-year-old Jack needed to blow away his midlife crisis.

Astor's divorce decree from Ava stated that he could not remarry in New York, so he and Madeleine arranged to wed at Beechwood, the 39-room 'cottage' in Newport, Rhode Island, that had belonged to Jack's mother. Known as *the* Mrs Astor, social arbiter of the Gilded Age, she most certainly would not have approved of young Madeleine – and neither did anyone else. Society was abuzz with the improbability of the match, not only in age, but in position; he was, after all, an Astor, she the daughter of a Brooklyn forwarding agent.

Because of adverse public opinion, Jack had great difficulty in finding a member of the clergy to perform the nuptials; eventually he offered a £200/$1,000 incentive, and a pastor was attracted to do the deed.

Beechwood's grand ballroom, a vast space with windows framing the North Atlantic, was the setting for an event attended only by the bride, groom, two attendants and the pastor. The ballroom was adorned with delicate murals depicting Poseidon, the God of the Sea, frolicking with water babies and dolphins – an ominous forewarning.

To avoid further scrutiny, the middle-aged groom and his child bride set sail for a honeymoon abroad. However, when it became apparent that Madeleine was carrying an Astor heir, Jack made arrangements to return to New York on the *Titanic*.

The couple occupied a suite of rooms, C62, and were accompanied by a maid, Rosalie Bidois, a nurse, Caroline Endres, and the Colonel's manservant, Victor Robbins. Their Airedale, Kitty, was in the kennel.

John Jacob Astor IV was the name above the disaster headlines as they flashed around the

Madeleine might have touched this bronze cherub at the foot of the aft Grand Staircase as she made an elegant descent on the arm of her husband.

This gold ring inlaid with one large diamond and over 70 smaller diamonds would have been the perfect gift for Jack Astor to give to his new bride.

world – the first tragedy to be made an international event by Marconi's invention. The reading public could not get enough of his last moments on earth as he sat with pregnant Madeleine in the gymnasium cutting open a lifebelt with a knife to show her its construction; how he assisted her through the open window on A Deck into Lifeboat 4, was barred from entering himself, handed her his gloves, then turned his lanky body in a gentlemanly fashion to help absolutely everyone else in sight to safety. It became a badge of honour among survivors to have been saved by the richest man on the ship, perhaps the richest in the world. His wealth of £17 million/$87 million, including 700 pieces of prime New York real estate, was itemised in the *New York Herald*, examined and drooled over, his children scrutinised, his marriages dissected, his will analysed for fairness, and his lack of charity duly noted.

Madeleine herself added to the myths surrounding him by saying that as she rowed away in the lifeboat she saw her dog Kitty running on the deck and assumed that Jack had gone to the kennels to release the dogs so that they, too, could have a fighting chance.

Madeleine's young life was forever altered by her short liaison with the Colonel. By a prenuptial agreement, £339,000/$1,695,000 was put in her account at the marriage. It was further stipulated that in the event of the Colonel's death, she would continue to have use of both the New York Fifth Avenue mansion

and Beechwood Cottage, plus a trust fund of £1 million/$5 million – forfeiting it all if she were to remarry.

On 14 August 1912 John Jacob Astor VI came into the world (John Jacob Astor V having been born to William Astor, John Jacob Astor IV's cousin), and Madeleine spent her time indulging him in unnecessaries like an ermine robe and a mink coverlet. Before the child was three she had spent almost £1,200/$6,000 on toys and clothing for him. But money was not as important to her as love, and in June of 1918 she remarried, eschewing her venerable Astor name and its millions.

Her second husband, William K. Dick, was a friend whom she had known since childhood, and not a poor man by any means (having inherited £600,000/$3,000,000 from his grandfather, a Brooklyn pioneer in sugar refining). They lived together for 15 years, had two sons, John and William (names curiously Astoresque), and were supposedly happy until 1933 when she surprised everyone by seeking a Reno divorce.

Mr and Mrs John Jacob Astor IV and their dog, Kitty, on a New York City street. (Author's collection)

John Jacob Astor VI, son of Madeleine and John Jacob Astor IV. (Author's collection)

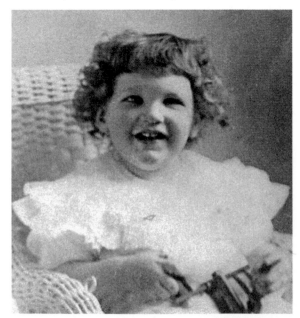

Somewhere near the Astor vault is the unmarked grave of Madeleine Astor Dick. (Author's collection)

Love had dictated her decision-making yet again. Now in her 40s, Madeleine had already been linked romantically with Enzo Fiermonte, an attractive 26-year-old pugilist with a wife back home in Italy. They had met when he had given boxing lessons to her sons.

Tongues wagged. Now *she* was the one involved with a younger, socially inferior paramour. Only half of those invited to a party in their honour attended, for Enzo was considered to be far too common. Nonetheless Madeleine married him on 27 November 1933 in, of all places, Doctor's Hospital in New York, where she was recovering from a shoulder fracture. In attendance at her bedside were John Jacob Astor VI, and his stepbrothers, John and William Dick. She relinquished all rights to any income she might have had from William Dick Senior in much the same manner as she had given up her millions from Astor 16 years before.

The Fiermontes had five tumultuous years

together before Madeleine secured a Florida divorce on the grounds of extreme cruelty. Short of funds and anxious to retaliate, Enzo wrote six revealing articles about his ex-wife for *True Story Magazine*. But by then Madeleine was too ill to care.

Always frail and with a heart condition, she died in 1940 at the age of 47, coincidentally the same age that John Jacob Astor IV had been when they married in 1912. Her access to vast wealth long past, she left £4,000/$20,000 to William and John Dick, but nothing to her son by Astor, as she felt that the £600,000/$3 million trust fund provided by his father was ample. (He disagreed, incidentally, and always felt cheated, eventually dropping the 'VI' from his name, claiming that his ancestors had never done anything for him, being known thereafter simply as John Astor.)

After her divorce from Fiermonte, Madeleine reverted to the name Dick and was buried under that name in an unmarked grave in

Trinity Cemetery, the burial ground of New York's rich and famous. Not far away was the Colonel. It was said that he had been the love of her life.

John Jacob Astor IV
13 July 1864–15 April 1912

Madeleine Force Astor Dick
19 June 1893–28 March 1940

John Jacob Astor VI
14 August 1912–26 June 1992

Ida Hippach (44)
Jean Hippach (17)

'Don't lower that boat until this woman gets in.'
Colonel Astor

BURNING BUILDINGS, sinking ships and crushed automobiles were to play a devastating role in the lives of the Hippachs. In fact, Ida and Jean had left the United States for Europe in January of 1912 out of concern for Ida's health, as she was unable to recover from the death of two of her three sons in Chicago's terrible Iroquois Theatre fire of 1903. Like the *Titanic* disaster, it was a headline-grabbing tragedy. And like the *Titanic*, the Iroquois had been advertised as the newest, the largest, the safest.

Ida's sons Bob (14) and Archie (11) had gone with 2,000 other Chicagoans to a holiday performance of 'Mr Bluebird'. It was 31 December and the audience was packed with students on vacation and families enjoying a holiday outing. An arc light was inadvertently knocked over during the performance, sending a tongue of fire up the canvas curtain, which turned into a blaze that killed 603 people. Trying to keep the audience calm after the fire curtain jammed, headliner Eddie Foy, the

Ida Hippach with her children, Jean and Howard, in early 1912. After Ida and Jean returned to Chicago in April 1912, Howard was killed in an automobile accident. (Author's collection)

famous vaudevillian, stood in the flames directing the evacuation. (Foy was one of the first artists who volunteered to perform at a theatrical benefit for *Titanic*'s victims in New York.)

Of course the Hippach family was devastated, and Louis Hippach thought that it would do his wife a world of good to get away, and Jean wanted to study music in Berlin anyway. The two were no strangers to transatlantic travel, having made the trip together four times before: Louis could not join them because he had his vast glass company, Tyler & Hippach, to run. Anyone engaged in the building industry in Chicago at the turn of the 20th century found themselves at an advantage – it was during this time that the Chicago School of Architecture produced the first new development in modern architecture, the 'skyscraper'. Steel beams and cast iron columns supported higher and higher structures built of masonry and glass, and Louis Hippach made a healthy living providing these innovative architects with his product. Among many of the famous structures in Chicago adorned with Hippach glass were the Civic Opera Building, the Field Museum, and the Merchandise Mart, then the world's largest building.

After the music lessons were completed Ida and Jean journeyed to Hippach, Austria, to visit family, then made a diversion to Paris for a look at the new fashions. Both were extremely well-dressed women whose social obligations required that they always appear in the latest styles. Hobble skirts were giving way to the pannier skirt and their wardrobes needed updating. To give themselves more time for the shopping expedition, they switched from a return on the *Olympic* to the *Titanic*, and boarded at Cherbourg with all of their latest finery.

In the only interview Jean ever gave on the disaster, recorded in *Wreck and Sinking of the Titanic* by Marshall Everett, which rushed into publication in 1912, she said:

'The *Titanic* was so huge that it is hard to give an idea of it ... The staterooms were like rooms in a hotel. We had regular beds and a handsome dressing table and chairs; and there was the lavatory with hot and cold running water and there were electric lights and an electric fan, and an electric curling iron and of course push buttons – everything you could think of. One of our friends, when her husband asked her if she could think of anything to add to the equipment, laughed and said,

An electric curling iron holder and hot and cold water taps from a First Class cabin. Jean Hippach mentions both in her account of the magnificence of the ship.

"Well, we might have butter spreaders. I can't anything else ..."

'If it had not been for Mr Astor I believe we would have been among the lost. The last lifeboat was being lowered when Mr Astor saw us. He ordered the boat raised so that my mother could get into it. "Don't lower that boat until this woman gets in," said Mr Astor. We were compelled to climb through a porthole in order to reach the boat, but mother would not get into it unless I joined her. Mr Astor again showed chivalry by pleading with the officers to permit me to get into the lifeboat, and they did.'

The facts in the book are not always correct, but in the case of Jean's account and her mention of the stars, we seem to find corroboration from her granddaughter, Caroll Scharin-Binotto. As a child Caroll remembers her grandmother, whom she called Ga Ga, always speaking of stars when remembering that night. Again quoting Jean's words from the Everett book:

'The water was very still and the sky – so many stars! You can't think how it felt out there alone by ourselves in the Atlantic. And there were so many shooting stars; I never saw so many in my life. You know they say when you see a shooting star some one is dying. We thought of that, for there were so many dying, not far from us.'

Jean and Ida were met in New York by Louis, who had taken the 'Twentieth Century Limited' to be by their side. They returned home only to be struck by tragedy once more in 1914. Howard, the remaining Hippach male heir, was in an automobile accident and died when his car overturned into a pond. Now an only child, Jean was extremely close to her parents, especially her mother, with whom she shared an interest in the arts (Ida was an authority on Flemish art) and in conducting a proper social and charitable life. Indeed, the two women were so close physically and spiritually that they were often mistaken for sisters.

Jean's marriage in the early 1920s to Hjalmar Unander-Scharin, a Swedish businessman with interests in the pulp industry, brought a new dimension and joy to their lives. Three children were born of that marriage, two daughters and a son, and the curse seemed to be lifted. Jean continued her social obligations and Hjalmar moved his business to Chicago. They lived near the Lindens, the Hippach family home, but also crisscrossed the Atlantic to their summer home in South Barrow, England, as it was closer to Hjalmar's primary investments in Sweden. But

Jean Hippach Scharin in later years with two of her three children. (Courtesy of Caroll Scharin-Binotto)

Jean's ties were with Chicago, and it eventually led to a divorce. In 1929 Hjalmar returned to Sweden and Jean to her roots in Illinois.

When Ida died in 1940 Jean moved to Osterville, Massachusetts, to a lovely home on a promontory surrounded by pine trees and ocean. She never remarried and would not allow any discussion of either her divorce or the death of her brothers, becoming more intransigent as she aged. (But she is fondly remembered by a now grown man who visited her when he was a boy of 6 or 7 to hear her *Titanic* stories; she was always very gracious and also told him about the stars that night.) In that vein she lived a life fast disappearing from the American scene, a life that included servants who knew their place and who ironed the newspaper each morning, where everyone dressed for dinner (which on Wednesdays was always calf's tongue), and where her dogs, Miffy and Sweda, sat in the front seat of her car on trips to the creamery for their ice-cream.

Ida Sophia Fischer Hippach
November 1868–1940

Jean Gertrude Hippach Scharin
30 September 1894–14 November 1974

Helen Churchill Candee (53)

'It was a fancy dress ball in Dante's Hell.'
Helen Candee

HELEN WAS CROSSING the Atlantic to attend to her son, Howard, who had been seriously injured in an aeroplane accident. Letting her home in Washington DC, she had spent the winter in Europe researching her latest book, *Tapestry*, which was to be published in the autumn and which was much praised for its scholarship. Passage on the *Titanic* was a sudden decision.

Travelling unaccompanied, Helen was quickly taken in hand by a group of unattached men who rallied round to see that she would not spend one moment on the crossing alone. By her side was Edward A. Kent, a Buffalo, New York, architect; Hugh Woolner, son of a famed English sculptor; Edward Colley, a jocular Irishman; Clinch Smith, a polo-playing American; Hakan Mauritz Bjornstrom-Steffanson, a Swedish military officer; and Colonel Archibald Gracie. The Colonel had just written his own not too exciting book on the Civil War, *The Truth about Chickamauga*, and, apparently, pestered many in First Class to read it.

This male attention must have been a bit excessive at times for Helen, who enjoyed a good read, but how could she resist the flattery, especially since one of the 'suitors' was a considerably younger man? Every day she took two deckchairs forward on the Promenade Deck, one for herself '... and the other for callers or for self-protection', whichever need arose first.

Colonel Gracie dubbed this group 'Our Coterie', and together they whiled away the hours of the journey testing the exercise equipment in the gymnasium, briskly walking the chilly decks followed by tea near the fire in the reading room, dining in formal wear, which Gracie called 'en règle', and thoroughly enjoying the luxury of the ship and the intimacy of each other's company.

Helen kept them all delighted with her witty conversation and suffragist opinions. She was truly an American original, descended on her mother's side from William Brewster, who arrived on the *Mayflower* in 1640 and was one of the first to plant British feet on venerable Plymouth Rock. And on her father's side she was related to Benjamin Hungerford, who had arrived in America 20 years later, but still early enough to be considered a settler.

This sense of exploration and adventure must

Helen Churchill Candee. (Michael Findlay collection)

have been in the genes for Helen was also well-travelled, and a published authoress with wide-ranging interests from decorative arts to politics. And she spoke her mind. One can just hear the gentleman callers asking about her book, *How Women May Earn a Living*, published in 1900. Considering the male-dominated times, they must have found it amusing that Mrs Candee presented practical advice to women on how to get along very well without a man. Her book was directed to 'all those women who labour through necessity and not caprice', of which she was one. Though not poverty stricken by any means, Helen had divorced her husband in a rather messy court case and was left with two children to rear on limited funds. She earned a substantial portion of the family income by writing articles.

In one such article for *The Illustrated American* of 6 November 1897, she took part in an enchanting discussion over the length of women's skirts on rainy days, observing:

'The gentle woman of the public is slow at throwing aside prejudice in favor of good sense ... fancy the relief to tired women if all skirts worn out of the house were shortened to six inches above the ground, and fancy the tons of bedraggled, germ-filled dry goods of which their delicate frames would be relieved.'

Women who adopted this attire were called 'Rainy Daisies', and no doubt Helen was among their ranks. (Cleaning garments was particularly difficult at the turn of the century, and mixing washing powder was a chemist's nightmare. One such concoction was a combination of soda ash, lime and rainwater, which had to be boiled. The clothes were then submersed in that vile liquid and soaked overnight.)

After dinner on the evening of 14 April 'Our Coterie' listened to an after-dinner concert in the Reception Room, then, wishing for their gay party to continue, adjourned to the Parisian Café for a hot toddy to ward off the drop in temperature. Helen, still chilled in her evening finery, decided to call it a night and returned to her cabin and the warmth of her electric heater at 11.40. But that was not to be for long.

Soon she was roused by Steffanson and Woolner who told her of the collision and urged her to dress and come on deck as quickly as possible. Later she fictionalised that night in a dramatic piece for *Colliers Magazine*:

Helen and 'Our Coterie' might have sipped cordials from these crystal glasses while listening to the after-dinner concert by Titanic's *orchestra.*

'Up the sweep of the regal stairway was advancing a solid procession of all the ship's passengers, wordless, orderly, quiet, and only the dress told of the tragedy. On every man and every woman's body was tied the sinister emblem of the sea and each one walked with his life-clutching pack to await the coming horrors. It was a fancy dress ball in Dante's Hell.'

Joining that throng, Helen climbed the stairs, meeting Edward Kent along the way. She entreated him to hold a small ivory miniature of her mother, which she prized dearly. Not being sure of his own survival at that point, he took on the task with some reluctance.

Helen was placed by Woolner and Steffanson in Lifeboat 6, and was joined there by Quartermaster Hichens, Lookout Fred Fleet, who had spied the iceberg that caused the disaster, and Major Peuchen, who was entreated to jump in and row. (Before he took on the task, Peuchen, mindful of his military reputation, supposedly had Second Officer Lightoller sign a quick note saying that he had asked the Major to take to the lifeboat and that he had not jumped ship in a cowardly fashion.) But Helen's most interesting boat-mate was undoubtedly the indomitable Molly Brown. Both of these ladies had a great deal to

Or perhaps, after a brisk walk on the open deck, they warmed up with chocolate poured from this silver pot.

say about the management of that boat during the long night adrift among the icebergs, and both later testified to the cowardice of Quartermaster Hichens, whom Captain Smith had placed in charge.

Life was to present Mrs Candee with many more adventures and a listing in *Women's Who's Who of America* in 1914–15. The First World War found her in Italy working with the Red Cross, for which she was decorated. Her cultural pursuits continued, with a position on the National Federation of the Arts, and of course she continued to write, lecture and travel extensively, especially in the Far East.

Of 'Our Coterie', only Gracie, Woolner and Bjornstrom-Steffanson survived, and Gracie not for long. Colley, Smith and Kent perished. When Kent's body was found by White Star's chartered search ship, the cable vessel Mackay-Bennett, *he had Helen's cameo safely tucked away in his jacket pocket.*

In 1924 she was again decorated, this time by the French Government and the Cambodian King for her book *Angkor The Magnificent, The Wonder City of Ancient Cambodia*. She travelled over 1,000 miles in Indo-China and passionately loved the Orient, living for a time in Peking. In a *New York Times* article in March of 1927 she wrote of the Chinese Civil War between the Nationalists and the Communists and was one of the first Westerners to believe that the Chinese National People's Party organised by Sun Yat-sen was the hope for China.

Feisty to the end, she died at her summer home in York Harbor, Maine, at the ripe old well-travelled age of 90.

Helen Churchill Hungerford Candee
5 October 1859–23 August 1949

Edith Corse Evans (36)

'I shall hold her memory dear as my preserver.'
Caroline Lamson Brown, survivor

EDITH HAD HAD A MARVELLOUS TIME in Paris visiting her cousins. And what would a trip to that capital of haute couture be without adding something new and delectable to your wardrobe? The brassiere was the dernier cri in 1912, and she most certainly must have been enticed to purchase one for her wardrobe. What freedom it gave her from the restrictions of the corset with its rib-piercing, breath-stealing stays.

Single, wealthy and self-sufficient, Edith had a presence that arose from having a family history dating back to the founding of the United States. Corse, her mother's maiden name, first appeared on the colonial scene in the late 1600s, etched into a Maryland tombstone. Hard-working Quakers, each generation worked to improve on the one before. The farmers became planters and the planters became businessmen, culminating in Edith's great-grandfather, Israel Corse, who came to New York as a young man, established a tanning business, acquired vast real estate holdings, and rose to become one of the wealthiest and most influential men in that city in the 1800s. Edith's grandfather, Israel Corse Junior, built on these foundations and collected fine art, loaning some of his more important pieces to the Metropolitan Museum of Art. His daughter, Edith's mother, Angeline, married Cadwalader Evans, a man of the same ilk.

Evans was a successful stockbroker, a prominent member of many New York social clubs and, according to a *New York Times* article, possessed of a 'charming disposition which made him a favorite of all who met him'. Sadly this bright light was not long an influence in Edith's life. At 33 he succumbed to kidney failure and died on a glacial winter's night in January 1880 with his wife, Angeline, and their two daughters, Edith, then aged 3, and Lena (6), by his side.

Angeline continued to rear Edith and Lena as generous, church-going souls – well-read, well-travelled and socially prominent. All were members of the Colonial Dames of America, a patriotic organisation whose membership was restricted to women directly descended from residents in the American colonies. The Evans women clearly qualified, as patriots dangled like apples from their family tree.

Edith had a bow knot broach with diamonds among her jewels – could this be hers?

Edith carried that legacy of strong moral character with her as she boarded the *Titanic* for the journey home from her continental holiday. She was a little tired after the six-hour train ride from Paris, then the tender transfer from the quay at Cherbourg, but she was also excited and anxious to settle in her cabin, number 29, on A Deck. It was a lovely room on the starboard side with a view through lace-curtained windows of the glass-enclosed First Class Promenade and the blue-black evening sea beyond. She shivered with anticipation, realising that she was the first to occupy this chamber, the first to sleep in this bed, the first to sit on the comfortable sofa, and – unbeknown to her – the last.

What pleasure she must have taken in seeing her garments placed in the ample wardrobe, their matching pointed-toed shoes in a neat row below. Carefully she laid her newly purchased lingerie and gold purse with the sapphire and diamond clasp in the drawers of the mirrored dressing table and arrayed her ivory brushes, combs and creams on its marble top.

Glancing appreciatively around, she stopped to straighten the feather on her new brimless hat and hurried off to take the electric elevator down to the purser's office on C Deck to deposit her jewels in his safe. She was travelling with 22 pieces, among them a diamond and emerald watch, a pearl necklace, a diamond bow knot broach, a locket with a spray of diamond lilies of the valley, and a platinum and gold bracelet. Edith's jewels were valued at almost £1,500/$6,000, and she was relieved to have them in safe keeping.

Conscientious by nature, Edith had in 1910, at the age of 33, executed a will. In it she had bequeathed not only these jewels, but also her books, laces, silver and clothing, to her 'dear sister' Lena and to her French cousins. Did she have a premonition? Or was she prompted by her own father's premature, and intestate, death at exactly that age – 33? We will never know. But certainly life, not death, was on her mind as, leaving her jewellery in trustworthy hands, she dashed off to survey the ship.

Edith was anxious to find her aunt by marriage, Malvina (Mrs Robert Clifford Cornell), and Malvina's two sisters, Caroline (Mrs John Murray Brown) and Charlotte (Mrs Edward Dale Appleton), who had boarded at Southampton earlier in the day. They were the Lamson sisters, returning on the *Titanic* after a sorrow-filled visit to London where they had attended the funeral of a fourth sister, Lady Victor Drummond. By the time Edith boarded, the three grieving women, all in their 50s, had been taken under the protective social wing of Colonel Archibald Gracie.

Gracie speaks of his gentlemanly offer in his 1913 book, *The Truth About the Titanic*: '... how little did I know of the responsibility I took upon myself for their safety!'

On Sunday evening, snug in her cabin high above the water-line, Edith felt little disturbance from the impact of the iceberg far below. And if she had, the fleeting 10-second jarring would most probably not have alarmed her as she dozed under her satin counterpane. In fact, she was not alerted until a little after midnight, when Captain Smith gave the order to uncover the lifeboats and the stewards began to rouse the passengers.

Edith hastened to the port side of A Deck where a small group of passengers had begun to gather, including the Strauses, the Astors, and her Aunt Malvina with her sisters and Colonel Gracie. They stood talking quietly in small groups, listening to a selection of lively tunes being played by the band in the First Class Lounge just aft of where they had congregated, waiting patiently for answers. Learning that the ship had struck an iceberg, the inevitable 'Don't worry, remember this ship's unsinkable' was bandied about in the freezing air to bolster their spirits.

A little after 12.25am Edith and the Mmes Brown, Cornell and Appleton were told by Gracie that there had been an exchange of wireless messages with passing ships and one would surely come to their rescue. Gracie jollied along his charges by leaning over the railing and pointing out the lights of one such vessel away in the darkness.

Edith watched as that ship's lights slowly disappeared from view. She felt her footing become more unstable as the *Titanic*'s bow began to dip further toward the surface of the sea. Seeing the possibility of rescue drift away, she confided softly to Colonel Gracie that a fortune-teller in London had warned her 'to beware of water', and she knew that she would be drowned. Gracie's 'efforts to persuade her to the contrary were futile'.

The grinding of the block and tackle heralded the arrival of Lifeboat 4 from the deck above. Now no different from the other passengers, this assemblage of the wealthy and influential were scared, cold and helpless in the face of the forces of nature and the efforts of an unprepared crew struggling to save their lives.

'Gentlemen, step aside,' commanded Sixth Officer Moody. 'Women and children first.'

Colonel Gracie relinquished his charges into

Moody's safe keeping and hurried off to help others.

In the ensuing frantic scramble to board a lifeboat, Edith and Caroline Brown were separated from Mrs Cornell and Mrs Appleton (who ended up in No 2). As Mrs Brown told a reporter from the *New York Herald* on 20 April 1912:

'… we were hurried from lifeboat to lifeboat by the men, but each was filled with passengers, mostly women and children, before we had a chance to board one. Meanwhile the scenes on deck, orderly at first, became more panicky. We found that there remained only three more lifeboats. In one of these each of us had

Caroline Brown, the woman for whom Edith gave up her seat in Collapsible D. (Author's collection)

a place, but we were ordered to leave as the boat was overcrowded. An officer shouted to us that there was another lifeboat being launched on the other side of the vessel, and we hurried to the place.

'There you may imagine our feelings when the officer in command said that there was room for only one more woman. The men stayed back and did not crowd. Miss Evans was by my side at the time. She pushed me toward the boat saying: "Please take this lady. She has children."'

Caroline Brown's boat was Collapsible D, the last boat lowered. It was 2.05am on 15 April. *Titanic* was to take its final plunge in 15 minutes.

Grace Church, New York City, as it looked on the day the memorial service was held for Edith Evans. (Author's collection)

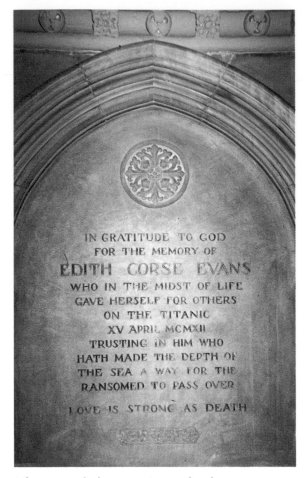

The memorial plaque in Grace Church commemorating Edith's heroism. (Author's collection)

What did Edith do with her last minutes of life? We know from Gracie that he came upon her near the end and she appeared 'perfectly calm'. Surely she prayed. Perhaps, resigned to her own fate, she walked the decks comforting others, or maybe she simply stood by the railing and waited for the inevitable end. Her body was never found.

On 22 April 1912 she was given a memorial service at Grace Church on Broadway at Tenth Street in New York. A plaque commemorating her heroism was presented to the church by three of her grieving friends. Caroline Brown tearfully spoke words of sorrow and gratitude to the weeping crowd: 'It was a heroic sacrifice, and as long as life lasts I shall hold her memory dear as my preserver, who preferred to die so that I might live.'

If only we had a photograph of the shadowy heroine to hold in our mind's eye.

Except for the newspaper articles from 1912 heralding her self-sacrifice, little remains of Edith today, even in the family papers donated by her sister, Lena, to The New York Historical Society.

In 1933 Lena was asked, as a direct descent of American patriot Andrew Hamilton, to speak at the Bicentennial celebration of the heroism of publisher John Peter Zenger. It was Philadelphia lawyer Hamilton who successfully defended Zenger against a case of seditious libel, stating in his defence that publishing the truth does not constitute libel, thus setting the precedent for freedom of the press in the United States.

At the end of her speech, Lena told the crowd, 'America has had suffering and sorrow, joy and gladness in her upbuilding, she has been lashed and wounded by the fury of a titanic storm, but the stripes upon her banner are outnumbered by the stars.'

Maybe, finally, this was her personal eulogy to Edith, a star who perished heroically in her own *Titanic* storm.

Edith Corse Evans
21 September 1875–15 April 1912

Margaret 'Molly' Tobin Brown (44)

'Get your facts first, than you can distort 'em as you please.'
Mark Twain

IF MOLLY WERE NOT INCLUDED in this narrative she would rise up and write a piece herself. Bright and ambitious, she went from shoeless country girl to satin-slippered grande dame. Hailing from Hannibal, Missouri, she was quick to align herself with another Hannibal citizen, the famous American humorist Mark Twain. She claimed that Twain had rescued her from a raging river and given her the advice to go west and marry a miner. Perhaps he did, although it is doubtful, as he had left Hannibal before she was born. But it made a whopping good story and that was what Molly was all about.

In one way it is fitting that she should claim Twain as a mentor, since he is known as a teller of tall tales, as was she. In another way it is an ironic misalliance, since Twain coined the term 'Gilded Age' to reflect his dismay at the era's conspicuous consumption, a pursuit Molly avidly endorsed.

Molly Tobin Brown in one of her fanciful ensembles. (Colorado Historical Society)

More than likely it was the Gold Rush that lured Molly west to Leadville, Colorado, and away from her poor family of 11 children. Always the dramatic one, she put on penny plays for the locals, prospecting during her performances for a rich husband. Along came unsuspecting James Joseph Brown, J.J. to all, the superintendent of the Little Jonny gold mine. Being the son of Irish immigrants himself, he was taken by Molly's Irish good humour, auburn hair, intense blue eyes and, lest we forget, ample bosom. He was 31 to her 16, and she thought of him as an old man, and a poor one at that.

J.J. may not have been rich, but he had ambition and determination, and, with some persistent courting, finally won Molly over. They settled in a log cabin near the mine and by 1889 had two children, Lawrence and Catherine Ellen, always called Helen. When the mine struck gold a few years later, the owners rewarded J.J. with an eighth interest, which Molly expanded to total ownership in her story-telling. Whatever, the Browns became rich and Molly immediately jumped on a fast track to refinement.

The prospects for social advancement in Leadville were limited, so the family moved from the log cabin to a brick mansion in Denver. Molly's flamboyant tastes now had the funds to support them and she decorated the house with gay abandon. In typical Victorian style it was chock-a-block with bear rugs, stained glass windows, tapestry walls, bric-a-brac, and, in a bow to the past, a welcoming moose head in the front hall. The pink-trimmed facade was embellished with lion heads and a plaque depicting Alexander the Great's triumphal entry into Babylon — a metaphor for Molly's desire to make a triumphal entry into Denver society. But Mrs Brown was turned back at the gates by Mrs

Caroline Hill, doyenne of Denver's 'Sacred 36', who felt the upstart too crass and unworthy to enter.

Molly therefore set out to 'show 'em'. First she studied languages, literature and dramatic arts at the Carnegie Institute in New York. Then she hopped over to Paris to improve her French accent, moved on to Spain where she learned the guitar, then headed to Switzerland for yodelling lessons. Along the way she collected people, and would say that she knew everyone worth knowing '... from Moscow to the Bosporus'.

Insistent that her children have all the advantages, Molly enrolled them in the finest European schools, then jeopardised their educations by withdrawing them at will to travel the world. Differing from his wife on almost everything, but especially on the rearing of their children, J.J. maintained that she had ruined them for any earthly use. But no matter how much attention she lavished on Helen and Lawrence, they became more and more alienated; especially Helen, who found her mother an outright embarrassment, particularly in the way she dressed.

This necklace with a drop of gold nuggets would have been the perfect piece for Molly to have been carrying in her jewel box.

Molly's flare for clothing was imaginative, to say the least, and she never let convention stand in the way of making a statement. For balls she wore Parisian gowns of satin, brocade and golden embroidery, and at one wound her hair with gilded snakes entwined with clusters of diamonds and opals. Always close by was her swagger-stick, which she claimed was for fallen arches, but may just have been brandished as its name intended.

Good-hearted to a fault, she and J.J. tirelessly devoted themselves to civic, religious and social causes and gave lavish parties to which they invited the immediate world. J.J., while agreeing in theory, was especially unhappy at these events and would disappear into the basement to smoke and sulk.

In 1909 they separated, but Molly, good Catholic girl that she was, continued to deny that they were divorced, telling people that she was a widow. In the settlement she was awarded the deed to the house, now called the 'House of Lions', and enough cash and stock options to allow her to pursue her quest for high society.

Finally unencumbered by a tag-along husband she could hobnob freely with the wealthy. In Newport, Rhode Island, and New York her yodelling sent the proper Gilded Age matrons into apoplexy. But in Europe she was welcomed with open arms for her wit and generosity. The French especially adored Molly for her flair and for her dramatic portrayal of their beloved tragedienne, Sarah Bernhardt, with which she was later to entertain the troops during the First World War.

It has been said that she wanted to be on the *Titanic* because it was the social thing to do that year. She did enjoy a good party, but in fact she was travelling home to see her grandson, Lawrence, who was ill, and to bring two cases of Carrara marble reproductions from the ruins of Rome and the basilicas of Florence to the Denver City Museum.

Her exploits on that crossing have been given mythic proportions by Broadway and Hollywood. But in all that hyperbole there is much truth. She saw to it that many women entered lifeboats with no thought to her own safety until two men picked her up bodily and tossed her in as well. Once there she sparred with Quartermaster Hichens over control of that boat, threatening to toss him overboard if he opposed her, making him 'shake like an aspen'. And she parcelled out bits of her clothing to others who were freezing, including her sable to an under-dressed stoker, and generally jollied everyone along until they were rescued by the *Carpathia*.

On board that vessel she comforted those who had lost loved ones, often speaking with them in their native languages, sent telegrams to passengers' families at her own expense, helped sew blankets into clothing for those in need, served on a committee to see that the White Star Line lived up to its obligations to the survivors, and helped draft a commendation for Captain Rostron and his crew. When the *Carpathia* arrived in New York harbour she stayed on board to help the Red Cross find shelter for the needy. Finally disembarking at 3am, the press swarmed round asking her how she survived. Her reply: 'Typical Brown luck. I'm unsinkable.' A legend was born.

Returning to Denver a heroine, the 'Sacred 36' were obliged to invite Molly into their midst, although it was never an easy alliance. No sooner was she in than she entreated them to petition Congress to reform maritime law, believing it immoral to separate women and children from their husbands and fathers. Next she tried her hand at politics, becoming a member of the National Women's Party and encouraging President Coolidge to lend his support to the Equal Rights Amendment to the United States Constitution. She even volunteered to serve as a 'soldierette' when there was talk of an American war with Mexico in 1914.

Molly was an outgoing individual and would have collected calling cards like these wherever she went.

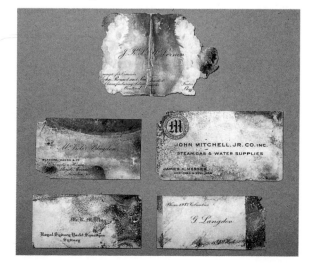

On the social scene, she continued to dine out on *Titanic* stories, boring the Newport crowd to the point where one sharp-toothed matron said, 'Mrs Brown's calling cards should read: "Survivor of the Titanic in Perpetuity".'

Travelling remained an important part of her life. In 1920 she characteristically booked passage on a freighter from Halifax to Denmark, a ship loaded with tons of coal but few passengers. Seven hundred miles out to sea, in a replay of the *Titanic*, fires started in the freighter's coal bunkers, raging out of control and almost burning through the hull. The ship returned safely to Halifax, and Molly, not pressing her luck, disembarked. While waiting for passage on another vessel, she visited the cemeteries where *Titanic*'s dead lay buried, placing handmade wreaths on their graves in remembrance. Then she was off again to far-flung places from Scandinavia to South Africa.

It is interesting that at that time she was travelling with a niece rather than her daughter. It is well known that Helen was growing more concerned over her mother's increasing peculiarities, but was helpless to do anything about it.

As the 1930s dawned Molly's trips abroad and to her beloved Denver became fewer as her funds and energy ran low. She became a parody of her former self. As a reporter from the *Denver Post* wrote in 1930 after seeing her on the street in front of the 'House of Lions', 'Heads turned at the sight of her, and as she passed by she left in her wake an essence of violets, rose-water and mothballs. Everything about her was amazing and fascinating ... I sensed that she was a brave and lonely woman probably living in the heyday of her past.'

On 26 October 1932 she died of apoplexy alone in her suite at New York's Barbizon Hotel. This hotel for young actresses was a fitting final dwelling place for Molly, whose flare for the dramatic made her a memorable character in the history of the 20th century.

Margaret Tobin Brown
18 July 1867–26 October 1932

Emma Ward Bucknell (60)

'Behave yourselves like men! Look at all of these women. See how splendid they are.'
Captain Smith

HAD WILLIAM BUCKNELL lived four weeks longer, it is unlikely that his wife Emma would have been on the *Titanic*, at least not in First Class. The year prior to his death in 1890 he had begun revising his will, dispersing his $7 million estate to charity and to his grown daughters from a first marriage, reserving for Emma and their four children only token sums.

His plan was to sign the will on 1 April 1890, his 80th birthday; it was his ritual to 'clean house', so to speak, each year on the anniversary of his birth. In Emma's case, however, his intention was to grab a new broom and sweep her right out of the door. Unfortunately for charity and, of course, for old William, he suffered a heart attack four weeks prior to the appointed day and died leaving his original will intact. Emma not only received considerable millions, but also the mansion in Philadelphia and the country house in Chestnut Hill, Pennsylvania. The story appeared in the West Chester, Pennsylvania, newspaper under the headline 'Bucknell Balked'.

Theirs had been a strange arrangement, the difference in their ages being far greater even than that of John Jacob Astor and Madeleine Force. Emma was an 18-year-old schoolgirl in New York State when she met Bucknell. She was the daughter of Reverend William Ward, a missionary, and a direct descendent of American Revolutionary War naval hero,

Emma inherited this mansion in Philadelphia from her husband, William, upon his death in 1890, even though he would rather it had gone to someone else. (Courtesy of Philadelphia City Archives)

General James Lawrence, remembered for another maritime incident and for uttering that famous phrase, 'Don't give up the ship'. William Bucknell, meanwhile, was 62, intensely religious, and intensely rich. Always a charitable man, he was a major supporter of a small Baptist college in Lewisburg, Pennsylvania, and served for years on its board of trustees. In 1887 the board changed the name of the college to Bucknell University in honour of his financial contribution, which it remains today.

William had been married twice before and had daughters, and probably shirts, older than Emma, which certainly did not bode well for the liaison, and it became more unpleasant as

the years went by. Emma was reduced to writing stories for magazines to earn pocket money, while her friends described her as 'an affable and most estimable woman and beyond reproach as a devoted wife and mother of four children'. Apparently William thought otherwise.

However, in the beginning he must have been taken with Emma, the pious, virginal daughter of a clergyman, which to thoroughly religious William was an attractive element. In 1867 he invited her to spend her school holiday at his home in Philadelphia. While out driving together one day he proposed to her, and before she knew what was happening arrangements for their wedding were under way. Lusty may also

Emma Bucknell. (Author's collection)

be added to the adjectives describing William, for in short order the new couple had a son and three daughters.

By 1912 all that was past history, and Emma Bucknell was 60 years old living the life of a wealthy Philadelphia widow, spending summers at her retreat on Saranac Lake in upstate New York, amassing a first-class art collection, and travelling First Class. The winter of 1911–12 found her in Rome with her daughter, the Countess Pecorini, and in April on board the *Titanic* on her way home to see her son, Howard, graduate from the College of Physicians and Surgeons in Atlanta, Georgia.

Boarding the ship with some trepidation at Cherbourg, she told her friend Molly Brown that she had an ominous feeling about the voyage. Since Howard was obviously on her mind, perhaps she was subconsciously thinking of his close encounter with an iceberg years before. In 1894, while a student at the University of Pennsylvania, he had joined a student polar

Sipping demitasse together may well have been an after-dinner event for Emma and her friend Molly Brown.

expedition with Dr Frederick Cook. While cruising the icebound regions of Labrador their vessel had been struck by an iceberg and completely wrecked, resulting in a terrible loss of life. Howard was one of the few to escape in a lifeboat and was picked up several days later by a passing steamer. All too soon she was to repeat his experience.

When the call came for women and children to take to the lifeboats, Emma met Molly Brown on the companionway and said, 'Didn't I tell you something was going to happen?' or words to that effect. She left the *Titanic* in Lifeboat 8 and soon learned that the assigned crew had no idea how to row. She herself took to the oars to teach them, together with other resourceful women. Emma was always proud to claim that she and her maid rowed the long night through side by side with the Countess of Rothes and her maid. But she and the Countess were not the only strong women in this boat. It also carried the two French chicken ladies (see Part II, Edwina Troutt), Miss Young and her companion, Mrs White. Miss Young also rowed and Mrs White provided the only light by swinging her electric cane, which she had also used to direct traffic during the loading of the lifeboats. Second Officer Lightoller had become annoyed: the cane's light caused him to see spots against the blackness of the night and he had sent someone to tell her to turn it off or he 'would personally throw the damn thing overboard'. Fortunately for those in Lifeboat 8, she had complied.

After the sinking Emma was most outspoken about the ill-prepared crew and the 'appalling unpreparedness of the lifeboat equipment'. As she told a reporter from the *Philadelphia Inquirer*:

'It is only the fact that no provisions of an adequate nature were made to safeguard the lives of the passengers of the *Titanic* that made me consent to this interview ... I have been across the ocean 30 or more times in the past four years and have seen many lifeboat drills, but I never saw one on board the *Titanic* ... They did not seem to understand how to operate the ropes, and the process of launching the lifeboat, which should not take more than two minutes, took ten.

'On the vessel there was beginning to be the signs of the great tragedy about to descend. Wives and husbands were separated when the women were placed in our boat. A few of the men grew seemingly desperate, and Captain Smith, who was standing by, cried out: "Behave yourselves like men! Look at all of these women. See how splendid they are. Can't you behave like men?"

'All of the women were calm, though they had just been torn from their beloved ones. There was only one little Spanish bride, who cried out hysterically for her husband, who was held back by other men.

'Then Captain Smith himself picked up a big basket of bread and handed it across to me in the lifeboat. That was all the provisions I saw. There may have been water on board, but I did not see it. I took the precaution to drink a glass of water just before I departed from my cabin.'

Thereafter Emma lived quietly, spending time in Clearwater, Florida, and at her lake retreat. She never fully recovered from the trauma of the wreck and spoke little of it after that interview. She died at Saranac Lake in her 75th year with her children by her side.

Emma Eliza Ward Bucknell
28 August 1852–27 June 1927

Helen Walton Bishop (19)

HELEN WALTON BISHOP'S short, tragic life is chronicled here in period prose exactly as it

This gold watch was a popular style in 1912 for more conservative ladies like Emma.

appeared in the newspaper headlines and stories that chronicled her every move.

Sturgis Times Democrat, 6 November 1911:

'MRS JOHN FLANDERS' HOME WAS THE SCENE OF A PLEASANT AFTERNOON CARD PARTY SATURDAY IN HONOR OF MISS HELEN WALTON

... The house was very prettily decorated with smilax and pink hearts, the same color scheme being maintained in the refreshments. The prizes, a bunch of roses and carnations, were given to the bride-to-be by the winners.'

The Dowagiac Daily News, 7 November 1911:

'DICKINSON H. BISHOP AND MISS HELEN WALTON WED TODAY IN STURGIS CHURCH

WEDDING CEREMONY IS PERFORMED AT ST JOHN'S CHURCH AT 2PM BY BRIDE'S GRANDFATHER

PROVES TO BE ELABORATE AFFAIR

The bride wore a gown of white satin made princess style, with court train. It was trimmed in Princess lace. Orange blossoms fastened her bridal veil, and she carried white orchids and lilies of the valley. A pearl necklace with an emerald and pearl pendant, the gift of the groom, was worn by the bride ...

The wedding is the most notable ever held in Sturgis. The bride is the only child of Mr and Mrs Jerold P. Walton. The father is one of the foremost business and manufacturing men of Sturgis. He came here a few years ago and patented and put on the market the royal push button chair ... every year 200,000 of the chairs are sold. For a wedding trip the bride and groom have planned to visit Egypt. They will not set sail until January 12. Upon their return they will take up residence in the handsome new

Helen Walton before she married Dickinson Bishop and tragedy struck. (Author's collection)

Bishop home on Main Street, Dowagiac, which has never been occupied since its erection ...'

The Dowagiac Daily News, January 1912:

'LEAVE SOON ON VISIT TO EGYPT

Next Sunday Morning Mr and Mrs D. H. Bishop will leave on a trip to Egypt, which before their return will take them also to some more interesting countries of Europe. They will go by way of New York City, sailing on the White Star Liner, *Adriatic*. En route they will make stops at the Azores and Gibraltar, reaching Egypt at Alexandria. After three months tour of Egypt they will cross over the continent coming home by way of Italy, Spain,

France and some of the most interesting points in Europe.'

The Detroit Free Press, 18 April 1912:

'MICHIGAN COUPLE ON WEDDING TRIP SAVED

One newly married couple, known in Detroit, Mr and Mrs Bishop, timed their return so they could come by the Titanic.'

The Detroit News, 19 April 1912:

'BISHOPS TELL OF TRAGEDY

"GO BACK TO BED, NO DANGER," STEWARD TOLD DOWAGIAC COUPLE'

The Detroit News Times, Sunday morning, 21 April 1912:

'BEG FOR NEWS OF MISSING

GRIEF-RACKED PEOPLE BESIEGE THOSE RESCUED FROM THE TITANIC

CARRY PHOTOS AND IMPLORE THE SAVED TO STUDY THEM

MRS BISHOP RECOUNTS HER PERSONAL PROPERTY LOSSES, A FORTUNE IN JEWELRY

Clutching at the last shred of hope for some word of their lost loved ones, scores of men and women are besieging Mr and Mrs Dickinson H. Bishop of Dowagiac, Mich, in their apartment at the Waldorf-Astoria ...

"We certainly are thankful to be here," continued Mrs Bishop, though we did lose about $20,000 worth of property, on which there was no insurance ... My three gold purses alone were worth $1,500. I had a platinum chain with diamond plaque, a pearl necklace with an emerald drop, 16 rings set with diamonds, sapphires, rubies and emeralds, a string of pearls. I lost my platinum bracelet, watch and diamond, a string of corals, two or three sets of emerald and pearl earrings. There were so many other things but I cannot remember them now ... I feel the loss of my little dog most of all. I will always remember how she tugged at my dress when I started to leave. She wanted to go with me so much.'

The Sturgis Times Democrat, 22 April 1912:

'STURGIS SURVIVORS TELL EXPERIENCES

MRS D. H. BISHOP RELATES IN VIVID MANNER HER IMPRESSIONS OF WRECK

New York, April 20: "When we got on deck there were few people there but there were tons of ice on the fore part of the ship. We were in the first lifeboat to be lowered over the side. Someone said, 'Put in the brides and grooms first.'

"There were three newly married couples who went in that boat. Altogether, there were 28 who went in our boat. There might as well have been 40 or 50, but the half hundred men on deck refused to leave even though there was room for them ...

"The water was like glass. There wasn't even the ripple usually found on a small lake. By the time we had pulled away 100 yards the lower row of portholes had disappeared. When we were a mile away the second row had gone, but there was still no confusion. Indeed everything seemed to be quiet on the ship until her stern was raised out of the water by the list forward. Then a veritable wave of humanity surged up out of the steerage and shut the lights from our view. We were too far away to see the passengers individually, but we could see the black mass of human forms and hear their death cries and groans.

"For a moment the ship seemed to be pointing straight down, looking like a gigantic whale submerging itself, head first ...

"After we had been afloat for several hours

without food or water and everyone suffering from the cold, I felt certain we should all perish. I took off my stockings and gave then to a little girl who hadn't as much time to dress as I had."

Seated in their apartment at the Waldorf-Astoria, Mr and Mrs Bishop, together with the bride's parents, discussed their plans of returning to Michigan. They expect to remain in New York a week, replenishing their wardrobes. Mrs Bishop playfully referred to her husband's ready-made suit, which had been purchased as an emergency outfit.'

The Dowagiac Daily News, 10 May 1912:

'BISHOPS ARRIVE HOME AND RELATE MANY THINGS ABOUT TITANIC NOT BEFORE TOLD

SHIP SLOWLY SANK TO WATERY GRAVE WHILE THEY WATCHED ONE MILE AWAY – DID NOT BREAK IN TWO

They arrived home this morning at 8.52 having made the trip aboard a train from Buffalo. They came that far from New York in their car, but such was the condition of the roads and the weather that they abandoned the auto and shipped it home ... "We waited over to take passage on this particular ship ... Up to the time of the wreck we had a beautiful passage ... I will never forget the sunset that night."'

When interviewed after the sinking, Helen spoke of losing an evening bag similar to this one.

The Dowagiac Daily News, 10 December 1912:

'INFANT SON PASSES AWAY

The infant son of Mr and Mrs D. H. Bishop passed away at 10am today.

The babe was only one day old. A private funeral will probably precede its interment.'

The New York Times, 6 November 1913:

'TITANIC SURVIVOR DYING – MRS BISHOP

FATALLY INJURED IN AN AUTOMOBILE ACCIDENT

To survive the Titanic disaster only to be fatally injured in an automobile accident was the fate of Mrs Dickinson Bishop ...'

The Dowagiac Times, Kalamazoo, 6 November, 3.30pm:

'AUTO ACCIDENT MAY RESULT IN DEATH

An operation was performed upon her by Dr Green and a number of Kalamazoo physicians, and portions of skull and brain were removed. It was found that paralysis had already set in, and that no definite hope could be held out that the injured woman would survive for many hours ...

The accident took place near a sharp turn in Lovell street, where scores of automobiles have been wrecked and a number of persons injured.

The machine in which Mrs Bishop and Mr Dickinson [the driver, and a cousin of Helen's husband] and Dr Eaton were riding skidded as it rounded the sharp turn and ran head on into a large tree close to the curb. Mrs Bishop was thrown completely over the front seat and windshield of the car, through the branches of the tree several feet above the ground, and struck head first on a cement walk 30 feet from the car ...

Mr Bishop had preceded the other members of the party to the city and when the accident happened it was some time before he could be located and when he was informed of the injuries to his wife he telephoned to Dowagiac for Dr G. W. Green, the family physician. The doctor was rushed to Kalamazoo at top speed in the Bishop automobile with Chauffeur Earl Patterson at the steering wheel. The doctor reached the bedside of Mrs Bishop in less than an hour after he first received the message.

Mr and Mrs Bishop were passengers on the steamship Titanic when it sank mid-ocean a year and a half ago. Their escape from watery graves was considered almost miraculous ...'

The Dowagiac Daily News, 18 January 1916:

'MRS BISHOP IS GIVEN DIVORCE

On Saturday Mrs Helen Walton Bishop, now of Sturgis, was granted a decree of absolute divorce from her husband ... Mr Bishop is at present at Palm Beach, Florida.'

The Detroit Times, 3 March 1916:

'PLAYS FAIRY GODMOTHER TO YOUNG MAN BUT SHE'S AS LOVELY AS CINDERELLA

Fairy godmothers are not always young, beautiful and very wealthy.

But Mrs Dickinson H. Bishop, who played fairy godmother to young Philip Edgar Grant, Cornell graduate and member of a prominent New York family, is lovely enough to play

(Author's collection)

Plays Fairy Godmother to Young Man But She's as Lovely as Cinderella

Mrs. D. H. Bishop

Cinderella rather than godmother and she has the wealth of a princess.

Mrs Bishop was on her way to Panama when she discovered that the steward in the steamer bathroom was the son of a family friend – a young chap who had strayed from home and "fallen from fortune". She urged him to return home and give up the bathroom job. Mrs Bishop was divorced in January from Dickinson H. Bishop, the Dowagiac "stove king".

He settled on her $100,000.'

Sturgis Times Democrat, 15 March 1916:

'HELEN WALTON BISHOP DIES SUDDENLY TODAY IN DANVILLE HOSPITAL

HER DEATH FOLLOWS AN OPERATION UPON HER HEAD WHILE SHE IS GUEST OF LADY FRIEND IN ILLINOIS CITY

OLD ACCIDENT TROUBLE IS THE MAIN CAUSE

REMAINS WILL BE TAKEN TO STURGIS – LIFE OF FORMER DOWAGIAC WOMAN, NOW A DIVORCEE, IS FULL OF EXCITING INCIDENTS

She wore a silver plate on her skull, placed there by skillful surgeons at the time of the operation which followed her automobile accident. It recently became necessary to submit to another operation, and this was undertaken in a hospital at Danville while she was visiting there …'

The Dowagiac Daily News:

'SAME PRIEST AT WEDDING, BURIAL

At the same altar of the same church, where four years ago Miss Helen Walton was united in marriage to Dickinson H. Bishop of this city, the Rev Frederick Patterson, the same priest who officiated at her wedding, is this afternoon reading the burial service of the Episcopal church for her … Two years ago in the same church the same rector conducted funeral services for the infant child of Mr and Mrs Bishop.'

On the same day that Helen's death was announced in her home-town paper, *The Sturgis Times Democrat*, Dickinson Bishop's home-town paper, *The Dowagiac Daily News*, ran the last front page story in which her name would appear. In prominent and poignant columns on the left and right of the front page, it announced:

Dowagiac Daily News, *15 March 1916. In a horrible journalistic coincidence the headline on the left announced Helen's death while that on the right announced Dickinson's marriage to another woman.* (Author's collection)

Randall Bishop, Helen's son who died at birth, is buried in the shadow of her grave stone, which bears the inscription 'God moves in mysterious ways his wonders to perform'. (Courtesy of Korkye and Joe Sternburgh)

Helen Walton Bishop
19 May 1892–15 March 1916

Dickinson H. Bishop
1887–16 February 1961

Lily May Futrelle (35)

'We used to cross the Atlantic at the drop of a telegram.'
May Futrelle, *Atlanta Constitution*,
12 December 1947

THEY WERE MADLY IN LOVE – and inseparable – for all of the 17 years of their

marriage. When May Peel met Jacques Futrelle he was a dashing young newspaperman about Atlanta, Georgia, with a round face topped by dark hair, a continental manner, and a zest for life. Soon after they met Jacques went off to Boston to work for the *Post*, but he missed May and returned home to set up the sports department at the *Atlanta Journal*.

Jacques was next offered a position with the *New York Herald*. But this time he was determined not to leave Georgia without May, and they were married on 17 July 1895. They began their marriage together in the artistic turn-of-the-century world of New York's Gramercy Park, socialising with literary luminaries like Wharton and O. Henry. Continuing to move up in his career, Jacques

May Futrelle. (Atlanta History Center)

was hired again by a Boston paper, the *American*, and the Futrelles moved to Massachusetts.

May was a true daughter of the South. She was what has come to be called a 'steel magnolia' – gracious and charming, but determined and unbending. She stood by Jacques's side, encouraging him, bantering with him, challenging him and still finding time to write on her own. She had been writing since she was a teenager and it was one of the things that had drawn them together in the first place. In 1906 the Futrelles collaborated on a story entitled 'The Grinning God', which May started and Jack finished. In 1911 they both had highly praised books published: May's

was *Secretary of Frivolous Affairs*, called 'a good hammock companion', and Jacques's was *High Hand*, promoted as 'a breezy, virile tale'.

In April of 1912 they were returning from Europe with £6,000/$30,000 in contracts, £3,400/$17,000 of it in cash, from publishers in Britain, France, Sweden, Germany and Holland for Jacques's 'Thinking Machine' mystery novels, which revolved around an irascible old professor named Van Dusen who did not believe in the impossible. The Professor had made his debut in Jacques's first mystery in 1905, *The Problem of Cell 13*, which his paper, the *Boston American*, agreed to publish in serial form. Jacques and the Professor were instant hits. On 45 further occasions between 1905 and

This was May and Jacques's first car and in it they made a trip from New York to Atlanta with the New York Herald–Atlanta Journal *Tour in 1909.* (Atlanta History Center)

1912 the Professor would come forth to solve yet another 'impossible' crime. This made Jacques ever more famous and later generations would credit him, along with Edgar Allan Poe, as a founder of the American mystery genre.

Wildly popular in the United States, these stories were now to be released in Europe and the Futrelles were ecstatic. In London they had celebrated Jacques's 37th birthday, and taking the *Titanic* was the culmination of all of their good fortune. Jacques commented to May that the only thing missing from this wonderful celebration were their children, Virginia (15) and John (13).

May and Jack were cruising on a tide of good fortune. They spent their last night together dressed in their finest, dining in luxury at a table graced by a fragrant bouquet of American Beauty roses and discussing the latest New York Broadway season with Henry and Renee Harris. Jacques retired early with a headache, and May went to the ship's library, which she thought filled with boring books, finally settling on one that she had already read and returning to her cabin. Being a writer, her descriptions of the hours between 11.30pm and the sinking, written for the *Boston Post*, are some of the best.

The Futrelles' stateroom was across the corridor from that of the Harrises. When the men went to investigate the stopping of the ship, they sent May to sit with Renee:

'Mrs Harris was pale and frightened. Our fear was increased twofold when we heard the harsh clanging of the great gong forward. I was afraid. The explanation of the reason for ringing the gong came to us in a flash. That very afternoon one of the officers had explained to us that this gong was only used as a signal for the closing of the watertight

This cut crystal vase with its fluted edge might have held the American Beauty roses at the dinner May and Jacques enjoyed on their last night together.

A gold fountain pen such as both May and Jacques would have used to correct their manuscripts.

compartments in case of emergency.

Mrs Harris was suffering from a broken arm, which she carried in a sling. I clasped her free hand and together we waited, fear-struck and silent for the return of our husbands.'

Their husbands did return and escorted the two women to the Saloon to wait for the call to the lifeboats.

'The first rush of men, with the fear of death in their faces, came when a group of stokers climbed up from the hold and burst through the saloon, their grimy faces appearing wild and distorted in the brilliant lights. The appearance of these stokers was the signal that the great heart of the ship had stopped beating, that the waters had reached the engines. In a moment we all understood that the situation was desperate, that the compartments had refused to hold back the rush of water ... At the moment the band was playing "Alexander's Ragtime Band".

I could not make up my mind to leave my husband, when I saw the lifeboat about to go down. I was afraid, the water looked treacherous. I ran back, threw my arms around his neck and said, "Jack, I don't want to leave you" ... The last I saw of my husband he was standing beside Colonel Astor. He had a cigarette in his mouth. As I watched him, he lighted a match and held it in his cupped hands before his face. By its light I could see his eyes roam anxiously over to the water. Then he dropped his hands and lighted his cigarette. I saw Colonel Astor turn toward Jacques and a second later Jacques handed the colonel his cigarette box. The colonel screened Jacques's hands with his own and their faces stood out together as the match flared at the cigarette tip. I know those hands never trembled. This was not an act of bravado. Both men must have realised that they must die ...

The *Titanic* was slowly sinking. Port light after port

May described the stokers rushing into the First Class Saloon with 'death in their faces' as the orchestra was playing 'Alexander's Ragtime Band'. (Irving Berlin Music Corporation)

light disappeared beneath the sea. All around us were great icebergs …'

May spent the next years of her life working to pay back the £3,400/$17,000 advance that had perished with Jack. She did so by serialising his books and by writing another novel of her own in 1916. In the 1930s she taught writing in Boston and New York and hosted a radio show on CBS called 'Do You Want To Be A Writer?' The American League of Pen Women made her national chairperson when she almost single-handedly caused a new Federal copyright act to be passed by the United States Congress in 1940.

Still the 'steel magnolia' in her later years, May became argumentative. There is some suggestion that Alzheimer's Disease was a factor here, which is a sadness for one with such a good mind. Through it all Jacques was never far from her thoughts, and every 15 April she would stand on the cliff at their home in Scituate, Massachusetts, and throw blossoms into the Atlantic as it crashed against the rocks below. She took a limited measure of peace in knowing that Jacques had hated cemeteries. He had always said that he wanted to be buried at sea.

Jacques Heath Futrelle
9 April 1875–15 April 1912

Lily May Peel Futrelle
26 May 1876–29 October 1967

Irene Wallach Harris (36)

'Mrs Harris was rich, racy and of infinite good humor.'
Moss Hart, Act One

'A NIGHT TO REMEMBER? No it wasn't,' Mrs Harris was often heard to say. 'It was a night to forget.'

Renee Wallach Harris did try to forget the incident, but with little success. She had lost her best friend and lover, Henry B. as she always referred to him. After the tragedy she cried for two years, then claims that her tear ducts dried up and she never cried again, returning, on the outside at least, to her old good-natured self.

In the best tradition of 'The show must go on', Renee did just that after she lost Henry B. She walked down the gangplank of the *Carpathia* full into the 20th century; no longer the woman behind the successful man, but the first woman theatrical producer of the American theatre.

Renee, born Irene Wallach in Washington DC, always pronounced her name in the masculine way with the emphasis on the first syllable. She met her 'boy' Henry in August 1899 while studying law in New York and working as a legal secretary at night. He was by then a famous and successful Broadway producer, credited with managing and launching the careers of such celebrities as Lillie Langtry and Ruth St Dennis. Finding her extremely competent, Henry asked Renee to read plays that were offered for his consideration. As their personal relationship grew, he also became more dependent on her theatrical instincts. A fellow theatrical producer quoted him as saying, 'I never take an important step without consulting Renee. If anything happens to me, she could pick up the reins.'

That she did, but it was a bigger challenge than anyone imagined. When Henry B.'s will was probated and all the debts paid it was discovered that he had died insolvent. Renee's father-in-law, a respected theatrical producer in his own right, surveyed the mess and advised Renee to call it quits. But she refused and paid back most of what was owed. She also put in a claim with the White Star Line for £206,105/ $1 million as compensation for the loss of her husband's earning power, more than the total ultimately paid to all the claimants; needless to say, she received only a small portion of her requested amount.

Her first theatrical production was a gutsy beginning: she mounted a production of *Damaged Goods*, a play about syphilis, and it was a success. She followed that with one hit after another, giving many young actors and playwrights their start in the theatre. Among them were Barbara Stanwyck (who later appeared in the 1953 movie *Titanic*), a chorus girl before Renee recognised her talent, and Judith Anderson, later Dame Judith Anderson, doyenne of American and British theatre.

Mr and Mrs Henry B. Harris. (Author's collection)

Moss Hart, the famed director of *My Fair Lady*, met Renee when he was young and an aspiring writer. She saw his potential and produced his first play, *The Beloved Bandit*, which was an unqualified failure. She stuck with him through out-of-town previews, and when the play flopped in Rochester, New York, Moss remembers her saying through a cigarette dangling from her lips, 'I'll tell you something, boys, the way it went tonight doesn't bother me a bit. Not a bit. You know why? First this is Rochester – what the hell does Rochester know about anything except Kodaks?' Eventually even she had to give up on the project, but Moss would for ever after be grateful to her for her belief in him. She was, in his words, 'Rich, racy and of infinite good humor'.

At that time it was a champagne and caviare life for Renee. She owned the Hudson Theatre (for which she had turned down a million-dollar offer), racehorses, a yacht and houses in New York, Maine and Florida. During the First World War she turned her considerable energies to bringing entertainment to the troops in France, and to collecting husbands – three more to be exact. But when the stock market crashed in 1929 her entire world came apart again. By 1940 she was living in a welfare hotel on 64th Street in Manhattan, playing bridge and writing an occasional article to keep body and soul together.

Walter Lord met her when he was writing *A Night to Remember* and they became firm friends. In 1958 she was invited to a showing of his book-turned-movie. She arrived in a wheelchair, having suffered a broken hip, and could not sit

A leather cigar case, a must for any theatrical producer.

This Autostrop safety razor and natural bristle shaving brush could have been among Henry B.'s personal belongings.

through the whole showing – not for the pain from her hip, but for the pain the movie caused her by being too realistic. While others sat through the screening, she retreated into her own memories of that night.

She and Henry were sitting in their stateroom playing the card game Double Canfield. Earlier in the day she had slipped on a teacake coming down the stairs to her cabin from the reading room and had broken her arm. The pain was intense and she was unable to sleep. As she sat with her arm in a sling across her chest, wrapped in two bathrobes to ward off the chill that had invaded the ship, she noticed that her clothing was swaying on the hangers in the wardrobe. Not thinking much about it, they continued to play until the engines stopped. It was then that she was overcome with a fear of 'appalling stillness'.

True to her tempestuous nature, she gave Henry B. a devil of a time when he tried to get her to leave in a lifeboat without him. They went from boat to boat watching them being loaded with women and children. To quote from her story of the event in *Liberty* of 23 April 1932:

'We crossed to the port side, passing through the bridge where the Captain was standing with Major Archibald Butt and the little doctor. I saw the clock – I can still see it with its hands pointing to 2.20.

The captain looked amazed when he saw me. "My God, woman, why aren't you in a lifeboat?" I kept repeating, "I won't leave my husband. I won't leave my husband." The little doctor said, "Isn't she a brick?" to which the Captain replied, "She's a little fool – she's handicapping her husband's chances to save himself."

"Can he be saved," I asked, "if I go?"

"Yes," he answered. "There are plenty of rafts in the stern and the men can make for them if you women give them a chance."

"Come along, Mrs Straus," I said. "We'll make it easier on our men."

Mr Straus spoke for the first time: "We've been together all these years, and when we must go we will go together. You are very young, my dear. Life still holds much for you. Don't wait for my wife."

I had no time to protest. I was picked up and I felt myself being tossed into the nowhere. I heard a voice saying, "Catch my wife. Be careful – she has a broken arm."'

Those are the last words she ever heard her Henry B. speak. Quoted later she said, 'If I had my life to live over, I wouldn't change it. After all, I had 12 wonderful, happy, superb, unforgettable years with my first husband. He spoiled me for any other man in the world. I have had four marriages – but really only one husband.'

Henry Burkhardt Harris
1 December 1866–15 April 1912

Irene Wallach Harris
15 June 1876–2 February 1969

Hélène Baxter (50)
Mary Hélène Douglas (27)
Quigg Baxter (24)
Berthe de Villiers (24)

'A woman who isn't loved is dead.'
Coco Chanel

ISN'T QUIGG BAXTER a fabulous name for a leading man? Join this name with blond good looks, money and athletic ability and you have the pivot around which spins this *Titanic* tale of women and children.

Our hero was travelling with his latest love, Berthe de Villiers, supposedly with the intention of entering into a marriage contract when they reached his home in Montreal. The trouble was, he was also travelling with his mother, Hélène, and his sister, Mary Hélène Douglas, better known as 'Zette, and there is some question as to whether they knew everything there was to know about Berthe.

There is a line from a song in the musical *My Fair Lady*, based on Shaw's *Pygmalion*, which says, 'The French don't care what they do actually, just so long as they pronounce it properly.' Much the same might be said of Edwardian morality. It did not care what you

Quigg Baxter during his days at McGill University. (Courtesy of Alan Hustak)

did actually, just so you did it with circumspection – and, of course, pronounced it correctly. To that end Quigg installed Berthe in cabin C90, far away from the suite he shared with Maman and 'Zette – B58–60 – one of the more costly on the vessel.

There is conjecture that Maman only learned of her son's friend when it was too late to do anything about the liaison dangereuse, which may not be true but makes a good story. Quigg was assisting her and his sister into Lifeboat 6 when he said something like, 'I've been meaning to tell you ...' With that he whipped out a flask and offered her a drink, whether to ward off the chill of the impending flight into the night in a leaky boat or to soften the blow of Madame de Villiers, we will never know. In any event, Maman chastised him for his drinking and he replied, 'Au revoir, bon espoir vous autres,' which essentially means 'goodbye and good luck to all of you'. Berthe, however, did not receive the same warm send-off.

In her story, which appeared in a Parisian newspaper soon after the event, Berthe claimed that she was forcibly removed from her cabin and only had time to slip into satin slippers and put a light travelling coat over her nightgown. In her haste she left behind several hundred thousand dollars in jewels. Molly Brown met her on deck moments later and talked her out of returning for the jewels, so that part of Berthe's story may have been correctly reported. With no time to find Quigg, she was directed to enter Lifeboat 6 where the Baxters were already seated. Looking across to the deck she saw him and their eyes met. With an almost imperceptible nod and a slight smile he bid her goodbye.

Maman Hélène had more to learn of her son's 'fiancée'. It seems that Madame Berthe was not what she advertised herself to be. This was no sweet young thing, and perhaps no Madame either. In real life she was a cabaret singer and courtesan, born Berthe Antonine Mayne in

Hélène Baxter and her daughter 'Zette Baxter Douglas on the porch of their Montreal home. (Courtesy of Alan Hustak)

Belgium on 21 July 1887. Always more ambitious than her two siblings, she pursued a life quite apart from the working class family of her birth. Like Shaw's Eliza Doolittle, Berthe recreated herself in an upper class image, adopting the name de Villiers, an aristocratic Belgian lineage, to match the persona, and dropping large hints that she was related to the Belgian Royal Family. What better way to gain access to the circles of the rich and famous than by making them think you were already there?

Her other manner of entry into that bastion was through the international world of entertainment. As a cabaret singer she was well known in the Brussels 'circles of pleasure', according to the Belgian newspaper *Nieuws*. Quite naturally she gravitated in the early 1900s to a Paris teeming with bohemians, cabarets and avant-garde luminaries with names like Picasso and Matisse. It was in this milieu that she met Quigg Baxter, young man about town.

From correspondence with Berthe's family we know that she thought her dreams of marrying a rich man were about to come true. Were it not for the *Titanic* disaster it is possible that her liaison with Quigg might have worked out — birds of a feather and all that. After all, the Baxters had a few skeletons of their own.

The Baxter family money had been made by 'Diamond Jim' Baxter, a parvenu from the Canadian hinterlands born into an emigrant family of what was derogatorily called 'Black Irish'. Being ambitious, Diamond Jim left his ten brothers and sisters early in his life and escaped from backwoods Ontario to the big city of Montreal. His charm, intelligence and zeal for self-improvement took him from jeweller's assistant to brokerage firm owner in 13 years. His attributes also secured for him a French-speaking bride 20 years his junior named Hélène de Lanaudière-Chaput, who had illustrious ancestors, a taste for the finer things in life and very little money. So Diamond Jim had the funds, Hélène had the flair, and it worked out well for both.

Driven by his new wife's desires, Jim built an impressive stone house in the sacrosanct enclave of Montreal's ruling Scottish Presbyterian families called 'the Square Mile'. The Irish Catholic, French-speaking Baxters did not belong among this social elite, at least according to the elite. Alan Hustak, Canadian newspaperman and *Titanic* enthusiast, wrote,

'Race and culture separated Montrealers at the turn of the century as deeply as religion.' But the Baxters held their heads high and Jim continued to expand the family fortune. Three children were soon born, William Antoine in 1883, followed by 'Zette in 1885 and Quigg in 1887. All were bilingual, well-educated, attractive and the family hoped for better social standing in the next generation.

Quigg and 'Zette's father established himself as 'the largest private banker in Canada' and as the builder of the first shopping mall in North America. Twenty-eight stores were gathered under one roof in what came to be called Montreal's Baxter Block, still in existence today. But all was not well. It seems that together with his charm and intelligence,

Berthe Mayne as Bella Vielly in an edition of Music-Hall Illustré. (Herman DeWulf/Michael Findlay collection)

Diamond Jim had a touch of larceny in his soul. In the same year that *Men In Canada* praised him for his Baxter Block and philanthropy, the United States accused him of violating currency exchange regulations. In 1900 Canada convicted him of defrauding his own bank (Banque Ville Marie, which failed in 1899) and off he went to prison – condemning the Baxters to yet a lower rung on Montreal's social ladder.

Berthe loved gold stick pins with diamond sprays.

Released shortly before his 66th year, beaten by his incarceration, Diamond Jim did not live to celebrate his freedom. Montreal newspapers had a field day printing stories that he died penniless – which may have been wishful thinking for his Scottish-Presbyterian neighbours, as nothing could have been further from the truth. The family fortune was reduced slightly, but Jim had cleverly hidden money in the banks of Europe, leaving his family in comfortable financial circumstances.

In 1911 Hélène sold the Baxter Block and left for Europe to avoid the autumn Montreal social season to which she was not invited. Quigg was also in Europe that autumn to accompany his mother as she sought medical help for a heart condition, and to check on his hockey interests. Always more athletic than academic, he had dropped out of McGill University in 1909 and had gone to Europe, where he organised an international hockey tournament in France and Switzerland. He had himself played stellar amateur and professional hockey, only stopping when a wayward hockey puck damaged his left eye.

Berthe may well have removed her make-up with the Elcaya cream from this jar.

In April of 1912 'Zette (married to Frederick Douglas, the doctor who cared for Quigg's injured eye) joined her brother and mother in Paris to celebrate her 27th birthday. Her marriage was not one of the best, due in part to her mother's meddling, and a separation was an indicator of things to come. The threesome decided to return to America aboard *Titanic* as much to impress the assembled Canadian passengers as for the experience. No one seems to remember much about them, however. Quite possibly extreme mal de mer kept Maman Hélène confined to her cabin.

She was, of course, roused on 14 April when Quigg carried her to Lifeboat 6 and deposited her in a seat. All that long cold night Madame Baxter wailed hysterically for her son, but she was left with only 'Zette and Madame de Villiers. Quigg had perished.

When they docked at Pier 54, 'Zette, Hélène and Berthe disembarked together, and 'Zette, fighting off the intemperate press and trying to keep intact what was left of the family dignity, told them that Berthe was a penniless widow whom they were taking to Montreal until she could gather her resources and return to Europe.

After a brief stay in Montreal, Berthe did return to Brussels, then on to Paris to resume her career in cabaret. In 1913 her picture graced the cover of *Music-Hall Illustré*, and her name had become Bella Vielly, as she did not want to use her real name, whatever that was at this point. Obviously still travelling in the 'circles of pleasure', she formed a long-lasting liaison with Monsieur Henri Cot, a steel manufacturer, and together they returned to Brussels in 1924. Monsieur Cot bought Berthe-Bella the house in which she lived out her days.

Because of her penchant for tall tales, Berthe's family never believed that she was on the *Titanic*, much less engaged to a rich Canadian. When she died in 1962 those relatives had a shock: in disposing of her belongings they found a cache of memorabilia including photos of Quigg and the Baxter house in Montreal, and hard evidence of her having been aboard the stricken ship. So Aunt Berthe had been telling the truth after all.

Hélène Baxter lived out her life in Montreal, dying in 1923 when 'Zette was finally free to divorce without causing further embarrassment to her mother. What remained of the Baxter fortune was split between 'Zette and her older brother William, aka James, but by that time it was considerably reduced. 'Zette married Edgar Richardson, a stockbroker, and moved to California, living in much reduced circumstances. Upon her death she willed her Baxter heirlooms to her Canadian family, but no one had the money to transport them back to Montreal. Quelle dommage.

Hélène de Lanaudière-Chaput Baxter
1862–18 June 1923

Mary Hélène Baxter Douglas Richardson
4 April 1885–31 December 1954

Quigg Baxter
13 July 1887–15 April 1912

Berthe Mayne de Villiers
21 July 1887–11 October 1962

Dorothy Gibson (22)
Pauline Boeson Gibson (45)

Her art imitated life.

A DERELICT SHIP bounced in frigid waters. On deck, Dorothy Gibson, struggling to keep her wits in the unfolding drama, played her part to the hilt. No, this was not the sinking of the *Titanic*; this was art imitating life. Dorothy, the actress, was re-enacting on celluloid a role that she had portrayed in life only a few short weeks before – Dorothy, the *Titanic* survivor.

First some necessary background. Dorothy was a daughter of Hoboken, New Jersey, where she lived with her mother, Pauline, and her stepfather, Leonard. Endowed with the quintessential American girl face and form, she became the model for one of the turn-of-the-century's most prolific illustrators, Harrison Fisher. As Fisher's favourite muse, illustrations of Dorothy appeared in hundreds of advertisements, magazines and newspapers, and she became known from sea to shining sea as the 'Original Harrison Fisher Girl'. But, alas, this was not enough for our heroine and in July 1911 she was wooed away by the French film company Société Français des Films et

Dorothy Gibson as depicted by illustrator Harrison Fisher in the early 1900s. (Author's collection)

Cinematographes Eclair to star on the silver screen.

The company had brought its expertise to Fort Lee, New Jersey, where it built a 40,000-square-foot state-of-the-art studio complete with glass-covered shooting stages, processing labs, dressing rooms, scenery storage and costume workshops. How could Dorothy resist? Especially since illustrator's model was not the highest paying of professions.

The American division of Eclair became known for its short films, which attracted the immigrant and the poor who, for a few pennies, could be made to forget the pressures of their daily grind. Dorothy performed in one after another of these reels until she became the company's star. In March 1912, after an exhausting year of shooting, Dorothy wrapped up her role in the production of *The Easter Bonnet*, which was to be released late in April, and left with her mother for a little relaxation in Genoa, Italy. All too soon the studio wired for her return.

Dorothy booked a passage on the *Titanic*, boarding at Cherbourg with her mother Pauline and full cinematic star regalia; nestled amongst the silk kimonos in her luggage were dozens of pairs of gloves (long and short), a $300 muff and a string of jet beads [could she be the one?]. When all were ensconced in a cabin on E Deck, Dorothy went off to enjoy the voyage.

On the night of the sinking she was engaged in a late game of bridge in the lounge on A deck with a new acquaintance, William T. Sloper, and Fred Seward, who knew the Gibson ladies from church. The steward asked them to stop, as it was time for the lights to be put out for the evening, but the card players persisted and finished their rubber. Later Dorothy was quoted in the *New York Dramatic Mirror* as saying, 'These ceremonies over I walked down to my room at just 11.40. No sooner had I stepped into my apartment than suddenly came this long-drawn, sickening scrunch.' Allowing

for Dorothy's sense of the dramatic, this may not have been the exact story, but it certainly made good press.

In any event, Dorothy hastily collected her mother, donned a white woollen sweater over her silk evening gown, slipped out of her white satin slippers with the rhinestone buckles into more serviceable black shoes and, gathering up two steamer rugs, hastened to the boat deck. Pauline and Dorothy were the first to board Lifeboat 7, but others were not so easily persuaded to follow suit. Dorothy used her feminine wiles to entice her bridge partners, Seward and Sloper, to hop in, but the boat was still lowered away with only 28 aboard.

Dorothy in a publicity shot for an Eclair film. (Corbis/Bettman)

Poor Dorothy. The lifeboat's plug would not stay fixed and her feet dangled in icy water all night. There was no water or food and no lantern, but our heroine found a box of matches in the pocket of her sweater for occasional illumination. She was quite perturbed when her lighted matches exposed a man, allegedly a French Baron, huddled in a corner of the boat under all of the available blankets, leaving the others to freeze. When finally rescued by the *Carpathia*, an exhausted Dorothy slept undisturbed for 26 hours.

A translucent glass jar with the face powder still waiting to be used. Certainly Dorothy powdered her nose before that bridge game on Sunday evening.

Meanwhile, back in New Jersey, Eclair went into action modifying a nautical script they already had in the works into the disaster film *Saved From The Titanic*, staring none other than their own little survivor, Dorothy Gibson. Contemporary audiences are very familiar with television movies of the week trading on a headline or tragedy, but in 1912 it was a new genre and Eclair had the publicity coup of the decade.

As soon as their star was back on terra firma, production began with Dorothy's expert technical advice. This was a plucky girl to say the least, exhausted from her ordeal, yet willing to relive it for her art. According to the Harrisburg, Pennsylvania, *Leader* of 21 April 1912, Dorothy's portrayal for the camera so distressed her that the production crew had to '... jump to Miss Gibson's rescue as she had practically lost her reason by virtue of the terrible strain she had been under in endeavoring to graphically portray her part.'

To its credit, Eclair did not claim that its masterpiece had actual footage of the wreck as did so many other film-makers of the time. There was no actual footage, of course; but newsreels were everywhere using footage of the *Olympic* and the *Lusitania* and passing them off as the *Titanic* to satisfy a public's insatiable thirst for the story. (Eighty-six years later technical wizardry would enable actual footage of the sunken ship to be used in James Cameron's blockbuster movie *Titanic*.) Instead Eclair utilised '... a miniature vessel and a studio-built ocean and iceberg, effecting a clever reproduction of the terrible affair as visualised through a nightmare of memory by Miss Gibson.' For further on-screen verisimilitude, Dorothy wore the same water-stained white satin evening dress, sweater and black shoes in which she had made her escape from the wreck.

The film was completed in less than three weeks and released on 16 May 1912. *The Moving Picture News* wrote: 'The startling story of the world's greatest sea disaster is the sensation of the country. Miss Dorothy Gibson, a heroine of the shipwreck and one of the most talked of survivors, tells in this motion picture masterpiece of the enthralling tragedy among the icebergs.' All this in 10 minutes and 1,000 feet of film.

The motion picture industry played a part in the lives of another First Class couple, Mary and Daniel Marvin, who were travelling home from their honeymoon abroad. Daniel's father was President of the Biograph Film Company. As a present for his son and new daughter-in-law, he had their wedding filmed — a most unusual occurrence for 1912. Daniel perished, but Mary, who was pregnant, survived.

On 25 July 1912 the film changed its name to *A Survivor of the Titanic* and opened in Britain to packed houses. But not much was heard from Miss Dorothy after that. Her last big scene came in 1913 when she killed a man while recklessly driving around New York City in an auto belonging to Jules Brulatour, an Eclair financier and holder of a patent on motion picture raw film stock. In the court case that followed, it became known to the world that Jules and Dorothy were engaged to be married, much to the shock of the reigning Mrs Brulatour. The publicity attached to stardom obviously had its drawbacks even then.

After securing a quickie divorce, Jules wed his star in 1917, but it was not a happy union, and the couple separated in 1919, perhaps due in no small measure to a question over the legality of Mr Brulatour's divorce. Facing a possible annulment of her own

The fragrance is gone but the memory lingers.

nuptials and the loss of any compensation, Dorothy settled the divorce proceedings by accepting a £2,000/$10,000 yearly alimony and £7,500/$15,000 in attorney's fees from Mr Brulatour.

Dorothy spent the rest of her life in Europe. Never remarrying, she kept the name Brulatour until her death of congestion in 1946 – alone – in her Paris hotel room.

Saved From the Titanic was lost to the viewing public in a fire that devastated the Eclair studios in March of 1914.

Dorothy Gibson Brulator
1890–20 February 1946

Pauline Boeson Gibson
1867–?

A publicity poster for the Eclair Film Company's movie Saved From The Titanic. *(Motion Picture News, 11 May 1912/John P. Eaton collection)*

Maria Josefa Peñasco (22)
Fermina Oliva y Ocaña (39)

'I feel so sorry for a little Spanish bride. She and her husband were just like little canaries. They were so loving, and were having such a happy honeymoon that everyone on the Titanic *became interested in them, but she was saved and he perished.'*
Helen Walton Bishop

MARIA JOSEFA, 'Pepita' to her family, screamed and sobbed all the night long for her Victor. But she knew it was no use. He was gone. Why had they ever decided to get on that horrible ship? Perhaps the sea would swallow her up too. It didn't matter any more.

When she married Victor on 8 December 1910 they had only wonderful things ahead: a grand honeymoon touring Europe and a magnificent mansion being readied in Madrid. With the optimism of youth they could never have imagined that in two years it would all be over. Victor's mother, Purificacion Peñasco, had warned them not to take an ocean voyage for it would bring bad luck. Agreeing, they had not given her admonitions another thought.

Victor was wealthy beyond belief. He had been left the fortunes of both his father, a famous author, and his grandfather; however, in accordance with a civil law harking back to Roman times, his wealth was held by his mother in a trust, and he had to solicit her every time he was in need of funds. She had sent the Señor and Señora Peñasco a constant supply of drafts during their two-year honeymoon — but money was not the object, fun and adventure were.

The emerald ring on Victor Peñasco's left hand was given to him by his mother as an engagement present. (Courtesy of Carles Bonet i Corbalan)

The newlyweds stopped periodically in Madrid on their two-year holiday to oversee the progress of their apartment, a palacete ('mini-palace') of three storeys and 44 terraces, but then they were off again to all the fashionable resorts, to London, to Vienna for the opera season in their own box, and on the 'King of Trains and Train of Kings', the 'Orient Express', to exotic Constantinople. Seventeen-year-old Pepita acquired jewellery wherever they went, which today, all things considered, would be valued at roughly £250,000/$400,000.

April 1912 found them in romantic Paris. Surrounded by advertisements for the *Titanic*, they hatched a plan to defy Mama Purificacion and sail on the magnificent liner without telling anyone back in Madrid. It would be delicious to think that they had stopped at Maison Lucile to outfit Pepita before the journey, perhaps being greeted by Madame Lucile herself, who told them that she too would be among the passengers.

Fermina, Pepita's maid, was to accompany them, but Eulogio, the lucky butler, though he must not have thought so at the time, was to remain behind in Paris. In his hands Victor and Pepita left pre-written postcards extolling the virtues of the French capital, and it was Eulogio's duty to mail them to the family each week to trick them into believing that their newlyweds where still in France doing what newlyweds do — in April in Paris.

Meanwhile the Peñascos were crossing the Atlantic in cabin C65 on *Titanic*'s starboard side, making friends, showing off Pepita's jewels and enchanting everyone with their love for each other. Fermina was berthed in C105, diagonally across from her employers, at the ready to sew a seam here and a tuck there on Pepita's luxurious wardrobe.

After dinner on the night of Sunday 14th, with Fermina in her cabin mending a corset, Pepita and Victor sat in the saloon deep in conversation with several gentlemen from

Uruguay. They returned to their cabin at 11.30 and Pepita snuggled into bed with a glass of warm milk to ease her to sleep. Victor had just put his shoes outside the door to be polished by the steward and was removing his tuxedo when the iceberg ground along the side of the ship in a collision so slight that it caused nary a ripple in Pepita's milk. But Victor thought it wise to investigate anyway. On deck he was told not to worry, but chose to ignore the cavalier attitude of the crew.

The postcards that Victor and Pepita bought in Paris were perhaps similar to this.

Jogging back down the Grand Staircase to C Deck, he roused Fermina to aid the Señora in dressing and accompanied the two women to the boats. No one knows exactly what happened to Victor after he placed Pepita in a lifeboat, but there is speculation that he returned to the cabin for his wife's jewels. Fermina looked everywhere for him, calling out frantically in Spanish in an attempt to convince someone that the lifeboat in which her mistress sat could not be lowered until the Señor returned. But no one understood her, and it would have been no consolation for Pepita to learn that Victor would have been barred from the boat anyway had he returned in time.

Did a steward use this brush to freshen Victor Peñasco's tuxedo before dinner on that Sunday evening? Silk men's hosiery – Victor's?

Lifeboat 8 held the Countess of Rothes with her cousin, Gladys Cherry, and her maid, and Mrs Bucknell and her maid, amongst others. All night as these women pulled at the oars (including Fermina, who laboured in a nightgown, her hair streaming down her back), 17-year-old Pepita cried piteously for her Victor. The Countess, who was doing a jolly good job of not only steering but also keeping intact the morale of the group, finally could stand it no longer. Turning the tiller over to her cousin she sat down next to the desperate bride, took her in her arms and tried to give comfort.

Meanwhile, the postcards kept arriving in Madrid announcing what a good time the newlyweds were having. Enterprising newspapermen determined that the young Spanish couple on the *Titanic* were indeed the Peñascos, and printed it in the local papers, much to the horror of their families who, postcards in hand, tried to believe it was a grisly mistake. Only Victor's mother had a haunting feeling that what the papers printed might hold some truth. For on the night of the tragedy, as she sat eating in her palatial dining room, a fly had fallen from the ceiling and landed in her soup. Looking up she had said, 'Something is the matter with Victor.' The Spanish Embassy in London soon confirmed her worst fears.

The Premier of Spain, Pepita's uncle, arranged to have her met on the *Carpathia* by the Ambassador of Uruguay and whisked to the Waldorf-Astoria Hotel to await further news. Her father, Manuel Perez de Soto y Tova, hurried to New York to be by her side. Tired of hearing nothing he and Fermina journeyed to Halifax to view the bodies, hoping to find his son-in-law's among them. Walking along row after gruesome row of victims' remains laid out for identification, Señor de Soto y Tova and Fermina could not find him.

Pepita's father was concerned with his daughter and her grief, but had another vital reason to find his son-in-law. Spanish law dictated that there must be a body for a person to be declared officially deceased. Without one, death was not official for 20 years. Pepita would have to wait until she was 37 to inherit from Victor's estate, and remarriage was out of the question. Something had to be done.

With the consent of Señora Purificacion, money changed hands and a body magically appeared under the name Peñasco in the Fifth Folio of the Halifax death certificates, attested to by the Vice Counsel of Spain in Canada. Señor Victor was officially buried in Fairview Cemetery and Pepita returned to Madrid one of the *Titanic*'s many widows.

After six years of mourning, Pepita married Baron de Rio Tovia, a man of many titles, had two sons and a daughter and lived the life of a wealthy and connected Spanish matron. Fermina, who never married, remained with

Pepita in later years. (Courtesy of Carles Bonet i Corbalan)

Pepita for a time, then retired to live with her sister, supporting herself by dressmaking. Life during the Spanish Civil War was very difficult and the sisters were forced to take in boarders, but they survived and remained together in that house for 46 years.

In 1962 a reporter found them there. He reported that getting an interview with Fermina was as difficult as getting a place in one of *Titanic*'s lifeboats, but he finally gained entrance. Then aged 92, she was thin, tall and agile with lively eyes behind glasses with nickel supports, and during the interview kept her hands busy with sewing. She told of those last minutes on deck as she dashed around trying to find Señor Victor for Señora Pepita and remembered that as the lifeboat was descending people were jumping in. She was terrified and turned her head away from the sight of the sinking ship but heard a loud noise 'as if a mountain went down'. When she turned back the ship was gone as if swallowed down 'a mysterious throat'. One of Fermina's prize possessions was the radio she was given as a guest of honour at the premiere of *A Night To Remember*. Seven years after the interview, at the age of 99, she died in her sleep.

Victor Peñasco y Castellana
24 October 1887–15 April 1912

Maria Josefa 'Pepita' Perez de Soto Vallejo
  Peñasco y Castellana
3 September 1889–3 April 1972

Fermina Oliva y Ocaña
12 October 1872–28 May 1969

Noëlle, Countess of Rothes (27)

'Grip Fast.'

WAY BACK IN THE 11TH CENTURY a dashing Hungarian knight named Barthoff distinguished himself in the service of the King of Scotland. As a reward the king bestowed upon him the title of Chamberlain and a substantial piece of land between a 'lesseley' (grassland) and the sea, and said, 'Lord Lessley shalt thou be and thy heirs after thee.' Now every lord needs a coat of arms befitting his station, and Barthoff's was emblazoned with a pair of gloves and the buckles of the belt worn as a symbol of his office.

He was a young Lochinvar, galloping around Scotland taking care of the king's business and acting as protector of the king's wife, Margaret. She was often seen riding behind him holding tightly to his Chamberlain's belt.

One day when the pair was crossing a flooded river, the horse stumbled and Margaret was close to being tossed into the raging current. In fear she cried, 'Gin the buckle bide?' ('Can the buckle hold?'). Barthoff in full manly pride shouted over his shoulder, 'Grip fast, my lady!' and spurred his steed to the safety of the far river bank. The Leslie Clan motto became 'Grip Fast', and remains so to this day. In 1445, Barthoff's descendent George Leslie was made the first Earl of Rothes.

In 1912 the 19th Earl was Norman Evelyn Leslie and his wife and Countess was the lovely Noëlle. Born on Christmas Day 1884, the baby girl was, of course, named Noëlle by her parents, land-owner Thomas Dyer Edwardes and his wife Clementina.

Following the disaster the popular press was absolutely enthralled by the idea of a young, pretty Countess who was not only saved from the disaster, but who had also distinguished herself in the lifeboats by gripping fast to the tiller and steering away. One of the more unscrupulous among them even went so far as to print that the Countess's hair turned from amber to pure white during the night of her ordeal. Hmm …

In April 1912 Noëlle was a young wife travelling from Leslie House, Fife, in Scotland

Noëlle, Countess of Rothes. (Author's collection)

to America to join her husband. Having wed on 19 April 1900, she a mere 16, they were to celebrate their 12th anniversary together. In addition, the Earl wanted to show his Lady what financial possibilities existed in America. He was seriously contemplating the purchase of a citrus farm in Florida to add to the income derived from his properties at home. His was one of the oldest and most respected earldoms in Scotland, but quoting a 1912 newspaper article on the subject:

'The Earldom of Rothes has for two or three centuries been financially embarrassed, the monetary straits dating from the reign of Charles II, while in more recent years the prolific nature of the family has not tended to lighten the load, for the income derived from its property has numerous calls on it in the way of jointures, annuities to younger sons, etc.'

The press, knowing their readers were as enamoured of the exploits of newspaper notables as we are today, were quick to jump on the family motto, Grip Fast, as a title for their articles on the 'plucky little Countess'. Family members denied that this petite, gracious lady was much of a sailor, but she did rally the morale of those in her lifeboat, did 'grip fast' to the tiller and did direct much of the conduct during the long night in Lifeboat 8, much to the admiration of Able Seaman Thomas Jones, who was ostensibly in charge of the boat. He sent her the number from the side of the craft as a token of his esteem and she good-naturedly quoted him as saying, 'I knew you wus a lady, m'm, because you talk so much.' They continued to correspond every Christmas for many years.

This silk necklace with circles of what could be diamonds looks very much like something the Countess might have worn on her slim aristocratic neck.

At one point during that interminable night, the Countess handed the tiller over to her cousin and travelling companion, Gladys Cherry, and slipped down next to the weeping Señora Peñasco, whose grieving for her husband was intolerable. The Countess recalled the incident thus: 'Poor woman! Her sobs tore our hearts and her moans were unspeakable in their sadness.'

Nöelle was met by her husband in New York and they remained in the United States for several months, finally returning home to their two children, Malcom (born 1902) and John (1909), and to their 9,000 acres in Fife. The citrus farm was never purchased.

A leather and velvet compact by Stewart Dawson & Cie.

Continuing the Leslie clan's service to the crown, Leslie House was turned into a military hospital during the First World War and Nöelle's husband served in active duty, twice sustaining severe wounds from which he never fully recovered, dying in early 1927.

Lady Rothes married Colonel Claud Macfie DSO, a big teddy bear of a man, in a quiet ceremony on 22 December 1927, but retained her title of Nöelle, Countess of Rothes. One evening, some years later, they attended a cocktail party and were announced to the assemblage by the butler as Colonel Claud Macfie and the Countess of Rothes. Sir Henry Darlington, a crotchety chap 'older than grim death', as the story was told, piped up loudly from a corner: 'Why the devil don't they just get married.' From then on apparently they were announced as Colonel and Mrs Claud Macfie.

The Countess and the Colonel settled in Fairford, Gloucestershire, near her family seat of Prinknash Park, which had been deeded by her father to a monastery, in whose care it remains today. She actively participated in the social life of the town and gave freely of her time to charities in that small corner of the world. The *Titanic* was not a topic of daily conversation for her, but it lingered in her thoughts. Walter Lord records an incident when she was overcome with a cold terror while dining out with friends. She could not imagine why this was happening until she realised that the orchestra was playing 'The Tales of Hoffman', the last selection played by *Titanic*'s orchestra on the evening of 14 April 1912.

Lady Rothes's family remember her as a petite, gracious lady, very much living the life of an Edwardian matron. In answer to a question concerning his grandmother's pastimes, the 21st Earl wrote:

'It should be remembered that although they [Edwardian women] were "ladies of leisure", they had a lot more to deal with and supervise than we might imagine now. They had a household to run, there were no labour-saving devices and as a result they had to organise the servants and their families as well as their own. Travel, even in this small country, was infinitely more complicated and a great deal slower, so again

The plaque in St Mary's Church, Fairford, Gloucestershire, placed there in Noëlle's memory by her husband, Colonel Claud Macfie. The Leslie coat of arms surrounds the plaque with its symbolic buckles and motto: 'Grip Fast'. (Courtesy of Reverend John Willard, St Mary's Church, Fairford/Graham Young)

took much more organising. Life was lived at a much slower pace because it had to be with nothing like the communications that we have today. They were certainly never bored, indeed they were much better read, better mannered and better educated in the arts and literature than … the present generation.'

Gladys Cherry wrote a letter to Able Seaman Jones in June of 1917 expressing her thanks for his splendid conduct on that night of nights. She wrote:

'The dreadful regret I shall always have, and I know you share with me, is that we ought to have gone back to whom we could pick up; but, if you remember, there was only an American lady, my cousin, self and you who wanted to return … I shall always remember your words: "Ladies, if any of us is saved, remember, I wanted to go back. I would rather drown with them than leave them." You did what you could and being my countryman, I wanted to tell you this.'

There is no account of the Countess ever having sailed again, much less at a tiller to which she would be obliged to grip fast. When she died in 1956, Colonel Macfie, to whom she had been married for 29 years, received special permission from the Bishop to place a plaque in her honour at St Mary's Church, Fairford.

Noëlle Lucy Martha, Countess of Rothes (Mrs Claud Macfie)
25 December 1884–12 September 1956

Gladys Cherry
27 August 1881–4 May 1965

Thomas William Jones
?–1967

Eloise Hughes Smith (18)

'We used to say that Eloise was probably the only woman in the world who in just a year's time made her debut, got engaged, married, survived the Titanic*, became a widow and then a mother.'*
Z. Taylor Vinson, relative

ALL THAT IS TRUE, and more. If Helen Bishop's life was a headline, Eloise Smith's was a soap opera!

Though born in West Virginia, Eloise Hughes spent much of her girlhood in Washington DC where her father, James, was the Republican Congressman to the House of Representatives. The family lived in the Willard Hotel directly across from the White House. Once, as a small girl, Eloise took her sister by the hand and they trundled across Pennsylvania Avenue to visit the President. Theodore Roosevelt graciously received the pair, comfortable in entertaining young people since he had a large brood of his own. He chatted with the two pint-sized Republicans, then sent them back across the street. Eloise had earned her stripes as a Washington insider.

Keen and inquisitive, Eloise attended exclusive Eastern schools followed by a year in Europe being 'finished' in the social graces. In January of 1912 she was presented to Washington society and barely one month later married Lucian Philip Smith, heir to a coal fortune.

Theirs had been a whirlwind romance. Smitten with her picture in the possession of a mutual friend, Lucian had come acourting. What a promising future they had, both from affluent families, both well-educated and well-connected. During their European Grand Tour honeymoon, a must for the wealthy in the early days of the 20th century, Eloise wrote to her parents: 'Lucian is getting so anxious to get home ... We leave here Sunday ... By boat to

Lucian P. Smith. (Courtesy of Catherine Gay/ Elizabeth McLain)

Brindisi, by rail to Nice and Monte Carlo, then to Paris and via Cherbourg either on the *Lusitania* or the new *Titanic* ...' (*The Huntington Quarterly*, Autumn 1997).

On the night of the 14th, Lucian saved his obstinate bride by tricking her into a lifeboat with the words, 'I never expected to ask you to obey, but this is one time you must. It is only a matter of form to have women and children first.' Leaning on the door of their stateroom in an outward show of calm, he munched on an apple and insisted that she dress warmly. But he would not let her delay by retrieving her jewels, calling them trifles. On the way out of the door Eloise did manage to scoop up a flawless diamond he had purchased for her in Amsterdam. With the words 'Keep your hands in your pockets – it is very cold weather,' Lucian sent her off in Lifeboat 6. That night the debutante bride became a widow – a pregnant widow.

This 18-carat gold pocket watch, made by Longines of Paris, survived in almost pristine condition.

On board the *Carpathia* she was consoled by Robert W. Daniel, a wealthy banker, luckier than Lucian. Clad only in his woollen undergarments, with his father's watch around his neck for good luck, Daniel had jumped overboard. After swimming among the ice floes he was picked up by a lifeboat and claimed to have been saved from freezing to death by his strenuous flailing around. Mr Daniel also claimed to have left £600,000/$3,000,000 in securities in his *Titanic* stateroom, but walked down the gangplank from the *Carpathia* with Eloise on his arm.

In full mourning regalia, Eloise returned home to Huntington, West Virginia, and the quiet stares of a thousand people who turned out to see her train arrive at the Chesapeake & Ohio station. Police were needed to escort her safely to her automobile then home to the seclusion of her grandmother's house.

On 12 May she emerged to attend the memorial service for her husband in the same church in which they had been married a scant three months before. Shortly thereafter she testified before the United States Senate Investigation into the causes of the wreck; she refrained from speaking of Bruce Ismay, but she was quick to condemn him to the press, claiming that the instant he reached the *Carpathia* he said, 'I'm Ismay. I'm Ismay. Get me a stateroom', leaving women to sleep on the floor. The *Wheeling Register* carried a banner

headline that screamed 'Congressman Hughes' Daughter Has Only Words of Scorn For The Creature Ismay, Who Lived While Hundreds Died'.

Eloise gave birth to Lucian Smith Junior on 29 November 1912 and slowly re-entered society. Robert Daniel began to call in January of 1914 and asked for her hand in marriage shortly before little Lucian's first birthday. Congressman Hughes was not at all happy about the request, but finally granted permission provided the engagement be kept secret. He was aiding his daughter with a law suit against her late husband's family, seeking child support, and it

Eloise with Lucian Junior. (Courtesy of Catherine Gay/Elizabeth McLain)

would not have been wise for Eloise to remarry in the process. Ultimately it did not matter, as the lawsuit was dropped; Lucian Senior supposedly had no money of his own and had lived off a family stipend.

On 18 August 1914 Eloise became Mrs Robert Daniel in a private ceremony in New York's famous Little Church Around the Corner. Daniel was leaving to check on his European investments and the couple agreed to keep their nuptials a secret until his return two weeks later. Due to the First World War and the number of Americans fleeing the continent, he could not book a return passage for two months, and Eloise was forced to keep her secret until then.

The Daniels moved to a home called Rosemont in Philadelphia and Robert became a surrogate father to Lucian. Eloise was active in the Red Cross, raising money for the war effort, and put her considerable speaking talents and political expertise into the campaign for women's suffrage. The marriage, however, did not live up to the rosy name of their residence, and Eloise and Robert separated as early as 1918, divorcing in 1923 when Eloise found her husband cohabiting in New York City with an attractive blonde.

Two serious surgeries and two marriages behind her, Eloise's third husband was Captain Lewis H. Cort, a handsome Virginia war veteran. While at their winter home in San Diego, California, in 1924 Eloise added another episode to her 'soap opera' life. One night, tucked safely away in their bedroom, she and Lewis were drugged by an intruder and robbed of £2,000/$10,000 in jewels. As Eloise struggled to consciousness she saw the thief escaping over the balcony with Lucian's diamond, the one she had saved from the *Titanic*. Due to war injuries Lewis Cort was unwell for the duration of their marriage and died in November of 1929. Eloise was only 36 and alone again.

Eloise with Robert Daniel, Lucian Junior and a prize French bulldog similar to the one lost on the Titanic. (Courtesy of Catherine Gay/Elizabeth McLain)

Robert Daniel and Lucian Smith Junior in matching First World War uniforms. (Courtesy of Catherine Gay/Elizabeth McLain)

Husband number four was C. S. Wright, the State Auditor of West Virginia, but that union, too, soon ended in divorce. With that Eloise dropped all recognition of previous marriages and took back the name Smith, the name of her only child and of the man who, it is said by her granddaughters, was her one true love. For the last ten years of her life Eloise lived in Huntington with her mother, dabbled in politics and researched the *Titanic* with thoughts of writing a book. She died of heart failure in a Cincinnati, Ohio, sanatorium in 1940 at the age of 46, after more than one lifetime.

Lucian P. Smith Junior was in many regards a *Titanic* survivor himself, having grown up in the shadow of his mother's grief over the loss of his father. He could only discuss the tragedy with great difficulty and then with tears in his eyes. In April 1966, almost 54 years to the day since the sinking, Lucian Junior had an experience eerily akin to that suffered by his parents on the *Titanic*. He, his wife and their two daughters were cruising the Caribbean when the ship caught fire. Hearing those tormenting words 'Women and children first', Lucian put his family in a lifeboat and stood back with the men. The evacuation effort was, however, well organised and all were saved, but it brought his family's tragedy surging back.

Robert Daniel loved French bulldogs and was bringing one back with him on the Titanic; *he had insured it for $750.00. In the early 1900s, learning that these bat-eared little animals were a favourite with the French 'Belles de Nuit', the international set adopted them as a fashion to illustrate how avant-garde they were.*

During the ups and downs of his mother's life Lucian always knew that he was her one constant. On his 21st birthday she wrote to him: 'Twenty-one years ago, I was waiting for you. When you did put in an appearance, you were the loveliest thing on earth. You were so adorable and such a gift from God to assuage all my grief and sorrow in those few seconds.'

Lucian Philip Smith
14 August 1887–15 April 1912

Eloise Hughes Smith
7 August 1893–3 May 1940

Lucian Philip Smith Junior
29 November 1912–24 October 1971

Robert Williams Daniel
1885–December 1940

Charlotte Drake Cardeza (58)

'For my part, I travel not to go anywhere, but to go.'
Robert Louis Stevenson

THIS IS THE LADY of the 14 trunks, numerous suitcases, three packing crates, two servants and a son by her side, who had taken the most expensive suite on the vessel, B51–53–55, with the servant room B101. These accommodations (depicted in the 1997 Cameron film *Titanic*) had the amenities of a small apartment, with two bedrooms, a wardrobe room, a sitting room, a bath and a 50-foot private promenade – all for the off-season rate of £660/$3,300. Her subsequent claim against the White Star Line of £35,470 11s 0d/$177,352.75 was the highest of any passenger, and the labels read like a who's who of the 1912 fashion and jewellery world.

Scanning down the list, the most expensive dress, at £180/$900, is a green and black lace example by Worth of Paris; the most interesting, a rose gown by Madame Lucile valued at a paltry £60/$350. (By comparison, Second Class passenger Jane Quick's entire

Charlotte Cardeza. (Courtesy of Cardeza Foundation, Thomas Jefferson University)

summer wardrobe was valued at £10/$50.) After all, Charlotte was travelling for protracted periods, so needed to be prepared for any climate and situation; she therefore also had 84 pairs of gloves, 32 pairs of shoes (in their own Louis Vuitton shoe trunk) and a £60/$300 white-lace-embroidered umbrella. To throw over it all she carried seal, ermine, chinchilla, silver fox, mink and white baby lamb coats. Her most expensive baubles were from Tiffany: a £2,800/$14,000 Burma ruby and diamond ring and a pink 7-carat diamond with the value of £4,000/$20,000.

But clothes alone do not the woman make. Charlotte's father, Thomas Drake, emigrated to America from Leeds, England, in 1829. Eventually settling in Philadelphia, he opened woollen mills producing hard-to-find print fabrics and pioneered the manufacturing of jean fabric. Soon he was manufacturing the jeans themselves under the trademark 'Kentucky Blue Jeans', and his wealth was secured. The United States Civil War found him in the propitious position of cloth supplier for the Union Army's uniforms, and from there he went on to increase his fortune by investments in real estate and banking.

Upon his death in 1890, Charlotte, his only surviving child, inherited millions and Montebello, a vast walled mansion in Germantown, Pennsylvania. It was a square block of turrets, gardens and splendour, but which she considered only her summer home, much preferring to globe-trot on her ocean-going yacht, the *Eleanor*. This vessel was, for its size, as luxurious and technologically advanced as *Titanic*, and could sleep 16 comfortably. On it she circumnavigated the globe several times, often eschewing the crew of 39 to navigate herself into exotic ports on every continent, except South America for some inexplicable reason.

Charlotte combined this rough-and-tumble life of outdoor pursuits with a love of opera and art, attending gala events with an armed guard to watch over the jewels she had chosen for the occasion. But again, to concentrate only on her appearance would be to sell her short, for according to one of her long-time associates, Dr Joseph Ullmon, she had a '... wonderful mind, a splendid knowledge of literature, was conversant with the best in music and art ... perhaps the most outstanding characteristic was her kindness, particularly to the poor and those in trouble.' She quietly gave boundless amounts of money to the needy.

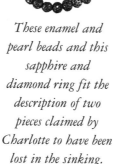

These enamel and pearl beads and this sapphire and diamond ring fit the description of two pieces claimed by Charlotte to have been lost in the sinking.

In 1874 Charlotte married James Warburton Martinez Cardeza, the grandson of a Portuguese Count, and in 1875 gave birth to her only child, Thomas. This marriage was not to last as James had a mistress (as was the tradition in his family, he himself being the progeny of such a liaison), and an illegitimate child. Charlotte, strong-willed and obviously not needing either his financial protection or his aggravation, divorced him and with her son took up in earnest the life of world traveller.

Mother and son were a strange combination of big game hunters and animal protectors. They bagged tigers, lions and wild boar on safari in India, Africa and the Orient, and Charlotte was known as the best female hunter in America; her various residences were adorned with stuffed examples of her expertise. But the Cardezas also maintained a small zoo at Montebello where animals roamed in a protected environment and where Thomas worked on breeding and protecting the fast-disappearing American buffalo.

In 1912 they had been on safari in Africa, also visiting Thomas's palatial hunting schloss in Hungary to see his wife, Mary. Charlotte and Mary had a tenuous relationship at best, not only because Mary's marriage to Thomas had been a secret one, of which Charlotte had learned from the *New York Times*, but also because both ladies were strong-willed and vying for Thomas's attention.

Charlotte had won this last round by persuading Thomas to return with her on the *Titanic*, since he was suffering from ill health and needed a visit to his American physicians. When the call came for women and children, Charlotte convinced those doing the calling

Charlotte Cardeza on her exotic travels around the globe. (Courtesy of Cardeza Foundation, Thomas Jefferson University)

that her son was ill and must accompany her into the lifeboat, which he did followed by his valet, a perfectly able-bodied individual named Gustave Lesnauer, and Charlotte's maid, Annie Ward. (Annie had terrible misgivings about the trip from the beginning, and subsequently refused to travel with her mistress after the sinking. She married William Moynahan, the Cardeza gardener, and stayed at home.)

Elizabeth Shutes, an articulate First Class survivor, may be referring to Thomas and Gustave when she wrote:

'… Two rough-looking men had jumped into our boat as we were about to lower, and they kept striking matches, lighting cigars, until I feared we would have no matches left and might need them, so I asked them not to use any more, but they kept on. I do not know what they looked like. It was too dark to distinguish features clearly, and when the dawn brought the light it brought something so wonderful with it that no one looked at anything or anyone else … The stars slowly disappeared, and in their place came a faint pink glow of another day. Then I heard, "A light, a ship …"'

Also in Lifeboat 3 with the Cardezas were the Speddens – Margaretta (Daisy), Frederic, and their six-year-old son, Robert. (The Spedden family account is told in the book *Polar The Titanic Bear*.) Mrs Spedden kept a diary of that night and it is the consensus of historians that she is referring to Charlotte Cardeza in the following passage:

'One fat woman in our boat had been a handful all along for she never stopped talking and telling the sailors what to do. And she imbibed from her brandy flask frequently, never offering a drop to anyone else … As we approached the ship [*Carpathia*] "our woman"

The number 3 from the lifeboat in which Charlotte and her son, Thomas, left the Titanic. *Above the number is a receipt for a Marconigram of 14 words that Charlotte sent on 10 April. Below is a receipt for 195 francs that Charlotte paid to transport her excess baggage from Paris to Cherbourg. (Courtesy of Cardeza Foundation, Thomas Jefferson University)*

promptly sprang up in order to get off first, when we had been warned to sit still, and it gave me the greatest satisfaction to grab her by her lifebelt and drag her down. She fell in the bottom of the boat with her heels in the air and was furious because we held her there till we were alongside the *Carpathia* when we were charmed to let her go up in the sling first.'

Charlotte kept to her peripatetic ways, only settling down at Montebello in the late 1930s when her health began to fail. When she died in 1939 she was very generous in her bequests: the Philadelphia Museum of Art received paintings by Rubens, Van Dyck, Holbein and Goya; daughter-in-law Mary, of whom she had grown fond, was bequeathed furs, clothing and a painting; and Annie Ward and her family were provided for quite generously with yearly stipends for as long as they lived. The residue of the estate was left in trust to her son Thomas, as

her father had left it in trust to her. With it Thomas and his wife Mary endowed the Charlotte Drake Cardeza Foundation at Thomas Jefferson University, its mandate to research diseases of the blood, which work it continues to this day.

Montebello was later sold to make way for an apartment block, and all the wondrous treasures that Charlotte had acquired during her travels were sent back out into the world.

Charlotte Drake Martinez Cardeza
10 April 1854–2 August 1939

Thomas Drake Cardeza
10 May 1875–6 June 1952

Annie Ward Moynahan
1 August 1876–25 December 1955

Edith L. Rosenbaum (Russell) (33)

'I'm accident prone ... I've had every disaster but bubonic plague and a husband.'
Edith Russell

EDITH MAY HAVE HAD every disaster, but she survived them in high style, and style she had in abundance. She was one of those self-sufficient women in First Class who, as a fashion correspondent, flitted back and forth across the Atlantic as though it were a Venetian lagoon; she was as comfortable in Paris and London as in New York or Cincinnati, Ohio, the town of her birth.

In the summer of 1911 she was motoring with friends through France to cover the fashions at the Deauville races for *Women's Wear Daily* and the *New York Herald* when the automobile crashed into a tree (which seems to

Edith and 'Maxixe'. (Private collection)

be a theme amongst *Titanic*'s passengers — Bishop, Ryerson, Hippach and Russell). That particular stretch of road was dubbed the 'Hill of Death' and Edith's companion, a Berliner called Ludwig Loewe, did indeed meet with his. Edith was lucky to be thrown into the tyre strapped to the back of the vehicle and survived, albeit 'severely shaken up'. The event was so traumatic that it erased itself completely from her memory.

Edith's mother, perhaps anticipating her daughter's penchant for disaster, and having heard that pigs are a good luck symbol in France, soon thereafter gave her daughter a small replica of one as a mascot, making Edith promise never to 'leave home without it'. Now this was no ordinary pig. It was adorned with white and black fur and, when its curly tail was wound, it played 'La Maxixe', a current popular tune. Edith had it with her when she boarded *Titanic*'s tender in Cherbourg and placed it on the dresser in her stateroom, A11, as a 'watch-pig'.

She felt particularly uneasy about this journey. It was one of her first attempts as fashion buyer and stylist (she anglicised Rosenbaum to Russell for business purposes) and she was travelling with trunks of valuable couture for her United States clients. When she had tried to insure these not-paid-for treasures, she was told that there was no need — the *Titanic* was unsinkable. Still feeling ill at ease, she made an attempt to leave the ship, but it was too late to retrieve her baggage, so she remained on board.

Edith had originally booked passage on the *George Washington*, but changed her plans when her editor wired her to cover the Easter races at Auteuil, France. There was also gossip that she

Edith might have used a pen similar to this to scribble notes on the fashions at the Deauville races.

This spittoon from one of Titanic's *masculine dens would not have intimated Edith in the least from entering and taking part in the gentlemen's conversation.*

changed vessels to sail with White Star's Managing Director Bruce Ismay, but that was never confirmed. She does, however, mention him frequently in a later account of that night, describing his attire of 'black evening trousers and a nightshirt with frills down the front'. Together with her pig, she credits Ismay with saving her life.

When the alarm was raised it seems that she, like so many others, was reluctant to leave the cosy ship for the uncertainty of the open sea. When she was told to put on a lifebelt and proceed to the boats, she methodically packed and locked every trunk, suitcase, bureau drawer and window in her cabin and went instead to the Saloon, where she lingered in an easy chair watching the goings-on. Seeing her cabin steward, Wareham, she gave him the keys and asked that since there was a likelihood the passengers were to be evacuated and the ship towed to Newfoundland, would he guide her trunks through customs there, then forward them on to New York? His response was, 'You go on and kiss your trunks goodbye.' Sensing that the situation may be more serious than she had thought, Edith sent him to fetch her good-luck pig, eschewing the more valuable items that she had deposited in the purser's safe.

When she finally wandered up to the Boat Deck, Ismay noticed her and said, 'What are you doing on this ship? I thought all women and children had left.' With that he practically threw her back down an iron stairway to A Deck where Lifeboat 11 was picking up more passengers.

Two burly crew members, seeing her reluctance to cross the chasm between the deck and the lifeboat, tried to manhandle her into the craft, in the process ripping one of the diamond buckles from her embroidered velvet slippers. With fashion always a priority, she spent valuable rescue time hunting for it in the gutter of the deck, never finding it, she was quick to lament. She was wearing her only warm dress – a woollen one with a 'hobble skirt' only 18 inches in circumference – and it should be noted for historical accuracy that she was also wearing a light broadtail coat, silk stockings and no underwear, not an ensemble in which to be tossed head first into an open lifeboat suspended high above a deep, dark ocean.

Sensing that a desperate situation might require desperate measures, one of the seamen, perhaps a little hysterical himself and thinking that 'Maxixe' was a baby, grabbed the pig from under her arm and threw it into the lifeboat, saying, 'If you don't want to go, we'll save your baby anyway.'

Edith followed. After all, she had promised her mother. Scrounging around in the bottom of the lifeboat she found the pig with two broken legs and no nose, but, always a trouper, he entertained the terrified children (Marion and Richard Becker and Winnie and Phyllis Quick) all night long with his music. The trauma of that ordeal jogged her memory and all the missing details of the motor accident in France came rushing back to add to her fears of the moment.

On 19 April, *Women's Wear Daily* carried an article by Edith in which she described members of the fashion world who were on the *Titanic*. Even during the tragedy her fashion eye was surveying the crowd, as she noted in the article:

'Lucile, Lady Duff Gordon, made her escape in a very charming lavender bath robe, very beautifully embroidered, together with a very pretty blue veil … we … exchanged compliments about our costumes and

"swapped" style information closely after getting on the *Carpathia*. All her models, as well as my own, had gone to the bottom of the sea, and we both acknowledged that pannier skirts and Robespierre collars were at a discount in mid-ocean when you are looking for a ship to rescue you.'

Edith continued to report on the fashion world and to bring garments into the United States for clients. Her claim to the White Star Line was for £2,913/$14,569.50 plus £400/$2,000 in cash left in the purser's safe. Only receiving 3 cents on the dollar, it took her four years of hard work (and she claims near starvation) to pay back her clients and recoup her losses. And as the First World War began, Edith, who had a tendency to be slightly foolhardy, traded her chapeau for a metal helmet and went into the trenches with the troops, whence she sent back reports to her American readers. Quite possibly

Edith Russell on the set of A Night To Remember *with producer William MacQuitty. (Courtesy of William MacQuitty International Archives)*

she was the first female war correspondent.

William MacQuitty, the producer of the film *A Night to Remember,* said that Edith '... was fearsome in her battle for her existence.' She regarded the *Titanic* as her prize and wanted to design the costumes for his movie, even though the studio had provided hundreds of professionals to do that job. It was her contention that she had been there, after all, and they had not. MacQuitty did use her for technical advice on the shoot and they became friends. As both lived in London, Edith was a regular guest in the MacQuitty home, spending holidays with them until her death in 1975.

'Maxixe' was left to Walter Lord and resides in a comfortable case in his living room in New York. People still ask to touch him for good luck.

Edith L. Rosenbaum (Russell)
12 June 1877–4 April 1975

Emily Ryerson. (Courtesy of Phyllis Ryerse)

Emily Maria Borie Ryerson (48)
Suzette Ryerson (21)
Emily Borie Ryerson (18)
John Ryerson (13)

'Swim'st thou in wealth, yet sink'st in thine own tears?'
Thomas Dekker

EMILY BORIE set her cap on being somebody early on. She was one of seven children and, although her family had impeccable social credentials dating back to the signing of the United States Declaration of Independence, they were short of money. There were three girls amongst the seven, and new clothing was always in short supply. One winter's evening, while dressing for a very important ball in their home town of Philadelphia, the sisters realised that they only had one proper coat. But that was not going to present an obstacle: when their carriage arrived at the event, Borie sister number one left the vehicle properly wrapped in 'her' evening coat, climbed the steps to the entrance, graciously greeted the hostess, then repaired to the ladies' cloakroom and passed the coat out the window to sister number two, and so on. Social inventiveness of this nature eventually led Emily to marriage with the highly eligible Arthur Ryerson, a Chicago lawyer and son of Joseph T. Ryerson, founder of the steel company that bore his name until it became a part of Inland Steel in the 1930s.

By 1912 Arthur had retired from day-to-day involvement in the law, and in February he accompanied his wife to Europe with three of their five children, Suzette, Emily and John (Jack). The purpose of the trip was to survey Europe's titled and wealthy young men as

The only surviving photograph of all five Ryerson children: (l to r) Arthur Jr, Emily Borie, Ellen, Suzette and Jack.
(Courtesy of Phyllis Ryerse)

possible suitors for their daughters. Besides Suzette and Emily, the Ryersons had Ellen (17), at home finishing her last year at school, and Arthur Junior, a 21-year-old Yale student.

It is this Arthur who would bring the family to the *Titanic*. With his family away and a long Easter vacation ahead, he had the choice of going to the Ryerson home in Chicago, their mansion in Philadelphia, or their summer home in Cooperstown, New York. All were lonely choices until his friend John Hoffman invited him to Philadelphia as a house guest. The weather turned unseasonably warm for early April and Arthur and John were out in an open car, enjoying their temporary freedom from studies, when the vehicle's tyre hit a rut, the steering wheel jerked out of control and the two

young men were thrown to their deaths.

The Ryersons received the devastating news on 8 April at their hotel in Paris. Cabling back and forth, the funeral was arranged for Friday the 19th in Philadelphia. Following that Arthur's body was to be taken by train to Cooperstown for burial in the family plot near Ringwood, their estate on Lake Otsego. Hasty plans were made to return to the United States on the first ship available, the *Titanic*, which would leave Cherbourg on Wednesday 10 April, getting them to New York on Wednesday the 17th, just in time. Luxury meant nothing to them — only speed. Emily's personal maid, Victorine Chandanson, packed the trunks with the help of the girls and a family friend, Grace Bowen, Jack's travelling tutor.

When they boarded the *Titanic* they were personally greeted by Bruce Ismay, who conveyed his condolences and insisted that they add another stateroom to the two they had already booked, further providing them with a personal steward for their every need. They were given three starboard suites on B Deck (believed to be 57, 59 and 63), which would provide three bedrooms, two baths and four large wardrobe rooms for their clothing. Victorine was given a room of her own nearby, and Miss Bowen stayed with Suzette.

In deep mourning, Emily rarely ventured from this suite, not wishing to endure the well-meaning sympathy of her many friends on board. She was acquainted with most of the

Victorine Chandanson, the Ryersons' French maid. (Courtesy of Phyllis Ryerse)

First Class passengers, many of whom were from Philadelphia, and with Ann Isham, who was the daughter of Arthur's business partner in his Chicago law firm. Late on Sunday afternoon, Marian Thayer, perhaps Emily's closest friend on board, persuaded her to leave the room for a walk in the fresh air. They took the elevator to the Promenade Deck, wandered in the cold and finally stopped to rest on two deckchairs in the pink glow of the setting sun.

Bruce Ismay happened by, very businesslike in his blue serge suit, and, much to Emily's annoyance, took up a position on the end of an adjacent deckchair. In the course of their conversation he waved a Marconigram from the SS *Baltic*, which mentioned their proximity to 'a large quantity of field ice' and that the German oil tanker *Deutschland* was out of coal and out of control. When Emily asked if they were going to aid the distressed vessel, Ismay left her with the impression that the *Titanic* would not do so, and that it was more likely that additional boilers would be fired up that evening and they would arrive in New York earlier than scheduled. (Emily would later testify to this conversation before the United States Inquiry.)

After the collision the Ryersons were in that group of passengers who were shuttled back and forth between the Promenade Deck and the Boat Deck while they waited to board Lifeboat 4. Lightoller had made the decision to lower No 4 from the Promenade Deck, forgetting that there were closed windows on that deck. It took over an hour from the time the boat was uncovered to get the windows opened and the passengers on board. By the time the group, consisting of the Ryersons, Astors, Wideners, Thayers, Carters, Hippachs and the Third Class Asplunds, were allowed to enter, it was 1.55am. The list to port by this time was extremely severe and the distance to the water a mere 20 feet. A chair was placed between the deck and the lifeboat as a makeshift ladder and the women and children were helped to board. Left behind to die were some of the richest and most influential men in the United States.

As the boat was lowered to the sea only two rows of cabin lights were still visible above the water. Emily was stunned into silence as she looked into the remaining staterooms with their gilt furniture, silken draperies and damask walls being consumed by the sinister green seawater. It was only a short time later that the sea finished its meal and the ship disappeared completely, taking with it Arthur Ryerson Senior.

On 22 April Emily, her daughters and Jack (the remaining male Ryerson heir) attended a church service in Philadelphia – now a memorial for two Arthur Ryersons.

Emily assuaged her grief by throwing herself into charity work. In September of 1912 she endowed a Yale scholarship in her son's name to be awarded to young men of promise. During the First World War she was appointed by President Herbert Hoover to work on a fund for the French wounded and fatherless children, and continued her efforts at his request after the war, for which she was awarded the Croix de Guerre. She travelled with the President on his goodwill tour of South America, and in fact spent most of her time abroad. She would come home occasionally to see her growing number of grandchildren, who thought her eccentric and affectionately called her Ri Ti Ti, Chinese for grandmother.

Emily particularly liked the Orient and at the age of 62, while on one of her many trips to Peking, she met and married 45-year-old Forsythe Sherfesee, who was serving as the financial advisor to the Chinese Government, and they made their permanent home in a villa on the French Riviera.

In December 1939 they were in Montevideo, Uruguay, when Emily suffered a fatal heart

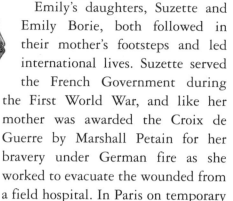

Emily took most of her meals in her room, and may have been served on a tray such as this silver one.

attack. Brought back to the United States on board the *Brazil*, she was buried near her son, Arthur, in the Ryerson family plot overlooking Lake Otsego.

Emily's daughters, Suzette and Emily Borie, both followed in their mother's footsteps and led international lives. Suzette served the French Government during the First World War, and like her mother was awarded the Croix de Guerre by Marshall Petain for her bravery under German fire as she worked to evacuate the wounded from a field hospital. In Paris on temporary leave from the war action, she met and married Lieutenant George Patterson, who served in both the American and French armies and who had also been awarded the same medal of honour. In January 1921, at the age of 30, Suzette underwent an appendectomy, but died from pneumonia following complications. Emily raced to her daughter's side but was too late to say her final goodbyes. Suzette was buried in the family plot near her brother.

Emily Borie, the child who carried her mother's name, married George Clarke, a gentleman farmer, and lived both abroad and in America until they divorced in 1932 after having seven children. She took up residence in the Ryerson family home, Ringwood, married Stephen Cooke of Cooperstown and lived there until she died in 1960.

The youngest Ryerson, Jack, who was 13 at the time of the sinking, accompanied his mother on sorrow-fleeing travels about the globe in those first years after the tragedies in their lives. He stayed home long enough to graduate from Yale in the class of 1921 and spent the rest of his life as an inveterate golfer. His goal was to play more courses than anyone else, and managed to walk the links of 1,400, but lost the title to a man who claimed to have played 3,000.

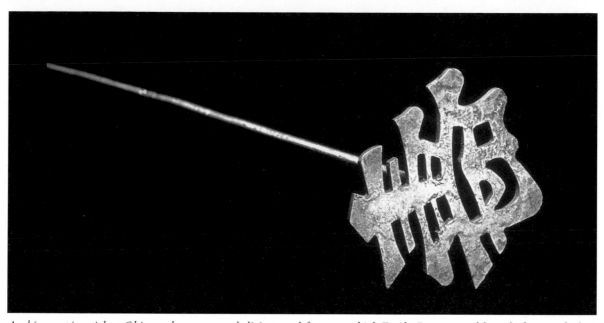

A chignon pin with a Chinese character symbolising good fortune, which Emily Ryerson could easily have picked up on a visit to Peking.

Jack never wanted to speak of the *Titanic*, saying that he had told everything he had to say to Walter Lord and that was that. He married in 1953 at the age of 54 and settled in Palm Beach; when he died he, too, was buried with his siblings and his mother in the family plot.

Victorine Chandanson married Henry Perkins, the Ryersons' chauffeur, and had one son. Pinned to her blouse until the day she died was the Swiss watch she had worn on the night of the sinking, and covering her legs was the navy blue and plaid rug she had taken from the *Titanic* on that fateful night. Grace Bowen continued to teach in private schools in the Cooperstown area, became the godmother to one of Emily's granddaughters, and when she died was buried near the Ryersons in Lakewood Cemetery, from which only Arthur Senior is missing.

Arthur Ryerson Sr
12 January 1851–15 April 1912

Emily Maria Borie Ryerson
10 August 1863–28 December 1939

Suzette Ryerson Patterson
3 August 1890–13 January 1921

Emily Borie Ryerson Cooke
8 October 1893–25 June 1960

John (Jack) Ryerson
16 December 1897–21 January 1986

Victorine Chandanson
1875–13 August 1962

Grace Bowen
9 March 1867–3 May 1945

Eleanor Elkins Widener (50)

'*Yesterday this Day's Madness did prepare;*
Tomorrow's Silence, Triumph, or Despair:
Drink! for know you not whence you came,
*   nor why:*
Drink! for you know not why you go, nor
*   where.*'
Rubáiyát, Omar Khayyám

PHILADELPHIA   SOCIETY   was   well

represented in First Class. They gathered together as if on an English country weekend. One of the wealthiest women in the group was Eleanor Widener, daughter of an American industrialist who had profited handsomely from the growth of the United States and its Civil War. As a butcher, William L. Elkins had taken part in provisioning the Union troops with mutton. Rich from his efforts, he joined forces with Eleanor's future father-in-law, P. A. B. Widener, to invest in trolley car lines just when public transportation was becoming a necessity in America's growing cities. In the right place at the right time, these two entrepreneurs made millions, not only from trolley lines but from a healthy interest in companies run by their friend, J. P. Morgan, whose Oceanic Steam Navigation Company ironically owned the

Harry Elkins Widener. (Michael Findlay collection)

Titanic. In the time before income taxes, Widener and Elkins were able to keep all of the wealth they accumulated, and Eleanor would inherit from both.

After attending one year at Vassar College, she left to marry George Widener, P. A. B's son, on 1 November 1883. The couple lived at the palatial 110-room Lynnewood Hall with George's father and their three children, George Junior, Harry and daughter Eleanor – in keeping with the society tradition of naming children after their parents. And they were a 'high society' family if ever there was one, leading the genteel life of horse shows, charity balls and the relentless pursuit of priceless objets d'art. Harry, the youngest at 27, commented to a friend, 'We are all collectors. My grandfather collects paintings, my mother collects silver and porcelains, Uncle Joe collects everything, and I collect books.' An understatement, as he was a noted bibliophile and had a 3,500-volume collection of rare first editions including all the great writers of the last four centuries.

In 1912 Eleanor and George were preparing to build a mansion on the Cliffs in Newport, Rhode Island, (Astor country) and sailed to Europe on 13 March to buy estate furniture for the project, among other things; accompanying them was Harry. Eleanor purchased items for her daughter's trousseau, George tended to business and Harry went book-shopping, acquiring a 1598 edition of Bacon's *Essaies*. Before taking their leave of London the Wideners attended the opening of the London Museum at which Eleanor presented King George V and Queen Mary with 30 silver plates once belonging to Nell Gwynne, mistress of Charles II.

It was on that now infamous Sunday evening that the Wideners gave the last dinner in the À la Carte Restaurant attended by none other than Captain Smith, Major Archibald Butt (aide to President Taft), John Thayer II, a Vice

President of the Pennsylvania Railroad, with his wife Marian, and beauty Lucile Polk Carter, with her husband William, scion of a coal and iron fortune. No doubt Eleanor's throat was swathed in her famous multi-strand of pearls valued at £150,000/$750,000 and which, by insurance agreement with Lloyd's, she had to keep within her sight during the journey.

China of this design was used in the À la Carte Restaurant and would have graced the table on the Sunday evening when the Wideners gave their famous dinner party.

Later that evening Eleanor would lose both husband and son. Harry ran back to the cabin to retrieve the *Essaies* before he went to his death, and Eleanor sent George for her pearls, which she had forgotten on her cabin's dressing table, before he was to perish as well. The volume of *Essaies* has become part of book-collecting lore, for it was reported that on the day he purchased the book Harry remarked to the seller, 'I think I'll take the little Bacon with me in my pocket, and if I am shipwrecked it will go with me.' And so it did, together with another famous book, the gold and jewelled edition of the *Rubáiyát* of Omar Khayyám being sent to Gabriel Weis of New York who had purchased it at a Sotheby's auction. The book had 1,051 semi-precious stones set in 18-carat gold, 5,000 separate pieces of coloured leathers and 100 square feet of 22-carat gold leaf in the tooling, and was originally valued at £1,000/$5,000 by its makers, Messrs Sangorski and Sutcliffe of London.

Eleanor returned alone to Philadelphia and seclusion to recover from her ordeal, which was similar in many respects to that of Emily Ryerson. But money can give a glorious expression to sorrow and Eleanor began the renovation of St Paul's Episcopal Church near her home as a memorial to her husband, and made plans for the Harry Elkins Widener Memorial Library at Harvard, her son's alma mater. Harry had left his huge book collection to her with the proviso that it be given to Harvard once a suitable location could be found. Eleanor went one step further. She gave the university well over £400,000/$2,000,000 for the project, tore down the old library, hired the architect for the new one, approved the plans and shovelled the first spadeful of soil.

In her conditions for the gift she requested that her son's collection, to which she added substantially over the years, be kept together in one room with its own curator, whose salary she

Illustrations of the lost Rubáiyát *from* The Graphic *of 29 July 1911. To quote the article: 'To find anything to approach it in sumptuousness, one has to go back to medieval days …'* (Author's collection)

put in trust, and that the room always be adorned with fresh flowers 'by the photograph of my dear son Harry'. She further stipulated that no brick or board be altered on the library and no structures of any kind be built in the courtyard surrounding the edifice, or it would revert to the city of Cambridge. In later years, when the library needed to expand, this presented a major problem. The university finally made an underground tunnel to another building by going through a window on a lower floor of the Widener – thus not disturbing a brick of the original structure.

At the dedication of the library in June 1915 Eleanor met Dr Alexander Hamilton Rice, whom she married in October of that year. Dr Rice was a physician and avid explorer and on their wedding trip he took Eleanor on a steam launch, outfitted with research equipment, for a 5,000-mile exploration of South America – the one continent missed by Charlotte Cardeza. They were to return to South America several more times searching for the source of the Orinoco River in an attempt to dispel the myth of a tribe of white Indians who ruled that region. With the blessing of the Brazilian Government, Eleanor studied the women of that country and funded schools for their children.

The Rices travelled and mapped much of unexplored South America and Eleanor penetrated further into the Amazon wilderness than any other white woman had done before. She was particularly interested in finding the mysterious tribe of warlike women who see men only once a year, kill their male children and rule like the Amazons of ancient Greek legends. She never did, but on one trip she was forced to defend herself against an attack of spear-throwing, blow-pipe-wielding cannibals. She returned to civilisation none the worse for

Eleanor Widener Rice with Dr Alexander Rice, and in an open touring car near her summer home in Newport, Rhode island. (Urban Archives, Temple University)

wear, only to die of a heart attack in a Parisian department store in 1937.

George Widener
16 June 1861–15 April 1912

Eleanor Elkins Widener Rice
21 September 1861–13 July 1937

Harry Elkins Widener
3 January 1885–15 April 1912

Ida Blun Straus (63)

'If you had a husband like mine you would do more than this for him.'
Ida Straus

IDA WAS DARNING one of Isidor's socks when a friend asked why a woman of her means would do such a menial task. Ida's reply was, 'If you had a husband like mine you would do more than this for him.' Mending was, however, a minor sacrifice compared with the ultimate one she made on the *Titanic*. That April night Ruth's words from the Old Testament must have guided her: 'Do not urge me to leave you, to turn back and not follow you … Where you die, I will die, and there I will be buried.'

Married in 1874, by 1912 the Strauses had been together for 38 years. Both were emigrants to the United States who believed in and prospered from the American dream. They felt a sincere obligation to give back. Nowhere was this more obvious than in their financial and emotional participation in the Educational Alliance of New York, an organisation that instructed Jewish immigrants in the necessity to be responsible citizens. The Alliance taught vocational training for independence along with American history, geography, and English.

But the Strauses' generosity was not confined to those of their faith, and it has been said that

Ida and Isidor in their younger years. (Straus Family Papers Manuscripts & Archives Section, The New York Public Library)

no worthwhile charity appealed to them in vain, from settlement houses, orphanages and hospitals to New York's firemen and historical preservation societies. Isidor served on his share of boards and banks, owned (with his brother) R. H. Macy's Department Store, counselled President Cleveland, and served in the Congress of the United States in 1894, while Ida confined herself to women's causes. Neither of them believed in luck and felt that success in life came from 'doing the right thing at the right time'.

Paradoxically, this philanthropy, which they extended to all, was not always extended to them in New York social circles. Anti-semitism was a fact of life in the early 1900s and no matter how wealthy or charitable, how kind or educated, the Strauses would have felt its sting. In the personal files of the family, now housed in the New York Public Library, a letter to Isidor Straus, dated 17 November 1909, makes that poignantly clear:

'Dear Mr Straus,
I thank you very much for your letter and I take it as a great compliment that you wish your grandchild to attend St Bernard's.

Though it is most painful to me, it seems only honest to tell you frankly that we dare not take a pupil of Hebrew parentage.

I cannot say anything in extenuation, except that we have reason to know that we should lose our gentile pupils were we to accept Hebrews ... I can only add that the writing of this letter to you gives me real distress.

Yours very sincerely,
Frances H. Tabor'

The Strauses rose above it all and lived within their devotion to each other and to their seven children. When separated, they wrote every day, calling each other Dear Poppa and Darling Mama.

'Sunnyside, Elberon, New Jersey
July 18, 1904

To: As good a wife as ever man was blessed with.

My Darling Mama,
In case I should die before you, I desire to give you a few suggestions for your guidance which may prove very welcome to aid you in what otherwise might be a puzzling proposition with which you may find yourself confronted.

By my will I have made ample provision for all my dear ones ...

You have an ample income, enjoy it; deprive yourself of nothing which can contribute to your comfort and happiness. I know you are fond of doing good, indulge yourself in this enjoyment without stint

These entwined cards accompanied the invitation to the wedding of Ida Blun to Isidor Straus on 12 July 1871. (Straus Family Papers Manuscripts & Archives Section, The New York Public Library)

and if you use up your entire interest it is the best use you can make of it.

Be a little selfish; don't always think of others. You have much left to live for, therefore don't be despairing but look forward to years of happiness with your children and grandchildren and instead of mourning disconsolately over our separation, be thankful for the happiness which was vouchsafed to us so many years. We have had more than our share of the blessings of life, therefore be cheerful and thankful and continue for many years to be the center of attraction to which your children will flock as the foundation of their family blessing.

Your devoted
Isidor'

(From *The Biography of Isidor Straus*, by Sara Straus Hess, 1955)

Ida died, not before but with Isidor on 15 April 1912, hand in hand, taken by the unforgiving North Atlantic. Having come into this world on the same birth date, it is biblically fitting that they should leave it on the same death date. Memorial services were held all over New York, and 40,000 attended one to pay their final respects, crushing a sidewalk with their weight. Mr Straus was praised for his business acumen and nobility, Mrs Straus for all that was brave and beautiful in womanhood. Quiet and unassuming, neither would have been comfortable with this lionising.

Mr and Mrs Straus will forever be entwined with the *Titanic* legend. On 1 May 1912 Isidor's body was taken from the sea by the search ship *Mackay-Bennett* and sent to New York for burial in Woodlawn Cemetery in the Bronx. Ida, his beloved Mama, was never found.

One of the many resolutions received by the children of Ida and Isidor expressing deep grief over the loss of their parents. (Straus Family Papers Manuscripts & Archives Section, The New York Public Library)

Rosalie Ida Blun Straus
6 February 1849–15 April 1912

Isidor Straus
6 February 1845–15 April 1912

PART TWO

SECOND TO SOME

TRAVELLING SECOND CLASS on the *Titanic* was, even by the most exacting standards, a comfortable, luxurious way to cross the Atlantic. Talk among frequent travellers was that Second Class on this White Star leviathan rivalled First Class on other vessels.

Second Class was entered through vibrant stained glass doors on the Boat Deck, aft of the midship entrance for First Class. The golden-oak-panelled vestibule, vaunted by White Star's publicity brochure as one of their ship's most outstanding features, was just a taste of the pleasures to come. From here passengers descended to their cabins via a rather grand staircase, which extended through seven decks of the ship and gave access to all Second Class areas. For the weak of knee or faint of heart, an electric lift, manned by a uniformed cabin boy, occupied the centre of the stairwell.

In the words of one observer, 'Lifts and lounges and libraries are not generally associated in the public mind with Second Class, yet in the *Titanic* all are found.' Due to the same social conventions found in all of the classes, one area, the gentlemen's clubby, beamed-ceiling Smoking Room, was off limits to 'ladies'. A liberated female with a craving for an after dinner cigar would have to sneak her puff behind the closed door of her cabin. More appropriately, she would have been encouraged to stroll with the other women along B Deck's open promenade or in the enclosed C Deck area reserved for those inclement days stirred up by the North Atlantic. On the *Titanic* this sheltered spot was appropriated soon after boarding by the 25 children in Second Class, left to entertain themselves as there were no organised activities on the crossing's agenda. Nannies were not common in this social strata so their mothers would be seated nearby keeping a watchful eye on the activities and the noise level.

Second Class cabins were much the same as standard First Class accommodations except that four instead of three berths occupied the space. Arranged in tandem style along the decks wherever possible, the goal was to provide natural light and air to as many passengers as design permitted. Each cabin was painted an enamelled white and provided seating upholstered in a thick velvety pile, mahogany bunk beds with electric reading lights for cosy evenings in, wardrobes and mirrored washstands.

Who were the Second Class women and their

families making the crossing? Individually they have become overshadowed by the glamour of *Titanic*'s First Class and the pathos of Third. Today we would refer to them as the middle class or bourgeoisie – a growing proportion of the population in Europe and the United States created by the Industrial Revolution with its greater distribution of wealth and diversification of labour. Their presence on the *Titanic* was prompted by a variety of reasons from holidays and business travel to emigration, like their below-stairs neighbours, with hopes of improving their lot even more.

While lacking the advantages of their better-travelled, better-educated upper class counterparts, these middle class women were still a most interesting lot, straddling the conventions and values of the 19th and 20th centuries. On the one hand they were still defined by the Victorian belief in family, religion and hard work, which dictated an almost total investment of their strength and intelligence in looking after their children and their pastor, craftsman, ship's captain or shop-owner spouses. On the other hand, looking through their well-ironed lace curtains, they may well have envied their more liberated middle class sisters who, turning their backs on convention, were tentatively raising their skirts and lengthening their sights on the expanding opportunities for women beyond hearth and home.

It was from these no-nonsense, meat-and-potatoes women that the suffragist movement sprang on both sides of the Atlantic, a movement that ultimately attracted the 'first class' lady and the 'third class' emigrant sweat-shop worker to its ranks in a united campaign for equal rights and freedoms in their not-for-long male-dominated world.

Michel Navratil ('Hoffman')
(32)
Michel Navratil (3)
Edmond Navratil (2)

'Orphans of the Deep.'

NEXT TO THE *Titanic* death of John Jacob Astor IV, no story created more worldwide attention than that of the 'Orphans of the Deep', 'Titanic Tots', or 'Titanic Waifs' as they were dubbed by the popular headlines. The press knew then, as now, what sold papers, and these cherubic boys enthralled readers from coast to coast and country to country. Their story had everything: mystery, mistaken identity, kidnapping, death and a fairy godmother, plus, of course, the toddlers themselves, with their chestnut curls.

When pieced together the story went something like this. Monsieur Navratil, an Austrian-born tailor living in Nice, France, was separated from his wife Marcelle, and divorce proceedings were in progress. Easter Sunday, 7 April 1912, was Navratil's day to visit his sons. Putting a well-thought-out plan into motion, he spirited them out of France, into England and on board the *Titanic* under the alias 'Hoffman', with a loaded revolver in his pocket in case of interference.

'Hoffman' isolated himself and his sons from the other passengers during the crossing, not wanting to explain the whereabouts of the missing mother and wife. Suspicious of everyone, he rarely let the boys out of his sight, sitting near them as they played on the deck, watching over them as they slept. At only one point, when he sought out adult company in a card game, did he allow them to be looked after by Bertha Lehmann, a Swiss woman on her way to Iowa, who shared their dining table and spoke French and German but not English.

His love for these boys was fierce, and no

Michel and Edmond Navratil, the 'Titanic Tots'. (Author's collection)

more so than when he handed them into the arms of strangers in Collapsible D to save their lives. He had wrapped them warmly in blankets against the damp chill, so much so that Edmond ('Momon') lay flat on the deck, swaddled into immobility like a papoose. Lovingly he kissed them goodbye and implored Michel ('Lolo'), the eldest, to convey his love to their mother and to tell her that all along his intention had been for the family to reunite in America. The strangeness and intensity of the situation and the anxiety provoked by the parting from yet another parent embedded the message in young Michel's memory, together with the fried eggs he had eaten one breakfast as through the dining saloon window he watched the ocean go by.

As Lightoller gave the order to lower away, Hoffman gave the boat a final salute and watched until it rowed out of sight, his face contorted in grief. It was then after 2am, and if he had looked to his right he would have seen water covering the ship's bow and creeping steadily toward the forward mast, and would have known that the rest of his life could be measured in minutes.

Perhaps he did love Marcelle, and in the certain knowledge of his death finally recognised it. In the real world, however, the couple had had a stormy relationship. There were so many reasons: he was 27 when they married, she perhaps as young as 15; he was Slavic, she Italian; he was methodical, she mercurial; and there was Marcelle's mother, who cared for the boys while her daughter supplemented the family income as a seamstress. Day by day she systematically undermined her son-in-law's standing in the household. It was an untenable situation and splintered the marriage.

At the end of the Easter weekend Marcelle went to collect her sons from their father, but they were nowhere to be found. Her desperate search began, but never in her wildest imagination or worst nightmare did she think that her search would take her to New York and make her name a household word on two continents.

Through this ordeal of being whisked away from their mother, then being awakened in the middle of the night to be given to strangers by their father, the tiny boys had each other for comfort — until they were hoisted in separate sacks to the *Carpathia*'s deck. Speaking barely understandable toddler French and with no identification, they were taken into the willing

Playing cards from the luggage of one of Michel Navratil's fellow passengers.

arms of different passengers — one to First Class and one to Third. Traumatised, they sobbed for each other until reunited with the aid of passengers Madame Laroche and Madame Mallet, who identified the 'Titanic Tots' with the only name by which they knew them — Hoffman. Enter the story's fairy godmother, New Yorker Margaret Hays.

Some of the *Titanic*'s more domineering passengers formed themselves into a committee on board the *Carpathia*, their goal to aid the more distressed passengers, send cables on their behalf and pledge funds for their use upon arrival in America. Margaret, who had been educated in Paris and spoke fluent French, approached the committee on behalf of the Hoffman children concerned that they might be taken to a welfare agency in New York and separated for ever. She was travelling alone, had not experienced a personal loss and was emotionally and financially able to take the boys into her home until their family could be located. The committee agreed.

She noticed that the boys looked Mediterranean and spoke with an accent from that region. When she reached New York she contacted the French Consul-General, Monsieur Lancel, whose office was the clearing house for the French citizens on the *Titanic*. He visited her and concurred with her assessment. Lawrence Beesley, a Second Class passenger who had seen the boys playing on deck, also visited Margaret and confirmed that the boys were the Hoffmans, as did Julian Pedro, who had the table next to them in the dining saloon. Pedro described Hoffman as a rather handsome man of 40, 5 feet 6 inches tall with a ruddy face, dark moustache and hair, who looked either English or French.

The White Star ticket agencies were canvassed and it was soon discovered that a man fitting this description named Hoffman representing himself as a German antiques dealer, had purchased tickets for himself and two children on the *Titanic* in March at the Thomas Cook offices in Monte Carlo. The net was closing. Right father, wrong name.

During Monsieur Lancel's visit he interviewed the boys and to put them at ease talked casually about their Easter. Lolo eagerly told of a feathered chicken he had received, which had laid a real egg. When pressed further, Lolo coyly admitted that the egg was only chocolate. That story, cabled around the world, was read by their distraught mother in Nice.

The pieces came together. She had given her two sons Easter chickens, which had delighted them by laying chocolate eggs. Her husband had a friend named Hoffman. Knowing that Hoffman was not on a voyage, Marcelle immediately sent a picture of her errant husband, Michel Navratil, to Monte Carlo, where he was identified as the ticket-purchasing Hoffman. Elated, she forwarded a complete description of the children to Miss Hays through the Paris Bureau of the *New York Herald*, confirming that she was their mother. That settled, the White Star Line gave her passage to New York on the *Oceanic*.

If there were any lingering doubts about the waifs' parentage, they were obliterated when the children raced sobbing into Marcelle's outstretched arms. Reunited, they returned to Nice, passing out of the public's consciousness, but not before a few more stories in the press. In the *New York Evening Journal* columnist Dorothy Dix lamented the boys' return to their 'poor' mother when they could have been adopted into a better life by a 'rich' American. She suggested strongly that Madame Navratil was being selfish by forcing her sons to grow up with little education and few advantages. These biases were no doubt Miss Dix's own, but they also mirrored the

First Class passenger Margaret Hays took the parentless boys into her home while the search for their identity went on. (Michael Findlay collection)

prejudice of the era against 'Italian' types.

Despite Miss Dix's predictions of doom, Michel became a scholar and teacher of philosophy. In 1952 he received his doctorate and served as a Professor of Philosophy at the University of Montpellier until he retired in 1969. In 1970 his wife of 33 years, also a student of philosophy, died, followed by his mother in 1974. His comfort for the loss of these two important women in his life came from his own children, all of whom had followed in their father's scholarly ways; his son was a doctor of urology, one of his daughters a psychoanalyst and the other a German translator and music critic. Take that, Miss Dix!

Titanic Waifs in Poverty, Mother Sues for $30,000

MOTHER AND WAIFS FROM THE TITANIC

(Author's collection)

Edmond also prospered, married and lived in Lourdes, where he was a builder and architect before the outbreak of the Second World War. He volunteered for active duty and was sent to the bloody combat zone in northern France. Under the German occupation, Edmond – who is rooted in our memories as that round-faced two-year-old – was captured and interred as a prisoner of war. He escaped, but never recovered from his ordeal, dying in 1953 at the age of 43.

Although Michel never forgot his father's final words, most details of that night remained vague. In 1996 he tried to recapture some of what he had lost by joining the RMS Titanic Inc expedition to the disaster site. Part of the trip included a stop in Nova Scotia and a visit to his father's grave. The body of 'Hoffman' had been picked up by the search ship *Mackay-*

Bennett with the revolver and his ticket still in his pocket, and had mistakenly been buried in the Hebrew Cemetery in Halifax when the White Star officials assumed from his name that he was Jewish. When the truth was revealed, the offer was made to remove his remains to the Catholic cemetery, but Marcelle requested that his body not be disturbed.

No member of the family had ever visited his grave until his namesake, now 88 years old, came to pay his final farewell. All those years the senior Navratil had not been ignored, however. Following the Jewish tradition, many visitors had honoured his memory by leaving stones on his marker to signify their having stopped to pay their respects.

Michel Navratil
1880–15 April 1912

Michel Marcel Navratil
12 June 1908–

Edmond Roger Navratil
January 1910–1953

Margaret Bechstein Hays Easton
6 December 1887–21 August 1956

Juliette Laroche (22)
Simonne Laroche (3)
Louise Laroche (1)

'The way in which people behave is all of a piece, their virtues and their sins, the way they slap the baby, handle their court cases, and bury their dead.'
Margaret Mead, anthropologist

BABY JOSEPH LAROCHE was not on *Titanic*'s passenger list, but Juliette was pregnant with him at the time. This places him in a peculiar hall of fame with John Jacob Astor

VI, Lucian Smith Jr, Randall Bishop and Betty Phillips Walker, to name a few. For several months Juliette Laroche and her husband Joseph had been discussing the benefits of moving from Villejuif, France, to Haiti, Joseph's country of origin. It was a great disappointment to him that having earned his engineering degree in France he could not find employment there. No matter how qualified he was, the blackness of his skin kept him from securing a position that paid his worth.

The pregnancy, confirmed in March of 1912, hastened their decision to make the journey before it became too difficult for Juliette to travel. Joseph's mother was so pleased that they were coming to Haiti that she prepaid their tickets as a homecoming gift on the French liner *La France* out of Le Havre. Juliette made preparations to leave, which was difficult because her father was a widower and she knew he would miss them terribly. During the months when Joseph had been unable to find work, Juliette's father had used his wine business to support them. But Juliette respected Joseph for wanting to care for his own family, and that would be easier in Haiti, especially since his uncle was the President of the Republic. The Laroche family had been prosperous on this West Indian island ever since the 17th century, when a French nobleman named Laroche, on military duty, married a Haitian girl.

It is strange that nowhere in the copious 1912 press descriptions of the ship and the interviews with the survivors was the presence of a black family among the passengers ever mentioned; indeed, this information has come to light only recently through the efforts of French researcher Olivier Mendez. It seems doubly strange in view of the keenness of the passengers and crew to take pot shots at other ethnic groups. This was done to such an extent that the White Star Line was forced to apologise for the derogatory statements made by *Titanic*'s crew about the 'Italians' (a generic term for all the darker-skinned passengers) and their behaviour during the last moments on the dying ship. Laroche must have escaped their vitriol and prejudice by acquitting himself at all times like the gentleman he was brought up to be. The only known mention of Simonne and Louise Laroche was made by Kate Buss in a letter home: 'There are two of the finest little Jap[anese] baby girls, about three or four years old, who look like dolls running about.'

Just prior to their departure, the Laroches learned that *La France* would not allow children to dine with their parents. Not wanting to separate the family and make the journey more unsettling for the girls, Joseph and Juliette returned their tickets and bought a passage on the *Titanic*. On the boat train from Paris to

The Laroche family in 1911. Simonne is standing on the chair and Louise sits on her father's knee. (Laroche/Mendez collection)

Cherbourg they met the Mallet family: Albert, Antoinette and two-year-old André. As the children played, their parents struck up a conversation; they shared destinations (the Mallets were off to Montreal where Albert was to sell French cognac), and continued their acquaintance on the tender *Nomadic*. All were a bit melancholy when at 5.30pm, with a blast from her whistle, the *Nomadic* headed towards the *Titanic* at anchor off the Grande Rade, to the strains of 'La Marseillaise'.

Monsieur Laroche spoke English as well as his native French, so on Sunday night he was quickly aware of the need to place Juliette and the girls in a lifeboat. Monsieur Mallet was doing the same with his wife and son. Both men were lost, but the women and children are believed to have left the ship in Lifeboat 10, launched from the port side at 1.20am. The following excerpts from the United States investigation testimony, reprinted in *The Truth About the Titanic* by Archibald Gracie, shed interesting light on the loading of this particular boat:

'Seaman F. O. Evans: "A young ship's baker (Joughin) was getting the children and chucking them into the boat. Mr Murdoch and the baker made the women jump across into the boat about two feet and a half. He threw them on to the women and he was catching children by their dresses and chucking them in. One woman in a black dress slipped and fell. She seemed nervous and did not like to jump at first. When she did jump she did not go far enough, but fell between the ship and the boat. She was pulled in by some men on the deck below, went up to

Juliette may well have been bringing her mother-in-law in Haiti a gift of French parfum like the one represented by this medallion from a bottle of La Rose France by Houbigant.

The Laroches chose to travel on the Titanic *rather than on a French liner so that their daughters could join them in the Dining Saloon. This blue and white dish in the Blue Delft pattern, still made by Royal Doulton today, was used in* Titanic's *Second Class.*

the Boat Deck again, took another jump, and landed safely in the boat … The only man passenger was a foreigner, up forward. He, as the boat was being lowered, jumped from A Deck into the boat …'

Juliette and Antoinette shared their sorrow on the *Carpathia* and reached out to the 'Hoffman' children who were parentless and frightened. They had another problem – there were not enough nappies (diapers) for the babies. Juliette handled the situation by hiding dinner napkins from the stewards by sitting on them until the meal was over, when they could be used where they were more urgently needed.

When they arrived in New York the Laroches and Mallets were taken to St Vincent's Hospital where their medical needs were looked after, especially Juliette's frozen feet. But this did nothing for their financial worries as two single mothers, destitute in a foreign country. After they posed for a photograph at the hospital with other French-speaking passengers, they said goodbye to each other, not to meet again for several years.

Fortunately, New York opened its hearts and pocketbooks to the survivors and the Laroches were taken under the charity wing of a Mrs Hugh Kelly, who moved them to the Lafayette Menhoff Hotel and provided money for food and clothing until Juliette could decide her family's future. Determining that a life in Haiti was out of the question now without Joseph, she returned with her daughters to France (on a French liner this time, the *Chicago*) and to her father's house in Villejuif.

The French-speaking passengers at St Vincent's Hospital. Standing are Matilde Weiss and Bertha Lehman. Seated from left are Antoinette Mallet with André, Simonne, Juliette and Louise Laroche. (Author's collection)

On 17 December 1912 Joseph Lemercier Laroche entered the world, none the worse for his travels or for the trauma his mother experienced. Grandpère Lafargue did the best he could, but his wine business declined when war erupted in Europe. He encouraged Juliette to sue the White Star Line for the damages that were rightfully hers, but unfortunately the case was filed too late. Lawyers came and went, no settlement arrived and Juliette with her three children lived in poverty through the First World War. Ultimately, in 1918 the White Star advocate Alexandre Millerand, who would become President of France in 1920, decreed that she would receive 150,000 francs. Six years after the death of her husband she could finally provide for the future of her children. She opened a fabric-dyeing business in a room of their small home. Hard work, yes, but it supported the family.

Occasionally Juliette would receive visits from Antoinette Mallet and André, who had returned to Paris to live with in-laws. But these visits ceased when Madame Mallet became Madame Rodomanowski in 1918. Not wishing to speak with anyone else of her *Titanic* nightmare, Juliette resolutely refused to grant interviews or to discuss it further. But when fellow survivor Edith Russell came to town and invited her and the girls to visit her at her fashionable Champs-Elysées hotel, the temptation was too great. Edith, though American, spoke fluent French and they got along famously. For many years thereafter on 15 April Edith would send perfume or chocolates to Juliette to commemorate not the sinking, but their friendship.

Louise and Simonne Laroche in their Grandfather Lafargue's garden in France after the disaster. (Laroche/Mendez collection)

Juliette, though ill, outlived Simonne by seven years. Haunted always by the *Titanic*, the following words were carved on her tombstone: 'Juliette Laroche, 1889–1980, wife of Joseph Laroche, lost at sea on RMS *Titanic*, April 15th, 1912.'

Baby Joseph grew to be a happy man surrounded by the love of his two sisters and mother. He was allowed the freedom denied his sisters and in 1945 married Claudine, a fellow worker at Electricité de France. They had two boys and a girl and the Laroche line was perpetuated in France where it had begun. He died in 1987, but his wife, Claudine, and his sister, Louise, remained together in the family home.

Louise carried on the tradition of not dwelling on her *Titanic* experiences, but accompanied by Claudine she paid a visit to the tender *Nomadic* in 1995 with French researcher Olivier Mendez. He walked with Louise through the boat pointing out what her family experienced in 1912, she surveying it all with sad eyes. It was an enlightening experience, but one she wished not to repeat. Near the end of the tour Mendez overheard Claudine whisper to Louise, 'Your mother would have liked to see all this.'

'No,' responded Louise. 'It would have been too much for her.'

Joseph Laroche
26 May 1886–15 April 1912

Juliette Lafargue Laroche
20 October 1889–10 July 1980

Simonne Laroche
19 February 1909–8 August 1973

Louise Laroche
2 July 1910–25 January 1998

Joseph Lemercier Laroche
17 December 1912–17 January 1987

The *Titanic* disaster scarred Juliette for ever. Living in silent fear of losing yet another member of her family, she held her daughters close, too close to ever give them the opportunity to marry. Louise gained a measure of autonomy by working as a clerk in the Justice Department, but Simonne never left home. She spent her entire life caring for her mother who, in later years, was completely paralysed on one side of her body. Always the creative one, Simonne took her pleasure from singing and making floral bouquets from the gardens surrounding their home.

Marion Wright (26)
Kate Buss (36)
Elizabeth Watt (40)
Bertha Watt (12)

'All is not lost ...'
Milton

MARION LOOKED THROUGH her kitchen window at the apple trees silhouetted against the distant Cascade Mountains. The smell of their blossoms each spring always brought back memories of her first April in Oregon with Arthur, 20 years before. Since then they had worked side by side to make ends meet and to rear their three sons. And now those sons were off to war – John to the Navy, Russ and Bob to the Air Corps. How lonely it would be when they were gone.

Turning back to the kitchen she knew that she must find something to keep her boys safe, to remind them of home and give them courage until they returned. Suddenly she was struck by an idea. For years her old mulberry woollen coat had lain at the foot of John's bed. It had been used in the lean years as an extra blanket and somehow had never been moved. When she thought of that coat it seemed to have a lucky quality about it. It was the coat that she had been wearing the night she escaped death on the *Titanic,* and the coat she had worn on the day she married Arthur Woolcott. Good things. The reason the boys were here at all.

Marion promptly cut three pieces of fabric from the right panel of the coat and fashioned them into small zippered bags into which she would place New Testaments. With these in their uniform pockets she knew her sons would be safe. Touching the worn fabric, Marion was overcome with memories, mostly of Arthur and their first meeting in England.

She had been visiting a friend in Yeovil, Somerset, when Arthur, her friend's brother, had burst into the room. He was back from America where he had gone in 1907 to find work as a draughtsman. Ending up in Cottage Grove, Oregon, he and a friend had jointly purchased an 80-acre fruit farm, but Arthur now had the opportunity to buy out his partner, so had come home to borrow money to keep the farm on his own.

He was filled with tales of the beauty of the Oregon countryside, how much it looked like

Marion's lucky coat that she wore on the Titanic *and at her wedding, displayed at the Cottage Grove Museum, Cottage Grove, Oregon.* (Author's collection)

England and the opportunities available to him there. But Marion was more enamoured with the man doing the talking than what he was talking about. She had known him slightly before he left, but had never realised how incredibly handsome he was until that day.

Arthur likewise must have thought that Marion had grown up rather well herself, for when he returned to the United States their letters sailed back and forth across the Atlantic. Soon they were engaged and the marriage was planned for a chapel in New York as soon as she arrived. Marion spent the months prior to her departure on the *Titanic* sewing her trousseau.

Second Class appears to have been a congenial mix of passengers; at least the British got along famously, and they were the majority. Marion was placed in a starboard cabin with the Watts from Aberdeen, Scotland. Older and already married, Elizabeth Watt, known as Bessie, was travelling with her 12-year-old daughter, Bertha. They were also on their way to Oregon where Mr Watt, an architect, was prospering from the influx of new settlers and businesses. Marion and Bessie had many notes to compare on their joint destination. Was this cabin arrangement the divine hand of fate or the practised eye of a White Star official accomplished at putting compatible passengers together?

Another British shipboard acquaintance with whom Marion became friendly was Kate Buss. Kate was also to be married in the United States; her fiancé, Samuel G. Willis, formerly of her home town of Sittingbourne, Kent, was waiting for her in San Diego, California. The excitement of it all must have been overwhelming for the two, who, incidentally, each had their own cabins as Second Class was not booked to capacity.

Kate and Marion shared a blanket as they sat in deckchairs looking at the passing sea and dreaming of their futures. Married life would certainly be different. Before the journey Marion had been the caretaker of her three younger stepsisters, while Kate, one of seven children, had earned her keep by working in her brother Percy's grocery store in Upper Halling. Both looked forward to having a home of their own and filling it with their trousseau items tucked away in the baggage hold.

So Marion, Bessie, Kate and young Bertha enjoyed their new friendships and settled into the ship's daily routine. At luncheon the first day Kate met her eight table companions:

'I found myself opposite two clergy, one quite a young foreigner and the other very ugly. I have an end seat. On my left is a mere boy; next [to] him a man whose acquaintance I have since made ... somewhat reduced in circumstances. He is bound for Toronto. Next to him is a lady, opposite her a Kentucky doctor.'

Dr Ernest Moraweck's seat at luncheon was a lucky thing indeed. It just so happened that he was an internationally recognised eye surgeon and Kate had a nasty piece of soot in her eye. In no time at all the soot was removed and the shipboard acquaintance begun. Moraweck, whom Kate called 'Doctor Man' (she nicknamed everyone on the ship – 'Sad Man', 'Cello Man', etc), told her that he was returning to his home in Frankfort, Kentucky. He had been in Vienna and Berlin on medical business and had stopped in The Hague to see a friend before coming to Southampton, almost missing the sailing. Widowed, with no children to encumber him, the doctor knew a pretty young thing when he saw one and invited Kate to tour New York with him when they docked. But she demurred. She was engaged after all, but admitted later that she found him 'very agreeable'.

This platter could have been in the household goods of any lady travelling in Second Class. It was not a White Star pattern.

Bertha, bored with her mother's adult conversation, soon teamed up with Marjorie Collyer, and the two girls roamed the decks entertaining themselves as best they could. Bertha knew a few words of school French and they spent time with the 'Hoffman' (Navratil) children who were playing under the watchful eye of their Papa, often on the enclosed Promenade Deck.

The two people that Marion, Bessie and Kate seemed to have particularly in common were the Reverend and Mrs Ernest Carter. This couple, devoted to each other and to their ministry, were on a well-needed vacation, paid for by their very poor parish in London's Whitechapel district, which had taken up a collection. Mrs Carter was exhausted and spent much of her time dozing in a deckchair, but she confided to Marion how she worried about her Sunday School class in her absence.

A souvenir from the Netherlands – might it have belonged to Dr Morwarek, who had been in The Hague just prior to the departure of the Titanic?

On Sunday afternoon, 14 April, after services conducted by the purser, many passengers retreated to the cosy library and away from the dropping temperatures. They were reading books from the selection in the glass-enclosed case at the end of the room and writing letters and postcards at the small desks placed along the gleaming sycamore walls. Reverend Carter had been told by several passengers, Marion and Kate among them, that it would be nice to have an evening worship service, so he arranged with the purser for a 'hymn sing-song' in the Saloon later that evening, and Mrs Carter bustled about inviting everyone to attend.

At 8.30pm a hundred or so passengers gathered in the Dining Saloon eager to sing their favourite hymns. At the beginning they sang together, then Marion sang several solos with Robert Norman, a Scottish engineer, accompanying her on the piano. After she finished 'There is a Green Hill Far Away' and 'Lead Kindly Light', Reverend Carter commented that this was the first time that hymns had been sung aboard the vessel, and expressed the wish that it would not be the last. With that the congregation sang 'For Those In Peril On The Sea', had coffee and tea, and dispersed to confront their own perils.

Marion, Kate, Bessie and Bertha were all saved in Lifeboat 9, launched at 1.20am from the starboard side by First Officer Murdoch. Robert Norman, the Reverend Ernest and Lillian Carter, and Dr Ernest Moraweck perished.

In her scramble to leave, Marion left her address book behind in the cabin and had no way of contacting Arthur when the *Carpathia* docked. She thought he was staying with a friend in Brooklyn, but did not know who or where. She searched frantically for his face at the Cunard pier but had no luck. The Watts were being met by Bessie's brother, Henry Milne, who lived a few blocks north on West 128th Street, and they insisted on Marion going with them. As they travelled uptown, Arthur was frantically searching Pier 54 and the hospitals downtown for his lost fiancée. He had been worried since he read of the sinking on the train from Oregon, when latest editions of the papers were brought on board at a stop in Buffalo. Marion's name was on the survivors' list, but that was not the same as seeing her face.

The next morning Henry Milne systematically began to call every hotel in New York hoping to locate Arthur. Fortunately, Arthur had registered at the Grand Union Hotel, not too far down the alphabet, and the couple were reunited.

On Friday 19 April they made a hurried trip to City Hall for their marriage licence, and on the 20th Marion and Arthur became man and wife in St Christopher's Chapel of the Trinity Church Mission House. Bessie was the bridesmaid and Milne gave Marion away. The chapel altar was decorated with white roses and asparagus ferns, which were hastily made into a bridal bouquet for Marion by the sisters of the mission who were touched by the story. The marriage photograph taken in front of the chapel shows a beaming Marion Woolcott standing next to her new husband, the roses clasped to the breast of her lucky coat. Outfitted with clothing from the Women's Relief Committee, £20/$100 and gifts from the church and others who had heard of Marion's plight, the Woolcotts left on 21 April for

Marion and Arthur on their wedding day at St Christopher's Chapel in New York City. (Author's collection)

Oregon and the farmhouse where she would live for the rest of her life.

Marion remained close to Bessie Watt and the two visited one another at Portland and Cottage Grove. Bessie attended the births of Russ, Bob and John, and to them she was always Grandma Watt. After she died in 1951 her daughter, Bertha, kept up the relationship.

By then Bertha had graduated from college and was married to a dentist, Leslie Marshall, with four sons of her own. In 1923 the Marshalls and the Watts had moved to Vancouver, and Bertha became a Canadian citizen. Undeterred by any lingering fear of water, she and Leslie sailed the coastal waters of the Pacific throughout their married life. She was one of those reluctant *Titanic* celebrities who would just as soon have forgotten the whole thing. When a *Toronto Sun* reporter called her in 1985 to say that the wreck had been found, her reply was, 'I don't give a damn.'

Meanwhile, back to 1912, on the same day that the *New York Times* ran an article on Marion's wedding under the headline 'Her Wedding Ends Saved Girl's Ordeal', it ran a smaller piece, 'Another Rescued Girl to Wed'. This was Kate Buss. *Carpathia* gossip had it that passengers who were not being met would be sent to immigrant processing on Ellis Island. That prospect struck fear into Kate's heart and she disembarked and melted into the crowd, hoping to avoid that dreaded possibility, which, unbeknown to her, had in fact been waived to prevent any further distress to the survivors. After a short stay in the Junior League House she moved in with friends from home, a Reverend Dalziel and his wife, for three weeks before she was strong enough to make the train journey west to San Diego. In July 1912 she wrote to Susan Webber, another Second Class survivor:

'I came by Pullman train special. It cost me a good bit extra but it was worth it … The scenery was lovely but

I never slept a wink. Every sound made me feel an accident had happened ... How are your nerves? ... I had a letter from Miss Wright [Marion] ... Everyone is asking me if the White Star have done anything. No, they haven't, nor can I hear that they have for anyone else. I was married directly when I reached here [to Samuel Willis on 11 May 1912 in St Paul's Church], only quietly indeed. My nerves were in an awful state again – so many foreigners made me feel so lonely.'

The new Kate Willis initially had difficulty adjusting to the strangeness of California, with its ethnic mix and frontier ways. She had several frightening experiences with trolley cars, on one occasion seeing a woman run over and, she claimed, nearly cut in half. Fortunately, one of her four sisters, who had also emigrated to the United States, arrived to give her comfort and a touch of home. It was the tonic she needed. With the help of £50/$250 from the American Relief Fund she began to replace the contents of her two large trunks and packing case that had been filled with a new bride's treasures: Irish linen sheets, hand-embroidered bedspreads, damask table clothes, solid silver table ornaments, a Singer sewing-machine, new clothing and an edition of Dickens's works, which she cherished.

She and Sam remained in California and had a daughter whom they named Sybil. When Sam died in 1953, Kate moved to Oregon (home of her *Titanic* shipmate Marion Wright Woolcott) to be near Sybil and her husband, the Reverend David Lane, and her grandson, Ronald. She was a member of St Hilda's Episcopal Church in Monmouth where her son-in-law was a clergyman and lived in a nursing home there until her death in 1972. On her headstone was inscribed 'Survivor of The Titanic'.

Marion Wright Woolcott
26 May 1885–4 July 1965

Kate Buss Willis
28 December 1875–12 July 1972

Elizabeth 'Bessie' Watt
1872–1951

Bertha Watt Marshall
11 September 1899–4 March 1993

Edwina Troutt (27)

'I felt I was saved for something.'
Edwina Troutt

EDWINA WAS NOT EXPECTED to live when she was born on 8 June 1884 in Bath, England. In fact she was so ill that her father, a brewer and part-time cabinet-maker, set aside wood for her coffin in anticipation of when – not if – her death occurred. That sickly baby developed into a sickly teenager plagued by pneumonia, which left her with only one lung. Legs incapacitated by inflamed joints and failing eyesight further complicated her daily existence. But Edwina, drawing on an indomitable spirit, flourished, sending the casket wood to another use. Not only did she flourish, but she married and buried three husbands in her long life, making her Edwina Troutt Peterson Corrigan MacKenzie. To *Titanic* enthusiasts she is simply the irrepressible Winnie MacKenzie.

But there was nothing simple about Winnie. Blonde, blue-eyed and rambunctious, she made her first crossing of the Atlantic in 1907 at the age of 23 on a dare from friends who goaded her into it by saying that she was not woman enough. They should have known better. By that time she had already taught pre-school children and worked as a clerk in her brother-in-law's tobacco shop. She knew life was for bigger and better experiences, and grabbed the opportunity. Giving herself five years in America, she worked as a waitress in New Jersey and as a domestic in Massachusetts. In 1911, six months short of her five-year goal, she returned to Bath, the New England winters having got the better of her already compromised respiratory system.

But that return was short-lived. Her sister, Elise, also living in Massachusetts during that period, was about to give birth, and Winnie was needed back in America. So she packed her navy blue serge suit, her blue straw and feather hat, her silk petticoat, her elastic stockings for aching-knees days, an outfit for the new baby, some family treasures her mother wanted to pass on, and a marmalade-maker, and off she went again – this time on the *Titanic*.

Edwina was assigned Cabin E101 with Susan Webber of Devonshire (of whom more in a moment) and Nora Keane, an Irish lady from Limerick who was returning to her current home in Harrisburg, Pennsylvania, where she and her brother had a store. Nearby was the musicians' cabin, and Winnie enjoyed hearing them practise each day as she passed by.

An earthenware Dundee marmalade jar. There were 1,120lbs of marmalade and jam in Titanic's *larder.*

These three single woman did not socialise much together on the ship, as Winnie was more gregarious than the other two. She commented that Susan spent most of her time talking over the gate between Second and Third Class to a fellow from her home town, while Nora, though more available according to Winnie, was too worried about sailing on the maiden voyage of a ship that may have been boasted unsinkable one too many times to be much fun. No matter, Winnie made friends elsewhere, gathering a laughing crowd wherever she went. People confided in her and she quickly learned the secrets of her fellow diners. Edgar Andrews, an 18-year-old from Buenos Aires, was secretly running away from his English boarding school to see his brother in New Jersey. Born of English parents, he did everything to annoy them, including refusing to speak their language. Jacob Milling, a Dane, confided that his wife did not know that he was on this quick trip to America to check out the railroads; however, at Winnie's suggestion he wrote to her. Edgar perished; Jacob's body was recovered and buried in Denmark.

Winnie's group loved card-playing, but on 14 April she retired early, thinking Sunday not the proper night to indulge. Preparing for bed, she did not undress completely, telling herself that there was the chill in the air, although she later admitted that Nora's pessimism may have coloured her thinking after all. Nora further disquieted Winnie by telling her that Nellie Hocking from Cornwall had heard a cock crowing earlier that evening, an omen of bad things to come.

(The crowing chickens were in fact an exotic French breed belonging to Ella Holmes White and Marie Grice Young of First Class, who were bringing them to their New York country home. Each day Miss Young would descend to the cargo area to check on the poultry and on one such visit she gave a crew member a gold coin for his care of the livestock. He thought it a lucky thing to receive gold on a maiden voyage. On Mrs White's insurance claim of £1,900/$9,500, she valued the chickens at £41 11s 4d/$207.87.)

Feeling the engines stop, Winnie, in a bottom bunk, was up and out in a flash to investigate. Returning with the urgency of the situation, she found Susan fast asleep and poor Nora in a dither. Susan quickly dressed and went on deck, but Nora insisted that she needed to don her corset before she could leave the sinking ship. In exasperation Winnie grabbed the wretched thing and tossed it out of the door. Nora got the message and they scurried to the Boat Deck.

Nora immediately entered a lifeboat, but

Marie Young (left) and Ella White (centre) with a friend at their country home. These First Class passengers had exotic French poultry in Titanic's *cargo area.* (Michael Findlay collection)

Winnie stood calmly watching the evacuation, resigned to dying, primed from an early age to believe that she would not live a full life. How sad, she thought, that newlyweds were being separated. If she ruled the sea it would have been married women and men first – then single women and men. As Lifeboat 16 (presumably) was hanging in the davits, a man, whom she later learned was Third Class Lebanese passenger, Charles Thomas, pushed forward with a baby in his arms. He had become separated from his sister-in-law Thelma, the mother of the infant. Prevented from entering a lifeboat himself, he begged anyone, anyone at all, to save his 3-month-old nephew, Assed. Winnie, shaken from her reverie by someone else's needs, readily took on the job. She entered the boat with a toothbrush, a prayer-book and the baby clutched to the unyielding cork of her lifebelt.

Winnie's life did an about-face that night. In an article written in later years, she said, 'I felt I was saved for something, so I vowed never to quarrel and always be kind to the sick and the elderly.' She went on to live her life under that banner, visiting the elderly and the ill long after she had herself joined their number.

In 1916 she moved to California and joined the Army Corps picking apricots used in making gasmasks for the First World War. She married her first husband, Alfred Peterson, in 1919 and together throughout the Depression they ran a bakery in Beverly Hills. In 1944 Winnie became a widow, but as you might expect, not an ordinary one. Besides marrying twice more, the last at the age of 79 to James MacKenzie, she became a citizen of the United States and added work for the Hermosa Beach Election Board to the list of her other civic duties. Redondo Beach, California, made her an honorary police chief and her city of Hermosa Beach, California, declared a day in July 1974 as Edwina MacKenzie Day, with a party in the town stadium.

That same year, Richard Nixon, the 37th President of the United States, sent Winnie a letter to commemorate her 90th birthday. She was thrilled, but quick to point out that she didn't agree with his politics. At that advanced age she was still motoring around Southern California in her red Pinto and ballroom dancing into the

These two toothbrushes would be similar to the one Winnie carried off the ship in her pocket.

night. Mischievously summing up the reasons for her long, zesty life she said, 'I drink plenty of whisky and keep late hours.'

She loved the spotlight and would break into song at a moment's notice, still remembering the waltz she heard *Titanic*'s musicians practising in 1912. And her sense of humour was outrageous. When she was 89 and Third Class passenger Margaret Devaney O'Neill was 82, they shared a hotel room at a *Titanic* survivors' reunion. One night Winnie jumped into bed with Margaret, teasing, 'Bet it's been a long time since you had a good hug from anybody.' The two octogenarians laughed like teenagers.

Winnie Troutt in later years. (Michael Findlay collection)

Winnie's infectious personality drew people to her like flies to the marmalade she still made, although without the aid of her sunken machine. She liked nothing better than to speak to groups about the *Titanic*, and continued to travel the globe, crossing the Atlantic by ship at least ten more times. Her last trip to England was made in her 99th year. On a stormy cruise to the Caribbean, another passenger asked Winnie if she was worried. Winnie's response: 'I've seen worse.'

Edwina Celia Troutt Mackenzie
8 June 1884–3 December 1984

Nora Keane
?–21 December 1945

Thelma Thomas
25 December 1895–7 January 1974

Assed Thomas
8 November 1911–12 June 1931

Ella Holmes White
18 December 1856–31 January 1942

Marie Grice Young
1876–27 July 1959

Susan Webber (37)

'Aunt.'

SUSAN WEBBER WAS SINGLE, well over 21, but not in the forward-looking, liberated 'modern' woman category. There is no evidence that she was interested in a career and she was not journeying to meet a husband. Her destination was the home of Charles Webber, her nephew, who lived in Hartford, Connecticut, and for whom she was to keep house. It conjures up a life lived in a period Edith Wharton novel in which a character past the marrying age and with no other means of support is forced – sadly – to live off the largesse of her relatives.

Her great niece, Kathleen Webber, well into her 90s when interviewed by Michael Findlay and Robert Bracken of Titanic International Inc, clearly remembered the night her Aunt Susie left Devonshire, England, for Connecticut. The family had a festive going-away dinner and after the meal Lewis and Owen Braund, who lived down the road, came by for dessert and to talk about the *Titanic*. They, too, were going on the ship, but in Third Class, and Susie promised to come down and visit them during the crossing. Also travelling in Third Class from Susan's area were William Dennis and his brother, Samuel. There was high excitement.

Susie is one of those passengers whose activities on the ship remain a mystery except for the brief references made of her by Edwina Troutt. From Susie's own writings, one page of which is reproduced here, we learn that she had no difficulty in entering a lifeboat, and that it must have been No 10 by her descriptions of the Japanese man who jumped from the deck and landed in it just as it reached the water. Of the *Carpathia* she wrote:

'I, with a great many others, slept on the dining room

Susan Webber. (Michael Findlay collection)

tables – and it wasn't soft wood, either. We didn't get much sleep, for the dinner hour lasted until nearly midnight, and they called us up before daylight to set the tables. For four days I lived in a nightgown, my hair trailing down my back and blowing in my face. Just before we reached New York on Thursday, a terrific thunder storm broke. It was night and pouring.

What did I think of New York? Well, I didn't much think of what I saw – I was in a sort of daze. In all that rain all we could see was a sea of faces. Anxious faces – waiting for news of friends. It was silent – you could have heard a pin drop. In all the rain there were ambulances, doctors, nurses, the Red Cross and everything to make us comfortable – clothes and food galore. I stood on the dock, waiting. When asked what I wanted most, I said. "A comb." I don't know why, when I was still hungry and didn't have a thing in America but a nightgown.'

Upon arrival in New York she was taken with Kate Buss, Amy Stanley, and Edith and

A page from Susan's hand-written account of the sinking. (Michael Findlay collection)

Elizabeth Brown to the Junior League House for women. She stayed there until her nephew, Charles, who was to have met her at Pier 54, but arrived 2 hours late, found her at 4 o'clock the next day through a list that Cunard had compiled.

Resting her frayed nerves in Connecticut, afraid to see people or to leave her nephew's home, Susie wrote to fellow survivors, most particularly Kate Buss. In a chatty return letter Kate mentions passengers they knew in common: Marion Wright, Lucy Ridsdale and Ethel Garside (who had been in hospital for two months after the sinking with a nervous condition). Near the close of Kate's letter to Susie she writes, 'I shall always be pleased to hear from you. As Miss Garside says, such an experience should make us lifelong friends.'

There is no evidence, however, that the correspondence continued and, regrettably, it sheds no light on Susie Webber, the person.

To retrieve some of her losses, Susie became part of the class action suit filed against the White Star Line by the Titanic Survivors' Protective Committee. The committee consisted of Archibald Gracie, George Harder, Henry Sleeper Harper and F. O. Spedden among others – influential First Classers who had taken the matter of passenger compensation in hand. Those survivors wishing to participate were obliged to contribute one per cent of the value of their claim to the committee for legal fees that would be incurred in the pursuit of the damages. Susan Webber sent 8 shillings/$2 to the committee based on her £40/$200 loss of baggage and personal effects.

In February 1916 Susan received a form letter stating that a settlement had been reached. After attorneys' fees and registration costs, £132,600/$663,000 was to be distributed in two payments to the claimants. What exactly Susie got from the suit is hard to ascertain, since each claim was appraised at approximate provable value. However, each claimant was reimbursed their fee for joining the suit in the first place. In Susie's case that was 8 shillings/$2. Lucky lady.

A tag like this would have been attached to Susan's limited amount of cabin baggage.

Susie went on to live a quiet life in Connecticut looking after her nephew's household and was an active member of the Grange and the Congregational Church. When she died in Hartford Hospital at the age of 77, her nephews and nieces placed a poignantly simple marker on her grave: Susan Webber, Aunt, 1874–1952.

Susan Webber
2 July 1874–29 January 1952

Mary Davis (28)

'I love America.'
Mary Davis

MARY'S STORY IS IMPORTANT to our narrative because it illustrates so graphically the class system prevailing in the world during the beginning of the 20th century. She was a single girl from England who earned her own passage on the *Titanic* by working as a vegetable cook in a London house. Her intention was to visit her sister in Staten Island, New York, then decide whether she would stay or return to England.

When Mary reached her cabin she situated herself in the bottom berth, having a fear that sleeping in the upper would make her dreadfully seasick. As she was finding spaces for the few possessions she had packed, her room-mate, Lucy Ridsdale, arrived. Seeing Lucy's age (50) and the fact that she was afflicted by a club foot, Mary transferred to the upper berth. Lucy was a retired nurse who had run a nursing home in London for many years, but had given up her position to emigrate to the United States where she had three sisters. Unlike Mary, she had all of her earthly possessions in the ship's cargo area and was nervous as to how they would fare during the crossing. Mary told her not to worry, bustled around repositioning both of their belongings, then went off to make friends.

Mary was quite used to making her way among strangers for she had had to do so since her teens when she first went into service. She was quick to introduce herself and was soon regaling her new acquaintances with her escapades as a servant girl in the kitchen of a 'titled lady'. It was a household with 22 servants, including liveried footmen in knee-breeches and velvet slippers, and she had soon learned her place in the hierarchy. She was known as a 'between maid' and reported to the housekeeper as well as to the head cook, both demanding souls. The kitchen was enormous with dozens of copper pans hung in gleaming rows along the stone walls, and the floor covered with sawdust to catch the drippings. Mary worked in a separate room devoted to the preparation and cooking of vegetables.

Her altercations with the Italian cook, who swore at her and spoke only limited English, made her fellow passengers laugh, especially her story of the day she under-cooked the cauliflower and he slid them back to her along the stone floor in their big copper pot yelling, 'Not done. Not done.' Holding her own, she slid them right back, yelling, 'No time. No time.' The lord and lady served their guests semi-raw vegetables that evening. She gave tempting descriptions of the enormous silver platters heaped with a formidable amount of wild game that made their way out of the kitchen to the elegant dining room above. Sometimes before her work was completed Mary would hide the dirty pans and sneak up the back stone stairway to watch as the lord and lady's guests arrived in their finery. She was particularly enamoured with the gowns and the tiaras worn to the dinners by the women guests, and would have found similar puffery at the tables in the First Class Dining Saloon on the *Titanic*.

From her days as a between maid Mary would have been familiar with items such as this silver-plated ladle from one of Titanic's *Dining Saloons.*

Mary was alerted to the danger on Sunday night by a steward who came down the passageway banging on the cabin doors with a stick, yelling, 'Everybody on deck — hurry or you will be locked in your rooms!' She did not need another reminder, but was slowed down by Miss Ridsdale, who required assistance in dressing and climbing to the Boat Deck. Once there the two of them realised how cold it

Mary Davis Wilburn at the age of 102. (Courtesy of Frederick Rueckert)

was and Mary scurried back to the cabin for blankets and Miss Ridsdale's heavy red coat. By the time she returned to the deck, Lifeboat 13, with Miss Ridsdale on board, had been launched. Seeing Mary standing there, a seaman said, 'You're a wee thing,' and with one hand picked her up and flung her into the descending boat. Flying through the air, grasping the coat and the blankets, Mary was not able to break her fall with her hands and landed in the boat squarely on her knees, which would trouble her for the rest of her life.

In the 102nd year of that life, still alert but frail and with elegant hands that belied her years of hard work, she was interviewed about her experiences by a young *Titanic* enthusiast.

She had never been comfortable talking to the press, but responded to the boy's interest. With a vestige of her English accent still in evidence, she spoke of the beauty of the ship, how the floors shone like glass and there was gold everywhere. Her memories of the night in the lifeboat and on the *Carpathia* had faded, but she did say, 'Half naked, most of us were.' She remembered putting on a heavy coat over her nightgown and jamming her bare feet into shoes. When asked if she saw the ship sink, she replied, 'First I knew of that. I'd a'thought she sprung a leak.' Age, thankfully, had taken some of the sting out of that night for Mary.

She did remember being met by her brother-in-law at midnight on arrival in New York and of being taken by train to Tottenham, Staten Island, to her sister. It was not long before she was introduced to her future husband, John Wilburn, and convinced to remain in the United States. Over and over in the interview she said, 'I love America. Don't have class distinction here. In England you better stay where you belong or they'll soon put you there. If you're a servant you're a servant.'

Mary gave up all rights to any compensation from the *Titanic* relief committees, requesting that they give her portion to the children who had lost their parents.

In America she was her own boss, working as a cook until she married and had a son. The Wilburns lived in Staten Island for years where John was a house painter, but eventually they moved to Syracuse, New York. John died in 1972 and Mary entered a nursing home. When asked why she was so lucky to have survived, she said, 'Never really gave it a thought, to tell you the truth.'

Mary Davis Wilburn
18 May 1883–29 July 1987

Lucy Ridsdale
1862–?

Annie Clemmer Funk (38)

'Our heavenly Father is as near to us on sea as on land.'
Annie C. Funk

ANNIE, A DARK-EYED, dark-haired woman with sweetness written all over her face, stood alone at the railing of the SS *Persian* as it manoeuvred out of Bombay Harbour. The 2½-day train journey from her mission at Janjgir to Bombay had been exhausting, but finally she was on her way home for her first furlough in six years.

Pastor Shelly's cable had such an urgency to it: 'Come home at once. Mother very ill. Have purchased passage on two ships.' Her mother's condition must be desperate. But how desperate? Annie would not be happy until she could see with her own eyes. Before that could

occur an arduous three-week journey lay ahead aboard this vessel to Marseilles, then by train and boat to England and finally the SS *Haverford* out of Liverpool across the Atlantic and home.

To divert herself from worries about her mother Annie thought of the first time she had seen this teeming harbour in December 1906. The mass of humanity swirling about in intense colour and pungent odours had made her dizzy as she stepped from the gangway. How quickly the exotic had become the ordinary. Even the steamy heat did not bother her as much any more, although she had to admit that it made her feel lazy at times and did little for her tennis game. What to others would seem hardship, to her had become a loved way of life, especially teaching the village girls. She regretted that with her abrupt departure she had been unable to say goodbye to them all.

This postcard was issued by the Hereford Mennonite Church in Bally, Pennsylvania, to honour Annie Funk's missionary work. (Courtesy of Hereford Mennonite Church)

But she would not be gone long. There was still much work to be done.

When she first arrived in Janjgir she was appalled that the only school in the village was restricted to boys. Girls were considered less than the oxen that pulled her cart from village to village. Annie was challenged. The girls must be taught to read and they would do it in a school of their own. Within two years the land for that school had been purchased and construction begun. Swaying the village elders to allow the girls to attend had been the last hurdle, and Annie had gone from door to door with her plea. By July 1907 that, too, had been accomplished, and Annie's one-room school, with its cow-dung floor, opened with 17 girls in attendance.

Annie admittedly was not the world's best disciplinarian, and her class was often unruly. She sought to balanced that by learning Hindi and grew closer to her charges every day. And they were now reading and had begun to take joy in the Bible and hymn-singing. As rewards Annie gave them gifts of sweets, a book or a sliver of hair-ribbon, especially at Christmas. Wouldn't the folks back home love to hear of these experiences doing God's work?

Home was Bally, Pennsylvania — affectionately called Butter Valley after the delicious spread churned there — with its green rolling hills and cool rushing streams turning the wheels of her father's grist mill — startlingly different from the parched golden terrain of India. Her ancestors had settled the valley in the late 1700s when religious persecution forced them out of Germany. They had been among the founders of the local Mennonite church, where she had been consecrated and her father had served as a deacon for 25 years.

Through the church's auspices Annie had attended the State Normal School at West Chester, Pennsylvania, and the Mennonite Training School in Northfield, Massachusetts. After graduation she had been sent to work among the immigrants in the slums of Chattanooga, Tennessee, and Paterson, New Jersey; but her dream had always been to become a missionary. In 1906 her prayers were answered when Pastor Shelly chose her to become the first female Mennonite missionary to India.

The increased speed of the *Persian*'s engines stirred up a breeze, making her lightweight skirt flutter and a shiver to run through her body. Annie smiled, thinking that it was a good thing her friend, Mrs Penner, had insisted that she borrow her heavy black coat for the journey. A gauzy cotton lawn dress would be no protection in the harsher weather of the Atlantic.

As the ship steamed though the Suez Canal, Annie wrote home to her sister, Cora:

'In three weeks time, if the weather or strikes do not prevent, I hope to be in Butter Valley. It does not seem possible but I shall be so glad ... PS Wrote to Aunt Lizzie to be ready to go with me to buy a suit. May try a skirt in Liverpool as the wind almost blows a light weight skirt away. A.C.F.'

That letter would prove prophetic.

Reaching England Annie learned that the *Haverford* was being held at the docks, a victim of a nationwide coal strike, and would not sail for at least six more days. Not knowing how threatening her mother's illness was, waiting seemed unthinkable. Thomas Cook & Sons provided what seemed to be the perfect option. For a few pounds more she could leave immediately on the new wonder-ship *Titanic* and be home before the *Haverford* left port. Annie changed her plans.

From Southampton Annie dashed off a letter to her fellow missionaries in India, sending it

A postcard taken on board the ship but never written or mailed.

with the pilot boat to be posted. She wrote: 'I had to get out a few more gold pieces to pay for passage on this boat but I gladly did that to get home six days earlier and will let my people know in New York.'

The luxury of the *Titanic* was an incredible contrast for Annie from the primitive life in Janjgir; there were no cow-dung floors here. Three days into the journey the trip was made even more memorable when Annie celebrated her 38th birthday. However, friends and relatives had sent birthday greetings to England care of the *Haverford*, and when Annie changed her sailing plans these messages, her final touch of home, never reached her.

Annie was asleep in her cabin when the steward's call came to dress warmly and don lifebelts. She slipped into her dress, added Mrs Penner's warm black coat, and dutifully proceeded to the Boat Deck where she was urged to take the only remaining seat in a lifeboat that was ready to go. As she was

climbing in a distraught woman burst through the crowds screaming hysterically, 'My children. My children.' The crew fought to restrain her, but the woman twisted out of their grasp and attempted to push past Annie to reach her children already in the boat. But she was pulled back – there was no room. True to her natural selflessness, Annie relinquished her seat without a moment's hesitation, allowing the woman to be reunited with her family. Annie was not afraid to die. She had accepted that possibility when she went to India.

No one in Pennsylvania knew that she was on the *Titanic* until the list of those who perished was published by the White Star Line. And even then they did not believe that it was their Annie. She was travelling on the *Haverford*. It had to be a mistake. Finally all had to accept the awful truth, perhaps comforted by the words Annie herself had written home when she began her final journey six years before: 'Our heavenly Father is as near to us on sea as

Annie's home survives in Butter Valley. (Author's collection)

The memorial to Annie in the Hereford Mennonite Church cemetery in Pennsylvania. (Author's collection)

on land.' No one needed to believe that more than Annie's mother, who lived on for a full year.

Annie may never have returned to her beloved Butter Valley, but a monument to her sits in the cemetery of the Hereford Mennonite Church, bearing the inscription: 'Her life was one of service to the master – not to be ministered unto but to minister.' The current Pastor, Reverend Robert Gerhardt, remembers being told stories of Annie by his own grandfather, who gave 10 cents towards that monument. There are others in the community who remember her also, and her family home still sits on one of the green, rolling hills looking as it did the day she left for India.

Annie's legacy, the school she nursed to life in Janjgir, was renamed the Annie Funk Memorial School in her honour. Over the years it has grown into a two-storey brick building

educating thousands of girls since Annie's original 17.

Annie Clemmer Funk
12 April 1874–15 April 1912

Marshall Drew (8)
Lulu Drew (34)

'Teaching I did on purpose. The Titanic *was purely accidental.'*
Marshall Drew

EIGHT-YEAR-OLD MARSHALL sat in the parlour of Blake's Hotel in Greenwich Village and pricked a picture into the hotel's stationery with a pin. When his hands ached to be creative, any instrument would do. Occasionally he would hold the project up to the light and check his progress, noting with satisfaction that his *Titanic* had a rather good likeness to the real thing. Marshall had been left to his own devices while his aunt went shopping to replace their clothing lost on the voyage. She guessed correctly that he would pass his time drawing, never imagining that he would also give the first of his many interviews to the press. A reporter, learning that there were survivors at the hotel, saw Marshall sitting there and the next day the *New York World* printed his story under the headline 'Young Drew's Account of The Sinking of the Titanic'.

Marshall, his Aunt Lulu and Uncle James were returning to New York from a visit to family in Cornwall. James had booked the

Marshall Drew, circa 1912. (Michael Findlay collection)

crossing on the *Titanic* as a perfect ending to what had been a most pleasant holiday. James and Marshall's father, William, were brothers. When Marshall's mother died two weeks after his birth, Lulu and James had become his surrogate parents; he lived with them, travelled with them and called Lulu 'mother'.

Before the *Titanic* left Southampton the Drews were invited, with the other Second Class passengers, to explore the ship's upper decks. Marshall remembered the gymnasium with its mechanical camel and rowing machine and his trip to the bridge in full preparation for the departure. When the tour ended they stood at the rail watching as the *Titanic* manoeuvred away from the dock and headed towards the sea channel of Southampton Water. They held their breaths as the force of the ship's passing in the narrow channel yanked the *New York*, docked nearby, from its moorings. Her manila ropes snapped and her stern swung out on a collision course with the *Titanic*. Marshall grabbed his uncle's binoculars and ran about the deck to gain a more advantageous look as the tugs came to the rescue, pushing the *New York* out of harm's way down river. A collision was averted, but this portent of things to come was high excitement for Marshall.

During his days on the *Titanic* the young boy, who had already cultivated the art of being independent and feisty, roamed the ship alone, exploring, getting lost and finding his way back again to his aunt and uncle. Most of the other children in Second Class were either younger or females, and as he said about that era, 'Boys didn't play with girls.'

On the Sunday Marshall and his aunt were in bed and James Drew was up on deck having a smoke and 'enjoying the pleasant breeze'. Marshall heard a scraping and felt a strange vibration running through the ship, but in a half-sleep did not give it much thought until his uncle returned with the news of the collision. Nonchalantly and with a smile in his voice, he told them to dress and put on their lifebelts as they were to be transferred to another ship while the *Titanic* was repaired. As they left their cabin Marshall noticed something different about the passageway, then realised that the watertight door at the end was closed. He did not fully understand the implications, but it gave him a funny feeling in the pit of his stomach. There was no confusion and no hysteria as they approached the lifeboats. James Drew kissed his wife and nephew goodbye and fell into line along the railing with a group of young men he knew from Cornwall who had escorted their own wives, mothers and sisters to boats in the same area.

Binoculars recovered from Titanic's *debris field.*

The lowering of the lifeboat was a harrowing experience. The ropes stuck in the pulleys and first the bow would jerk down, then the stern. In this unsettling manner it lurched its way to the surface of the sea and was rowed a safe distance from the foundering liner. Uncle James perished, and Marshall sensed it as he watched row after row of portholes go black, but to quote him, 'This was 1912. Little boys didn't cry. You were a little man. You kept a stiff upper lip. I went to sleep on the life preservers. I woke up in daylight and 360 degrees there were icebergs. You would think you were in the Arctic Circle. They couldn't miss.'

The workings of this pair of heavy-duty metal pulleys would have fascinated a young boy like Marshall Drew.

Soon after waking, Marshall saw the *Carpathia* steam into view and hoped with his Aunt Lulu that by some miracle Uncle James had been rescued and was already on board. Marshall watched as the other children were hoisted from the lifeboat to safety in a canvas bag. He remembered them crying, but when his turn came he thought it was great fun and would have tried it all over again if allowed.

His eight-year-old's recollection of the journey to New York was one of quiet, extreme quiet. He slept in the lounge and all night long the ship's fog-horn blew an ominous rhythm through the thick dense air. During the day the passengers were huddled together inside because of the damp weather, so Marshall escaped the crowd by going outside to watch the seaman constantly swabbing the deck to keep ahead of the condensation collecting underfoot. With its passengers in shock and its flag at half-mast, the *Carpathia* was on a funeral march to New York.

While the rest of the family was on holiday, Marshall's father had remained at home to look after the Drew monument business in Greenport, Long Island. He was a talented marble sculptor and undoubtedly the source of Marshall's artistic talent. When the first news of the sinking was telegraphed around the world, William read with horror that both his brother's and son's names were absent from the list of survivors. He fully expected Lulu to be the only one he would bring home to Greenport. When Marshall's face came into view on Pier 54, William dropped to his knees and wept. Marshall's name had missed the list because running off for hot chocolate and doughnuts was much more important to an eight-year-old boy, who had spent five freezing hours in a lifeboat, than giving his name to some grown-up with a pad and pencil.

After his press encounter at Blake's Hotel, Marshall returned to Long Island and continued to live with his Aunt Lulu until he was 10 and she remarried, becoming Mrs Richard Opie. Apparently there was no room in that relationship for Marshall, and he was shuttled across town to live with

Lulu's father and mother, the Henry Christians. What could have been a traumatic upheaval seems to have been a positive experience for Marshall. Grandpa Henry was a Civil War veteran and spun tales of his battle adventures to a fascinated Marshall. In addition, another of grandpa's relatives had been a captain in George Washington's artillery and there were stories there to be told as well. In the process Marshall added a love of history to his artistic interests.

His was a dual existence: teacher and *Titanic* survivor. In 1928 he graduated from Pratt Institute, a prestigious New York art school, with a variety of experiences and a talent that would enrich his life. He taught fine arts in a New York public high school for 36 years, married in 1930 and had one daughter, Betty, and four grandsons. He was relentlessly interviewed about the ship, and researched the event until he had the facts well in mind before he spoke. Always the optimist, he chose to look at the positive side of the experience, stressing the changes it brought about in ice patrols and lifeboat regulations. He believed that his survival obligated him to help others and in his retirement he fulfilled that mandate.

His distinctive craggy face and flowing white hair were seen everywhere from Long Island, New York, to Westerly, Rhode Island, where he eventually moved to be near his daughter and grandchildren. In Westerly he taught art classes at the local community house, chaired the Westerly Arts Festival, which showcased new artists, served on the board of the local Audubon Wildlife Refuge, and continued to paint, draw, and take stunning photographs of nature, which he showed to hospitals and churches in an inspirational presentation titled 'The Wonders of Creation'.

But what he most wanted to be remembered for was his teaching, always saying, 'Teaching I did on purpose. The *Titanic* was purely accidental.'

To that end, Titanic International erected a memorial stone in his honour, which reads:

Marshall B. Drew
Teacher-Artist-Friend
'Survivor RMS Titanic 4-15-1912.'

James Drew
4 May 1869–15 April 1912

Lulu Christian Drew Opie
19 March 1878–3 June 1970

Marshall Drew
30 March 1904–6 June 1986

Charlotte Collyer (31)
Marjorie ('Madge') Collyer (8)

'I cried hardest when I thought of my dolly back there in the water with nobody to mind it and keep it from getting wet.'
Marjorie Collyer

HARVEY COLLYER gathered his daughter on his lap and asked, 'How should you like to go to America?' Eight-year-old Madge thought that she should like it very much, especially if the new climate helped her mother's health. Her parents did not speak of it much, but she knew what trouble her mother had breathing and it was frightening.

Madge learned that they were going to join their friends who had bought a fruit farm in Payette, Idaho. It was exciting, even though leaving behind the people and places they held so dear was not an easy thing. Despite being plagued with epilepsy, Harvey had made a success of his grocery shop in Bishopstoke, Hampshire, and served as the verger of St Mary's Church where Charlotte had been housekeeper to Vicar Sedgwick. It was their fervent hope that America would provide an even more comfortable life.

Marjorie Collyer in 1912 with a new doll given to her by children who heard of her plight. (Author's collection/*Brooklyn Eagle*)

On the day before the Collyers were to depart, the villagers turned out in droves to bid them goodbye. In honour of Harvey's dedication to the church, an hour-long concert was played on the carillon. Charlotte later commented, 'It was almost too much of a farewell ceremony.' She would rather have concentrated on where they were going and not on what they were leaving behind.

The next day bright and early the Collyers left for Southampton, stopping off at the bank to withdraw the money earned from the sale of the shop – their nest egg for a new life. Harvey tucked the notes into his breast pocket for safekeeping, against the warnings of the bank clerk who thought a draft might have been a better idea.

When the *Titanic* hit the iceberg Charlotte said that it was '... as if the ship had been seized by a giant hand, shaken once, twice; then stopped dead in its course.'

Harvey returned from investigating, pale and shaken, and seeing the fear in his eyes Charlotte put on a dressing gown and light coat and quickly tied her long hair at her neck with a ribbon. Harvey wrapped Madge in a White Star blanket and the three left their cabin for the Second Class Promenade Deck, only to realise that Harvey had left his watch on his pillow and Madge her favourite doll, but there was no thought of going back. Besides, the important thing, their money, was safe in his jacket pocket.

There was little excitement until a stoker emerged from the lower decks. The fingers on one of his hands had been severed in his escape from the rising waters below and he was bleeding profusely, the red of the blood streamed ominously down the black of the coal dust that covered the rest of his body. When Charlotte asked if there was any danger, he shouted at her as if she were an idiot: 'Danger! I should just sye so! It's 'ell down below. Look at me! This boat'll sink like a log in ten minutes.'

That memory, together with the seaman shouting over and over, 'Lower the boats. Women and children first! Women and children first! Women and children first!' would never leave her.

The Collyers went to the Boat Deck but still clung together watching as the lifeboats were loaded and sent away. Charlotte was unwilling to part from her husband. In desperation to his duty, a seaman wrenched Madge from her mother's side and threw her into Lifeboat 14. Next he grabbed Charlotte around the waist and forced her to follow, with Harvey shouting after, 'Go, Lotty! For God's sake, be brave and go! I'll get a seat in another boat.' But, of course, that was not to be.

Soon after reaching New York, Madge was

interviewed by the *Brooklyn Eagle*, and a heart-tugging photograph of her clasping her new dolly named Eleanor appeared with the following story:

'My father raised me in his arms and kissed me, and then he kissed my mother. She followed me into the boat. The women in one of the other boats said that they wanted somebody to row for them and father got in that boat. [At this time she still did not know that her father was dead. Perhaps her mother had told her this to explain his absence.] The stars were shining and it was just like day. Some sailor put a rug around my mother to keep her warm. There were so many in our lifeboat that we had to sit up all the time. Nobody could lie down. My mother was so close to one of the sailors with the oars that sometimes the oar caught in her hair and took big pieces out of it. There was one officer in our boat who had a pistol. Some men jumped into the boat on top of the women and crushed them and the officer said that if they didn't stop he would shoot. Another man jumped and he shot him. My mother says I called out "Don't shoot!". But I don't remember it … While we were rowing away we heard a lot of people crying and the women in our boat asked the officer what that noise was and he said that the people on the decks were singing … We rowed around for 7 hours. All the time I was frightened a whole lot and sometimes I cried. I cried hardest when I thought of my dolly back there in the water with nobody to mind it and keep it from getting wet.'

There were 58 women and children in Lifeboat 14 with Madge and Charlotte, including Eva Hart and her mother, and an eight-man crew with Officer Lowe in charge. After the *Titanic* disappeared and the terror of their situation took root, Lowe ordered lifeboats 12, 10, 4 and Collapsible D to be lashed to No 14 to prevent their being lost in the dark open sea. That accomplished, he shifted a goodly number of the women and children from No 14 into the other boats, freeing space to return for survivors still struggling in the water.

Chamber pots like this one with the White Star logo were used in even the most luxurious cabins.

This lid from a toothpaste jar is embellished with a profile of young Queen Victoria. The cherry-flavoured paste inside would have appealed to a little girl like Marjorie.

Most of the passengers thrown into the water at the end had succumbed to the cold before Lowe got to them, but he managed to save four (one subsequently died in the lifeboat). One of the saved was an oriental man who had lashed himself to a door in a desperate attempt at survival; cleverly he had anchored the ropes through the hinges for security. As the icy water washed over him he appeared if not dead, then certainly half frozen. Lowe hesitated to save him, stating that there were '… others better worth saving than a Jap!' (The man must in fact have been Chinese, as the only Japanese passenger was Mr Masabumi Hosono, an official of Japan's Transportation Ministry, who left in Lifeboat 10.) Common decency prevailed, however, and the man was hauled on board. Passengers joined in an effort to revive the poor soul by rubbing his hands, feet and chest — and it worked. He rallied and insisted on taking his place at the oars, pushing an exhausted crew member aside. Properly chagrined, Lowe said, '… I'd save the likes o' him six times over, if I got the chance.' Seeing this, Charlotte could only pray that her Harvey had been as lucky.

She and Madge arrived in New York destitute but still hopeful, but reality soon began to creep in, as seen in this letter she wrote home to her mother-in-law on 21 April:

'My dear Mother and all,

I don't know how to write to you or what to say, I feel I shall go mad sometimes but dear as much as my heart aches it aches for you too for he is your son and the best that ever lived. I had not given up hope till today that he might be found but I'm told all boats are accounted for. Oh mother how can I live without him. I wish I'd gone with him if they had not wrenched Madge from me I should have stayed and gone with him ... I lived for her little sake otherwise she would have been an orphan. The agony of that night can never be told. Poor mite was frozen. I have been ill but have been taken care of by a rich New York doctor and feel better now ... Sometimes I feel we lived too much for each other that is why I've lost him. But mother we shall meet him in heaven. When that band played "Nearer My God to Thee" I know he thought of you and me for we both loved that hymn ... I will work for his darling as long as she needs me. Oh she is a comfort but she don't realise yet that her Daddy is in heaven. There are some dear children here who have loaded her with lovely toys but it's when I'm alone with her she will miss him. Oh mother I haven't a thing in the world that was his only his rings. Everything we had went down. Will you, dear mother, send me on a last photo of us, get it copied I will pay you later on ... God Bless you dear mother and help and comfort you in this awful sorrow. Your loving child Lot.'

Charlotte received £40/$200 from the American Red Cross Emergency fund, and £90/$450 from another fund to fulfil Harvey's dream of living in Idaho. But his loss was too much to bear and after a brief stay in the West she returned home to Bishopstoke with the aid of an additional £400/$2,000 raised by friends in New York and £60/$300 she earned writing an article entitled 'How I was saved from the Titanic' for the *Semi Monthly Magazine*.

For two years Charlotte and Madge struggled to bring some order to their lives. Charlotte remarried with the hope that things had finally changed for the better, but in 1914 she succumbed to tuberculosis and died. Madge was now ten, unwanted by her stepfather and reduced to the state her mother had feared, a ward of court, an orphan. There was a small weekly pension from the British Titanic Relief Fund, to which she was entitled until the age of 18, but that did not provide her with a family or a place to live.

There is conjecture that after her mother's death Madge was sent to a boarding school for a time, then went to live on a farm in East Horsley with her father's brother, Walter, whom she called Uncle Wad. Stories of her childhood are sketchy, but it was not pleasant. Madge's face staring out from the *Brooklyn Eagle* of 25 April 1912 was disquieting in its

Marjorie Collyer Dutton and her husband, Roy. (Courtesy of Derick Shonfeld)

maturity, and encouraging in its strength, a strength on which she would have to draw repeatedly in her lifetime. For dollies are easily replaced, parents not quite so.

Late in the 1920s, in a Christmas wedding, she married Roy Dutton, the motor engineer for a fleet of grocery store delivery vans, and finally had a home of her own and stability for the first time since she was eight years old. But that stability was shattered when their new-born child died unexpectedly. They never had another, and Madge filled her time with gardening and the dogs and cats she loved. Roy died in 1943 at the young age of 41, leaving Madge alone again.

For 20 years she lived the widow's life, working as a doctor's receptionist and maintaining her cottage in Chilworth. In the early 1960s, too ill to function on her own, she was moved to a nursing home at Alverstoke, Gosport, where she died of a stroke.

Charlotte Collyer
1880–1914

Harvey Collyer
1881–15 April 1912

Marjorie Collyer Dutton
1904–26 February 1963

Eva Hart as she would have looked on the Titanic. (Courtesy of the executors of Eva Hart's estate)

Esther Hart (49)
Eva Hart (7)

'If only there had been enough lifeboats.'
Eva Hart

SOMEWHERE IN THAT CROWD of 58 in Lifeboat 14 with the Collyers sat seven-year-old Eva Hart huddled next to her mother sobbing uncontrollably for her father.

Back home in Seven Kings, a developing suburb of Ilford, Essex, east of London, her father Benjamin had been a reasonably successful master builder, but had recently experienced financial reverses. On the urging of a friend, who was having success in a booming Winnipeg, Canada, Ben sold his business and prepared to enter into a building partnership with the man.

The Harts boarded the *Titanic* in Southampton and took up temporary residence in a comfortable Second Class cabin on the port side. Eva thought it all quite wonderful:

'As it was a four-berth cabin, we only had three of the tiered bunks lowered and this made it much easier for moving around. We had ample cupboards for all our clothes and the cabin had its own wash hand basin and a dressing table as well as a couple of comfortable chairs. My bunk was beneath the one used by my father, and much of the time it was occupied by my doll and teddy bear which I had taken to keep me company.'

Esther Hart might have had these glasses perched on her nose as she sat up all night reading and listening for danger.

Eva soon discovered six-year-old Nina Harper, who was travelling with her father, Baptist minister Reverend John Harper, and her Aunt Jessie Leitch, from Britain to Chicago, Illinois. The two ran around the decks dragging Eva's teddy behind.

One of Eva's fondest memories of the *Titanic*, if there can be such a thing, is her attachment to a friendly scrunch-faced bulldog. After a hurried breakfast she would visit the kennels on F Deck, tucked next to the Third Class Galley, to see how her small friend had fared during the night. Seeing this attachment, her father promised her one of her very own when they were settled in Canada. That promise was not fulfilled until 44 years later, and then by someone else.

Esther Hart had grave misgivings about sailing on the good ship *Titanic*. In fact, consumed with premonitions of disaster she sat up each night reading to watch over her sleeping family, ears strained for any sign of danger. Her erratic behaviour became the talk of the Second Class passengers. Her routine was to take breakfast with Eva and Ben, then retire to her cabin to sleep the day away, comfortable that others would keep her vigil during the daylight hours. Awake and refreshed she would rejoin her family for the evening meal.

Eva was not troubled in the least by her mother's bizarre conduct because that left her beloved father to be hers alone. They explored

This bundle of postcards must have belonged to an inveterate writer like Esther Hart. Notice the stamp on top.

the ship and visited the barber's shop where Ben, being less strict than Esther, bought Eva toys to add to the collection on her bed in the cabin. She knew that both of her parents adored her, possibly because she would be their only child, having been born so late in their lives (Ben was 40 and Esther 41). Esther's strictness may well have come from the fact that in a previous marriage she had nine children, all of whom died within a few months of birth from a combination of her husband's physical abuse and her own rare blood type. Esther's current family was of the utmost importance to her, and the care with which she watched over them each night undoubtedly aided in saving at least her daughter's life, if not that of her husband.

Hitting the iceberg was felt as a minor jolt in the Harts' cabin, but Esther woke her not too happy husband anyway and was insistent that he go on deck to explore. Grumbling, he pulled his trousers over his pyjamas and did as she asked.

He returned white-faced and shaken, and Esther knew then that her premonitions had come true. Ben gave his heavy sheepskin-lined coat to Esther and, grabbing a blanket from the bed, wrapped Eva up warmly and led his family to Lifeboat 14, which was boarding on the port side of the ship. There he waved goodbye with a smile and turned to assist other women and children to safety.

Eva clung closely to her mother in the lifeboat, frightened and cold until they somehow became separated during Officer Lowe's mid-ocean boat transfer. At that point Eva wrote that she '… started screaming … and no doubt added to the level of misery around me.'

From that night forward nothing was ever what she and Esther thought it should be. Winnipeg became a forgotten dream and the two returned to England to patch together the remnants of their old life. They were able to survive on £205 13s 3d/$1025.65 left by Benjamin and on a sum of £1 1s/$5.25 for Esther and 3s 6d/.85¢ per week for Eva provided by the Titanic Disaster Fund. With this money they bought back one of Benjamin's houses and lived there together until Esther's death in 1928.

The fund also paid a small portion toward Eva's education, although she never felt that it went far enough due to faulty administration. Possessed of an excellent soprano voice she was given piano and vocal training out of her mother's paltry resources, and at 16 opened a small music school of her own, teaching the children in her village. Concurrently, she began to dabble in politics, becoming eventually the Conservative Party Chairman for her area.

During the Second World War Eva worked in various capacities, ranging from entertaining the troops with her singing to distributing emergency food and shelter coupons for those who had lost everything in the bombing raids. While always working to support herself, Eva was still a ready volunteer and founded the Women's Junior Air Corps among other efforts.

One of her greatest achievements came on 30 May 1956 when she was sworn in as one of Her Majesty's Justices of the Peace. Her good common sense helped her to adjudicate matters from burglary and shoplifting to marriage separations. This led to her mediating in problems that arose behind the barbed walls of local prisons, and to a seat on the parole board. Her list of volunteer activities is endless and her dedication to helping others was recognised in 1974 when she was made a Member of the Order of the British Empire (MBE).

In her 20s and 30s she concentrated on work and on travelling and spoke little of the *Titanic*.

Eva in her teen years, perhaps on her way to music lessons. (Courtesy of the executors of Eva Hart's estate)

But as her life progressed she became a frequent guest on radio and television and appeared in several documentaries of the event. She never, however, got over the loss of her father, and in her memoir, *Shadow of Titanic*, wrote: 'If only there had been enough lifeboats.'

Esther Hart
1863–September 1928

Benjamin Hart
1864–15 April 1912

Eva Miriam Hart MBE JP
31 January 1905–14 February 1996

Elizabeth Brown (40)
Edith Brown (15)

'A Lifetime on the Titanic.*'*

IN 1996, a few months shy of her 100th birthday, Edith Haisman sat in her wheelchair on the deck of the *Island Breeze* at the exact spot where the *Titanic* had foundered. She had not seen this spot since 1912, but it was never far from her thoughts. The memories of that night had given her nightmares for a good part of her life, causing her to wake with the screams of the dying ringing in her ears. One of those dying had been her father, Thomas.

Thomas Brown had been a successful hotelier in Cape Town, South Africa, but business had declined and he had decided to give the booming American Pacific Northwest a try, encouraged by his wife Elizabeth's sister, who had already settled in Seattle. The hold of the *Titanic* held linens, tableware and furnishings – all uninsured – for the new hotel he hoped to build.

They had lived a comfortable life in Cape Town and their daughter Edith had grown up adoring the kind, gentlemanly father who doted on her. Edith's mother was 20 years younger than her husband, and his second wife. They had a loving marriage and Edith was the only child from the union, a younger sister having died at the age of 8 from diphtheria.

This was by no means the first sea voyage for the Browns, who had taken frequent trips from South Africa to Southampton and on to London to purchase fixtures for the various hotels Thomas had owned. They regularly stayed at the Russell Hotel and Elizabeth would shop with Edith and search out the latest in women's wear. It was essential that she keep abreast of

Mr and Mrs Thomas Brown in 1912. (Author's collection/*The Seattle Intelligencer*)

the styles, for in Cape Town she created fashionable plumes from ostrich feathers for elegant ladies to wear on their hats. She would have been jealous to know that George Rosenshine, an ostrich feather importer, was also to be on board the *Titanic* – in First Class.

Thomas had bought Second Class passage for Edith and her mother in a four-berth cabin with two other ladies, while he was accommodated in another. This seems to have upset Elizabeth, who would have preferred First Class, but the family's tenuous economic situation caused Brown to be more economical than usual. Second Class proved quite enjoyable, however, and they mingled with the other passengers, chatted with William Harbeck, also Seattle-bound, and attended the Reverend and Mrs Carter's 'hymn sing-song' on the Sunday night. A few hours later Mr Brown would show his daughter and wife into Lifeboat 14 and stand back to await his fate, smoking a cigar. In later years Edith would have him wearing a smoking jacket and sipping a brandy; but foggy memories aside, her consistent lament was that she never gave him a proper goodbye.

After a brief sojourn at the Junior League House in New York, Edith and her mother made the 4½-day journey by train across the United States to Seattle. In her biography, *A Lifetime on the Titanic*, Edith is quoted about this experience:

'I think this journey is one of the most interesting in the world. It's similar to the journey from Cape Town to Johannesburg at the Hex River portion – not that we were in any frame of mind to appreciate it. At all

A Thomas Cook & Son receipt (in rupees) for baggage from Colombo, Ceylon, and a letter on Rosenshine Bros letterhead belonging to First Class passenger George Rosenshine, explaining that the business for ostrich feathers was going to be slow because of the newer shaped hats.

the major stations along the way, as soon as our identity was know[n], we were given clothing and other useful items.'

Despite the presence of family, Edith and Elizabeth did not stay long in Seattle, opting to return to South Africa. On reaching there, they went off on another journey to Melbourne, Australia, as much as anything to erase the memories of the *Titanic*. Out for a stroll one evening they happened into a spiritualist meeting where the medium asked if anyone in the room had an association with a shipwreck. Elizabeth raised her hand. After the meeting the medium invited them back to her home, saying that she had a message for them from someone. Entering a trance, the medium, through automatic writing, conveyed a message from Thomas saying that he had died holding the Reverend Carter's hand and that he was now in a beautiful land. The message also said that the spirit message-giver would come to Edith that night and give her a kiss. Then the spirit signed his name, T. W. S. Brown – according to Edith and Elizabeth, in Thomas's very own handwriting. Since Elizabeth had told the medium no more than that she was Mrs Brown, how did the medium know to sign the message with Thomas's full initials? How could she have duplicated his signature, not having met them before? And how can it be explained that Edith got her kiss that night?

Returning to South Africa, Elizabeth took up her ostrich feather business again. She remarried and moved to Rhodesia with her new husband, but it was not a good match. Edith, not caring for the man's treatment of her mother, stayed in Cape Town with relatives. In May 1917 she met Frederick Thankful Haisman, a shipbuilders' engineering draughtsman, and a friend of Robert Hichens, *Titanic*'s quartermaster. It was love at first sight, and they were married six weeks later on 30 June. The Haismans began their family with a son born in August 1918, and they would continue to produce little Haismans until there were ten.

That many children presented a challenge in maintenance. The situation was further complicated as the Haismans moved during those years from South Africa to Southampton

Edith Brown Haisman at a Titanic International event. (Michael Findlay collection)

and back again. Times were often lean – very different from those comfortable years before 1912 when Edith's father was alive. Sixty years went by in the blink of an eye. One son died, four others went off to war, their children married and Edith and Fred were blessed with 30 grandchildren and great-grandchildren. Two of the brood moved to Australia and Edith and Fred followed. But by that time England was more like home and they finally moved back to Southampton for their retirement.

George Rosenshine was travelling on the ship with his mistress, Maybelle, as Mr and Mrs George Thorne to keep tongues from wagging over their arrangement. They had been on a protracted voyage around the world and the trip from Cherbourg to New York was the last leg of their adventure. Maybelle was saved in Collapsible D, but George perished and his body was the 16th found by the Mackay-Bennett, *claimed by his brother and forwarded to New York for burial. During a dive to the wreck site several of Mr Rosenshine's papers were retrieved and restored, including a Thomas Cook receipt and a letter on a Rosenshine Bros letterhead, the family firm that specialised in importing ostrich feathers.*

Over the years Edith had participated in some *Titanic* events, but in her 90s she became more involved. She was on hand in October 1994 with Millvina Dean to cut the ribbon when the National Maritime Museum in Greenwich, England, opened its exhibition of Titanic artefacts, and she participated in the dedication of the Titanic Memorial Garden in the Museum's grounds. By her side always was her daughter, Dorothy, named after the little sister Edith lost to diphtheria.

That brings Edith full circle to her journey

on the *Island Breeze* with RMS Titanic's 1996 memorial expedition. It was a time of tears and reflection. To the strains of 'Nearer My God To Thee' she tossed a wreath into the sea and said at last her final, proper farewell to her father. Then she wept in her daughter's arms. Six months later, at the age of 100, she died. By her bedside was a picture of her father wearing the bowler hat, stiff collar and bow-tie he had purchased to travel on the great ship *Titanic*.

Thomas William Solomon Brown
1852–15 April 1912

Elizabeth Brown
1872–29 June 1925

Edith Eileen Brown Haisman
27 October 1896–20 January 1997

Elizabeth Ramell Nye (29)

'You will like to hear the truth of the wreck from me, for the papers never tell the right news.'
Elizabeth Nye, in a letter to her parents,
16 April 1912

LIZZIE, as she signed that letter, went on to say that she was all right but had been left with only 'scanty clothes' and a big coat. And with characteristic strength she continued, 'I am amongst the fortunate, for God has spared my life when I was so near death again,' referring to a severe attack of appendicitis when she was a young girl. Adversity seemed to plague her, poor dear.

Her first love was lost when he was washed off Folkestone Pier, Kent, during its construction. She found love again when she was 22 and in 1904 married another Folkestone native, Edward Nye. The couple emigrated to New York and Lizzie got her first job with the Salvation Army in the uniform department, no

Elizabeth Nye early in her Salvation Army career. (The Salvation Army National Archives)

doubt with the help of her father, who had formed the Army in Folkestone in 1883. In 1911 she suffered another devastating loss when her husband and child both died. Her voyage on the *Titanic* followed a protracted stay with her parents and sisters in England where she had gone to mourn.

Lizzie shared her cabin, 33 on F Deck, with

Mildred Brown (the Allisons' cook), Amelia Lemore and Selena Rogers Cook. The latter was listed on the passenger list as Selena Rogers, but she had recently married.

When Lizzie was greeted at Pier 54 by her Salvation Army compatriots she fainted at the sight of their welcoming faces. She awoke to the sympathetic eyes of Captain George Darby, national headquarters bandmaster. There is debate as to whether his band played that night. Given the strong belief held by the Army that music is a means to the soul, it would seem likely, but no contemporary reports exist to confirm the fact. Captain Darby was there more for assistance to the survivors than for music, and who knows, maybe he was sent there by some divine intervention to meet Elizabeth.

After all, this woman had had enough of life's tragedies and it was time for her luck to change. Prior to the *Titanic* disaster she had not yet dedicated her life to the Army's work, but when iceberg and ship collided she promised herself, if she were to survive, that she would take up the cause. Seeing Captain Darby may just have sealed that bargain.

The Salvation Army had a regulation: there could be no marriage between a commissioned officer and one who is not identified with the movement. Elizabeth therefore entered the officers' training school and was herself commissioned as a Lieutenant on 9 June 1913. She worked at the Boston and Philadelphia Rescue Homes until her marriage to Darby, now a Colonel, on 26 November 1913, when they both were assigned to the New York area. Elizabeth worked tirelessly in the Home League and the League of Mercy Ministry and gave birth to a son, George Ray.

She and the Colonel, who was then secretary to the Salvation Army's National Commander,

Elizabeth had been home to Folkestone and perhaps was bringing this souvenir pitcher back to New York as a present for a friend.

retired from the Salvation Army in 1948 and eventually moved to the Salvation Army Retired Officers' Residence in New Jersey. Elizabeth died there on 22 November 1963. To quote from her burial service:

'Ungrudgingly, she gave her strength to the weak, her substance to the poor, her sympathy to the suffering, and, moreover, gave it with a graciousness which added much to its influence.'

Lizzie will also be remembered for two stories that have become part of *Titanic* lore. Recovering from her fainting spell at Pier 54 she ran back to the *Carpathia* to collect something she had left behind. Incredibly, she emerged with a yellow canary in a brass cage, bedraggled but still singing. Did this smallest of God's creatures go through the whole ordeal with her from *Titanic* to lifeboat to *Carpathia*? Lizzie does not make this clear in her detailed description to the Salvation Army reporter taking notes on her story for *The War Cry*. What she did say quite emphatically is that from her position in Lifeboat 11 she saw Captain Smith jump from *Titanic*'s deck into the water to rescue a little child. When several men on a raft tried to pull him to safety, he said, 'No boys, I am going back to my ship.'

She is also one of the passengers who said about the ship, 'She did not sink flatly, like boats sail the ocean, but tipped up on end, and when she was half-submerged she broke completely in two and the lights went out.' This was a belief not taken seriously until 73 years later.

Elizabeth Rammel Nye Darby
27 May 1882–22 November 1963

Jane Quick (33)
Winifred Quick (8)
Phyllis Quick (2)

'My missus is the most wonderful woman in the world. And those two children are the finest you'll ever find ... there are none who will beat them.'
Fred Quick, *The Detroit News Tribune*, 1912

JANE RICHARDS had a certain glamour, with her natural rosy cheeks, deep dark eyes, and a chin with a kissable cleft. No wonder Fred Quick has fallen in love with his 'Jennie', and

no wonder she was a magnet for the photographers milling around Pier 54 the night of the *Carpathia*'s arrival in New York. And she had two adorable girls in tow, Phyllis, a curly-haired blonde moppet of nearly 3, and eight-year-old Winnie, who had inherited her mother's dark good looks.

What a poignant sight they were in their donated clothing: Jennie in a stylish second-hand grey coat with a lighter grey collar and cuffs, and a face-framing hat; Winnie wobbling about in much too large, high button shoes, being tripped up by a trailing feather boa; and Phyllis carried aloft on the shoulders of a seaman. Fred, who had frantically paced the

Mrs Fred Quick and her experiences as interpreted by a 1912 sketch artist for the Detroit News Tribune. (Author's collection)

MRS. FRED QUICK

pier blowing his old courting whistle to attract Jennie's attention in the throng, was beside himself with joy at the sight of them, and vowed that they would never be parted again. Even so, an enterprising newsman managed to separate them in the crowd at the pier when he linked his arm in Jane's and pulled her away for an exclusive interview. Fred rescued her in the nick of time.

It had been wrenching when he had left his 'girls' in Plymouth, England, to try his hand as a plasterer in Detroit, Michigan. He and Jane had been married for ten years and the flame of their relationship was still aglow. Before he left, Fred had pin-pricked 'I love you' into a leaf and Jane carried it with her always in a small metal box once containing wax friction matches. This box and a small gold bag with four English sovereigns, which hung around her neck, were the only possessions Jennie carried with her into Lifeboat 11 – besides her precious daughters, of course.

This story and Jane's other remembrances were to be told over and over again until she tired of hearing herself. Vaudeville was in vogue in the United States in the early 1900s and an enterprising agent from King Amusements talked Jane into sharing her story

These bottles may very well be from the Titanic's *dispensary, which perhaps Jane visited to get help for her daughters' sea-sickness.*

with paying audiences at Detroit's Palace Theatre. His offer of £1 8s 6d/$7.14 per show, eight shows a day, went a long way to convincing the Quicks to take to the boards. This money would replace their possessions, which now lay on the ocean floor.

Sandwiched between singers, comics and acrobats, Jane relived her *Titanic* experiences dressed in the same skirt that she had thrown over her nightgown to escape. Fred, not letting her out of his sight as promised, stood in the wings ready to push Winnie and Phyllis, giant bows atop their heads, on stage for a brief appearance. Audiences were mesmerised.

She always started with how beautiful the ship was and how new. Their cabin had been painted so recently that it still had a paint odour and they slept with the door open because Winnie was sick from the smell. Jane's first indication of danger came when a woman in the next cabin told her that something was amiss. Not too alarmed, she slowly pulled a dark skirt over her nightgown, but was in no hurry to disturb her sleeping children. When a crew member poked his head in the open door and indicated the seriousness of the situation, she sprang into action, dressing Winnie as best she could and wrapping Phyllis in a shawl. Carrying Phyllis, who was heavy with sleep, and their lifebelts, and dragging Winnie by the hand, she climbed up the red-carpeted Grand Staircase to A Deck.

Two male passengers saw her juggling all of this and one held Phyllis while Jane put on her lifebelt, and another strapped a crying Winnie into hers.

Almost separated from her daughters during the loading of the boats by an over-anxious seaman, Jane agonised as she sat in Lifeboat 11 suspended between heaven and the deep dark sea, and witnessed a horrific scene that would never leave her. A seaman grabbed a small baby from the arms of its mother and tossed the child over the ship's railing into her boat. Jane could

Jane Quick and her daughters, Winnie and Phyllis, stand to the right in this picture taken at Pier 54. Next to Jane is Leah Aks holding Filly, the 'Titanic Baby'. (Author's collection)

see the anguished mother leaning over the side of the ship and hear her screaming in despair. It was one of her most vivid recollections, together with the death cries of the passengers, which the crew in her lifeboat tried to pass off as cheers for an impending rescue.

Winnie's hysteria added to the clamour. She had started screaming on the *Titanic*'s deck when she was strapped into her lifebelt, convinced that she would have to make the jump 60 feet into the Atlantic. Matters were not improved when she lost her slippers as she was tossed into the boat and found her bare feet dangling in freezing water. Phyllis, a sleepy toddler, slumbered though the whole ordeal, much to Jane's relief. Her major concern upon waking was the whereabouts of the miniature White Star flag her mother had inadvertently brought on board in the pocket of her raincoat.

During the night on the open sea Jane sat freezing so near the oars that she was hit in the back each time they were pulled in her direction. Winnie was enfolded in the coat of a German lady and eventually her hysteria subsided and she slept. Another survivor gave her coat to Jane to cover the sleeping Phyllis. And so it went that night, each survivor comforting the other in their despair. There was

no singing as in other boats, just prayer.

Later Jane was to tell the same story in Grand Rapids and Battle Creek, Michigan, borne along by the post-trauma excitement, the sights of a new country and the need for money. But soon the terror of what actually had happened and the realisation of how close she and her girls had been to death crippled her and stopped her show-business career.

Jane presented Winnie and Phyllis with two more sisters, Vivian in 1916 and Virginia in 1918, and was devoted to Fred until his death. She remained a very strong woman, still lovely at 84 with beautiful white hair and that rosy glow in her cheeks, though it may have been given a little boost in later years.

Phyllis continued to be the calm one, working for a telephone company until she married Austin Murphy and had four children. She was totally fulfilled by keeping house for her family and died in 1954 at a much too young 44. Winnie, who was described as more highly strung than Phyllis, dropped out of school after the eighth grade and went to work in a chocolate factory, then a bakery. One evening at a party she spied a young man who caught her fancy, 19-year-old Alois Van Tongerloo. During the course of the evening they learned that both had emigrated to the United States in 1912. Winnie let Alois know that night, in no uncertain terms, that she felt an attraction to him. Alois felt the same, but when he learned that Winnie was only 14 he put a halt to the relationship. Being a wise older man, he told her that he would see her in a few years.

And so he did, behind the counter of the bakery one day when he stopped to buy bread. They courted, married, had three sons and two daughters and camped their way through every state in the Union but Hawaii. To reach that island state would have meant crossing another large ocean, and Winnie was not taking any chances – even in an aeroplane.

Today she lives in a nursing home in Michigan having weathered the death of her mother, sister, husband and two of her sons. But she still holds dear the physical remembrances of the past: the four gold sovereigns her mother wore in the purse around her neck the night of the sinking, the matchbox that held her father's leaf of love, and the bedraggled White Star flag she and her sister, Phyllis, had played with as children.

Jane 'Jennie' Richards Quick
31 August 1878–27 February 1965

Phyllis May Quick Murphy
26 July 1909–15 March 1954

Vera Winifred 'Winnie' Quick Van Tongerloo
23 January 1904–

Kate Phillips (19)
Ellen Phillips

'Last Sad Survivor.'
Daily Mail, Friday 26 August 1994

ELLEN PHILLIPS WALKER'S birth certificate states that she was born on 11 January 1913 to Kate Phillips, a confectioner's assistant. There is a blank beside her father's name. Ellen was supposedly conceived on the *Titanic*. There were babes in arms and pregnant ladies, but surely this makes Ellen the youngest and possibly most sorrowful survivor.

The story is ages old. Kate Phillips grew up in Worcester, England, and at 19 began to work for Henry Morley in his sweet shop. Morley was many years her senior with a wife and 12-year-old daughter, but that did not keep him from eyeing Miss Kate. Amongst the bonbons the two concocted plans to run away together. Henry sold his share of the business to his brother, Arthur, and with the money bought two tickets to San Francisco. Leaving a paltry income for his wife and daughter, he and Kate boarded the *Titanic*, using the pseudonym Marshall to cover their highly illegal tracks.

Henry was one of the 154 Second Class male passengers who perished, leaving Kate with dashed dreams and no place to go but back home. While she waited for a ship to take her there, she was looked after by the American Red Cross, which gave her £20/$100 to supplement the £40/$200 and clothing she had received from other American relief funds. (Morley's widow only received £25/$75 from the British relief fund.) On 2 May Kate boarded the *Adriatic* bound for Liverpool, together with the crew of the *Titanic* and Bruce Ismay, finally released from giving testimony in Washington DC before Senator Smith's *Titanic* investigating committee.

Kate was not looking forward to facing the animosity that awaited her, but she felt that it would pass in due course. But, alas, she soon discovered that she was pregnant, and the now simmering scandal came to a roaring boil all over again. Kate stuck it out until the birth, then left, giving baby Ellen over to the care of her parents. They reared Ellen as their own, together with their other daughters whom Ellen thought for years were her real sisters.

When Ellen was two her grandparents moved their girls to another town to spare Ellen the whispers and stares (which she did not know until much later) and she remembers her childhood there quite clearly. She recalls hand-crocheted dresses and lace petticoats being part of her wardrobe, which she liked, and a lady who would sweep in now and again to shower her with kisses and cuddles, which she did not like. In her ninth year that lady swept in and took Ellen with her when she left. Kate had married Frederick Watson from South Ealing, London, had given up her position as a shoe and hat saleswoman, and thought she would now have the time and the resources to bring up her own daughter.

This Gladstone-type travelling bag could have been carried by Kate as she ran away with Henry Morley.

Ellen admits that it must have been a life-altering experience, but remembers it only as a time when she had to adjust to an entirely new way of life and a new mother. Her grandparents had treated her as if she were a little princess, but with her mother she became Cinderella. '... [S]he rejected me and used me as a sort of servant. I did all the housework, while she spent her time in bed with imaginary illnesses.'

It was not long before Kate, more as the wicked stepmother in the tale than the loving mother, started locking Ellen in a closet, depriving her of food and beating her with a cane until her legs were raw and bloody underneath the harsh flannel of her knickers. A playmate's mother told the authorities and the court intervened. Ellen's stepfather became her Prince Charming, guaranteeing the officials that he would protect her from her mother, and the beatings stopped. In return Ellen helped him to eke out a living

Any Second Class baggage not needed in the cabin would have been labelled with this sticker and stowed in the baggage compartment.

in a small café where he cooked and she served.

Ellen believes that her mother was mentally unbalanced due to Morley's loss on the *Titanic*. Her dreams of living as a rich American lady were part of the debris left by the sinking ship together with the human wreckage, deckchairs and window frames. In that era before psychoanalysis was commonly practised, when the prescription for handling trauma was a stiff upper lip, Kate was as much a victim as Ellen or Henry Morley. Eventually she gave in to her misery and drank acid in an attempt to end it all. When that failed Kate simply stopped getting out of bed. Ellen's stepfather did the best he could, but finally left, and Ellen was forced to care for her mother alone.

When Ellen was 17 her aunt had told her the sketchy details of her birth, her father's name and that she had a stepsister named Doris. But the subject only came up once with her mother. It was midday and the café was full of customers. Ellen was exhausted from serving them and from running upstairs to see to her mother's incessant sickbed demands every time she thumped on the floor with her walking stick. In frustration Ellen shouted, 'We're busy. For goodness sake, put your head under the cover and die.'

Kate's response was, 'Don't look at me like that. That's how your father looked at me, with the same eyes, the day I was dragged off the *Titanic* and thrown into a lifeboat.'

Years passed. Mother and daughter went their separate ways and Ellen did nothing to find out more about her father, except to send for her birth certificate and cry over the blank space where his name should have been. Living the present was more important than exploring the past. She worked in a florist's shop and in the passport office in London and worked as a railway porter during the Second World War. She married twice, having a son of her own. Kate died in 1958 and Ellen did not know until months after the funeral. One of her deepest regrets was that she and her mother did not talk more about Henry Morley. She believes that if they had, her mother would have been much less disturbed.

Ellen was left a widow in 1971 by her husband, Frederick Walker, and returned to her roots in Worcestershire. In April 1990 the local history magazine ran a story about three men in the community who had been on the *Titanic*. Ellen devoured the article, coming to an abrupt halt at the photograph of her father, the first

she had ever seen. There he was – a dark-haired, good-looking fellow with intense eyes and a well-groomed moustache. Staring at his face she decided that it was time to find out about her heritage. Fortunately, a local paper printed her story and distant relatives came forth to help with the details. A second cousin filled in Morley's birth date and another told her that her uncle, Arthur, had sent £1 per week for her schooling and that her half sister had moved to India. One day she even visited Morley's confectioner's shop where it had all begun and stood outside imagining those halcyon days in 1912 when her mother and father had fallen in love.

But bits of information are not what Ellen wants. Now in her 80s, her goal is to be officially recognised as Morley's daughter – to

Kate Phillips and her daughter Ellen in 1913. (Courtesy of Ellen Walker)

place his name in the blank on her birth certificate marked 'father'.

Henry Morley
3 May 1873–15 April 1912

Kate Phillips Watson
1893–1958

Ellen Phillips Walker
11 January 1913–

Two rather different views of sea travel, the sentimentalist's postcard (below) and from a cartoon of the day, Humanity adds the word 'safety' to a list of Titanic's attributes. (Author's collection)

PART THREE

SAVE OUR SOULS

'SOS' WAS USED for the first time on board the *Titanic*. Harold Bride, the wireless man, suggested it to his colleague John Phillips as a jest, saying that it might be the last chance he would have to send it. It had evolved as an easier way to call for help on the telegraph than CQD, the established international distress signal, and had no specific meaning. 'Save Our Ship' was often suggested as a mnemonic for the letters, but 'Save Our Souls' is far more appropriate when thinking of *Titanic*'s Third Class women and children. Fewer than half of them survived.

Which brings up the poignant and painful question, why? Was it their location deep in the ship? Were they locked in Third Class until it was too late? Did they get lost on their way to the Boat Deck? Did their lack of English make it impossible for many to understand the seriousness of the situation? Did their anxiety to try and save their belongings as well as themselves slow them down? Were there too few lifeboats? Had the available lifeboats been sent away only partially filled? Yes, to all.

They were in essence double victims, at the mercy of an unanticipated sea tragedy and of a social hierarchy that, however vehemently denied, valued the lives of those on the upper decks more than those on the lower. *Titanic*'s Third Class were not just on a lower deck, they were a lower class. And was this not what these emigrants were coming to the 'New World' to avoid?

Emigration to the United States in the four years prior to the First World War averaged one million people a year. Transporting them was a lucrative business and the White Star Line was in heavy competition with its rivals Cunard, Hamburg-American and North German Lloyd for a slice of the people pie. Without this base and constant non-seasonal flow of emigrant revenue to offset their costs, ferrying the mails and the moneyed would not have been possible. To entice that population White Star had ticket offices in strategic locations in Europe. Their aggressive advertising campaign promoted the *Titanic* as not only the best and the most affordable, but as the most attractive and comfortable as well. The 'floating coffins' raging with 'ship fever' were a thing of the past. White Star had provided service that could no longer legitimately be called steerage.

Depending on finances the Third Class passenger had a choice of two-, four- and six-berth cabins, together with the less costly dormitory-style area for the men forward on D Deck. Women and children would not have been welcome in that area or in the men's smoking room or bar, but they had the use of a simply furnished General Room and the open areas forward on D Deck and aft on B Deck. The children played wherever they could find an open space (cranes, companionways, passageways and cabins) without creating too much noise.

Long gone were the days when steerage passengers had to bring their own supply of food for a journey. Meals on the *Titanic* were jolly boarding house affairs served in two dining rooms, which sat midships allowing access from both fore and aft, and may just have been the most ample and varied food many of the passengers had ever eaten. To add to the festivities, they were served by uniformed stewards at long tables covered with crisp white cloths. On the bill of fare for the main midday meal were such hearty dishes as steak and kidney pie, ragout of beef, corned beef, fish, rabbit, a variety of soups, vegetables, puddings, fruit, and always butter and freshly baked bread.

The majority of this class of passengers had boarded in Southampton and were, of course, from Britain. But a large contingent also came from Sweden, Norway, Denmark and Finland by boat to Hull, then by train to Southampton. There they were joined at the White Star docks by the Austrians, Belgians, Bulgarians, Croatians, Russians and Swiss who had chosen to cross the Channel rather than board at Cherbourg. At that French port passengers who had made the long trek from Greece, Turkey, Syria, Lebanon, Armenia and Italy via Marseilles joined the French and other continentals. And lastly, the Irish (111 strong) boarded at Queenstown. This polyglot of nationalities and religions was going to America under the general umbrella of desire for a better life. For most this meant economic betterment, but for some it also held out the promise of religious and political freedom.

The emigrant women had courageously said goodbye to the only lives they had ever known. Some were brides-to-be, others were re-uniting with sorely missed husbands, and oh, so many, were young girls on their way to independence in positions as maids and nannies, waitresses and shop girls. They travelled alone or with friends and family and 39 boarded with the responsibility for their small children. In all, 262 Third Class women and children walked up *Titanic*'s gangplank, bringing with them not only their personal belongings but also their passionate and joyful hopes and dreams – which only 121 survived to fulfil.

Emily Goldsmith (31)
Frank Goldsmith (9)

'So long, Frankie. See you later.'

FRANKIE WAS A TYPICAL nine-year-old boy thrilled with his journey on the *Titanic*, racing around Third Class exploring every nook and cranny. Soon after boarding he had joined seven other curious lads and the little posse had a wonderful time hanging from baggage cranes, climbing ladders and engaging in good clean mischief.

The proximity to the engine room was a particular attraction for Frankie, who was fascinated with the firemen stripped to their undershirts, black with soot and shiny with sweat, labouring to throw shovel after shovel of coal into the fire-breathing boilers. To him this was more magic than labour, and in his autobiography, *Echoes In The Night*, he remembers the workers singing and striking their shovels on the grates of the furnaces in time with the music; a similar incident is romanticised in the Broadway musical *Titanic*. If Frankie were alive to see it, his reaction now would most likely be horror rather than fond remembrance.

Frankie was travelling with his mother, Emily, and father, Frank Senior, to their new home in Detroit, Michigan. Emily was the only one of nine Brown child who had not left England; her entire family had emigrated a few years before, and had written, often and passionately, of their good life. The death of Frankie's baby brother, Bertie, from diphtheria just before Christmas 1911 may have been the catalyst for the Goldsmiths to finally make the decision to leave, as a diversion from the

This jar of olives was retrieved intact from the ocean floor. Twenty-five cases of olives were listed on the cargo manifest and carried in the ship's cargo holds along with Emily's sewing-machine and Frankie's cap gun.

A spool with the thread still wrapped around it.

wounds of so recent a death.

Frank Senior quit his job as a tool and dye maker and Emily packed up her precious Singer sewing-machine and Frank Senior's tools in a large wooden crate destined for the ship's cargo hold. Frankie smuggled in his cap pistol just before it left the house. From Strood, Kent, they travelled to London, then on by boat train to Southampton. Along for the ride of a lifetime were two other Detroit-bound passengers, Thomas Theobald, a close friend of Frank Senior who was going to establish himself before sending for his wife, and 15-year-old Alfred Rush, whom the Goldsmiths had promised to deliver safely to his brother. Alfred was to celebrate his 16th birthday on board the *Titanic* and was extremely proud that he could then discard his infantile knee-breeches for the long trousers and the grown-up activities of a man.

The journey, which held so much promise, would bring only sorrow to all involved. When the women were separated from the men and sent to the boats, Alfred, who might have been spared due to his small stature, chose to stay behind. Proud of his newly acquired manhood he said, 'No! I'm staying here with the men!' and retreated behind the barricades.

Thomas Theobald, fearing the worst, pressed his wedding ring into Emily's hand as he said goodbye and asked her to give it with his love to his wife should he not survive.

Frank Senior kissed Emily and, patting Frankie on the shoulder, said, 'See you later.'

Frankie never forgot climbing a steel ladder to the Boat Deck and being hurried along a narrow path formed by a human chain of seamen, their arms linked to prevent a rush on the lifeboats. One man broke through and charged in front of his mother, but she pushed him aside – if her husband could not come along, this nasty chap was not going to either. The seaman cheered her bravery as they hustled her and Frankie toward Collapsible C.

As the boat was winched down past the various decks Frankie peered into the recently vacated, brightly lit staterooms; saw couples walking the decks arms entwined; and young cabin boys, freed from their duties, playing a game, while others stood smoking a normally forbidden cigarette. What would have been frightening to an adult aware of the gravity of the moment was to Frankie just another

Emily and Frankie soon after the disaster. On Emily's finger are two wedding rings, hers and Thomas Theobald's, which he asked her to return to his wife should he not survive. (Author's collection/Detroit Free Press)

adventure on this journey to America. His thoughts were on the Eno's fruit salts tucked in his pocket in case the sea became rough, and it never entered his mind that he had just seen his father for the last time. 'So long, Frankie. See you later,' meant just that.

Emily, too, held on to the hope that Frank Senior had been saved by another rescue ship. On the *Carpathia* she set her sewing talents to use by fashioning clothing from blankets for the women and children who had left the ship with nothing but their nightwear. Frankie was placed under the watchful eye of Fireman Samuel Collins whom he had watched stoking the enormous boilers on the *Titanic* only days before. Emily wanted Collins to keep Frankie entertained, his mind off the whereabouts of his father. Samuel did a great job, even taking the boy to visit *Carpathia's* stokers to share in their camaraderie. They rallied round, offering to make Frankie an honorary seaman provided he would drink a nasty concoction of water, vinegar and whole raw egg called a Bombay Oyster. Frankie, thrilled with the honour, swallowed it in one go and forever after considered himself part of that crew.

In New York the Salvation Army's Major and Mrs Thomas Cowan and their 12-year-old daughter, Eva, took the Goldsmiths under their protective wing. Eva took Frankie for his first ice-cream cone and to Seigel & Cooper's Department Store for a ride on the only escalator in the city. Mrs Goldsmith was outfitted, given railway tickets and pocket money and sent with Frankie to Detroit and the waiting relatives.

Not one to depend on others for long, Emily soon took a job for £1/$5 a week as a dressmaker, and Frankie began his life as an American boy. It took six months for him to realise fully that his father was gone. Even in later years he half expected him to walk through the door at any minute.

Emily became fast friends with other

survivors in those few days on the *Carpathia*. Over the years she corresponded with Amy Stanley, Rosa Abbott, Sarah Roth Iles and exchanged letters and visits with Samuel Collins. Eventually she married again, becoming Mrs Harry Illman, but Frankie always thought another good choice would have been his hero, Fireman Collins.

As Mrs Illman, Emily continued to give of her time to those less fortunate. Always indebted to the American Red Cross for their assistance in 1912, she donated over 5,000 hours to their cause during the Second World War, and countless pints of blood. In 1942 she took on the task of air raid warden for her district in Michigan should the war raging in Europe transfer to her adopted homeland. In 1955 she died quietly on a train in Ashland, Ohio, as she was on her way to visit Frankie, who by then had a family of his own.

After completing a night school course in business, in 1926 Frankie married Victoria, who was to be his companion for 55 years. They had three sons and bought their first house in Detroit with money from *Titanic* relief funds, which Emily had been diligent in pursuing. Unfortunately for Frankie, the home was located near Navin's Field where the Detroit Tigers played baseball. Every time the crowd roared over a great catch or a batter's long hit, the sound would drift over the field's walls into the surrounding neighbourhood. To Frankie's ears those cheers sounded like the moans of *Titanic*'s passengers as they froze to death in the frigid Atlantic, and he would relive the nightmare.

The Second World War found Frank employed as a civilian in the Photographic Division of the United States Air Force. He was the author of a manual for Kodak used by the troops in the South Pacific to assemble their aerial cameras. After the war he put this knowledge to use when he and Victoria opened a photographic and art supply store in Mansfield,

Ohio, which they operated for 27 years.

As with other survivors, sharing his *Titanic* story was not uppermost in Frank's mind as he went about supporting his family. He left the task of telling his sons to their grandmother, Emily. But eventually, when he retired to Florida in 1979 and the pain of the memories was less intense, he was able to begin speaking about it. He and Victoria criss-crossed the United States meeting with other survivors, and eventually Frank gained enough perspective to set his experiences on paper as a legacy for his sons. He completed his book just before his death on 27 January 1982 – Frank Senior's birthday.

Two and a half months later, on 15 April, the ice patrol unit of the United States Coast Guard scattered Frank's ashes over the site where his father had perished 70 years before, along with a commemorative wreath for all of *Titanic*'s victims. 'See you later' had finally become a reality.

Frank John Goldsmith
27 January 1879–15 April 1912

Emily Goldsmith Illman
October/December 1880–22 September 1955

Frank Goldsmith
19 December 1902–27 January 1982

Rosa 'Rhoda' Abbott (35)
Rossmore Abbott (16)
Eugene Abbott (14)

'Salvationists on the "Titanic" – "Mother Spends Five Hours on Raft and sees Sons Drown – Died like True Soldiers".'
The War Cry, 27 April 1912

THE SALVATION ARMY, as we have already heard, was ready and waiting at Pier 54 for the

Rosa Abbott. (Eaton-Haas collection)

arrival of the *Carpathia*. They had been hard at work setting up beds in their shelters for the homeless survivors and collecting food, clothing and money to sustain the needy. Identified by their uniforms and special yellow badges, they cut through the throng of 30,000 gathered in the rain and made their way to the receiving area. Evangeline Booth, Commander of the Salvation Army in the United States, was in charge. By her side were Major and Mrs Cowan, Captain George Darby (staff bandmaster) and a platoon of officers and soldiers.

Several of the arriving passengers had an affiliation with the Corps, but Rosa Abbott ('Rhoda' in many accounts), a Salvationist travelling in uniform, was by far the most seriously injured. She was suffering from exposure and her legs were so frost-bitten that they appeared burned. But Commander Booth had only to look at her to know that her bodily

injuries paled in comparison to her psychological ones. The poor soul had seen both of her sons die in the shipwreck. Hastily an ambulance was summoned from the queue and Rosa was hurried to St Vincent's Hospital and a private room away from prying eyes.

Lying in her hospital bed, Rosa mourned her sons and relived the terror of her last moments with them. They had made their way from Third Class to the Boat Deck and had watched as lifeboat after lifeboat was sent away. Rosa knew that she would be turned back if she attempted to enter one with her sons. Aged 14 and 16, Eugene and Rossmore were children to her, but men to Second Officer Lightoller loading the boats nearest to where she stood according to the 'Women and children first' rule. Eugene, sensing their fate, had fallen to his knees in prayer, not for his survival or for his brother's, but for hers. It broke her heart to think of it. She had nothing left now. She was alone.

When the water was closing in on the bridge and the ship was 'well down at the head' there was still one more boat to be launched, Collapsible A, sitting on top of the officers' house. Rosa and her sons watched as all available hands worked the boat off the roof and into the davits. Edward Brown, a steward who had been pressed into service as a seaman, climbed into the boat and called out for the falls to be cut at the exact instant that the *Titanic* took its final dive into oblivion. A bone-crushing wall of water washed him, the collapsible, and the remaining passengers into the sea. Rosa frantically clasped her sons hands as they were swept from the deck. Vainly she struggled to hang on, but they slipped from her grasp, first Eugene and then Rossmore — swallowed into the swirl of the black sea.

Gasping for air, she fought through the humanity thrashing around her, tearing at her clothes and trying to pull themselves up on her body. Flailing through the wreckage and debris littering the sea, she searched for her sons, calling their names over and over. But it was fruitless. At some point, it could have been minutes or hours, strong hands dragged her into Collapsible A.

Thirty other survivors (all men) clung to the collapsible or hauled themselves on board to stand for hours thigh deep in icy water waiting rescue. August Edvard Wennerström and his friends Gerda and Edvard Lindell swam to the boat and remained in the water clinging to its sides because Gerda did not have the strength to climb over the gunwale. Eventually August and Edvard found the strength to pull themselves in, but Gerda could not and Wennerström continued to clasp her hand to keep her afloat. But she soon slipped away. Turning, August saw that Edvard had

'... aged from a man in his 30s to a man between 90 and 100. His face had sunken in, hair and moustache turned grey, his eyes had changed and he no longer knew who he was, he just stared into space, he did not move, he did not say a word.'

Wennerström knew then that his friend was dead and eased him over the side to join his wife.

'All the feeling left us. If we wanted to know if we still had legs left, we had to feel down in the water with our hand. The only exercise we got was when someone gave up hope and died, whom we immediately threw overboard to give the live ones a little more space and at the same time lighten the weight of the boat.'

Finally only 12 or 13 of the original 30 remained.

Shortly before dawn, with the boat riding lower and lower in the sea, those few spied another lifeboat, under sail, heading in their direction. In unison they shouted to attract attention to their plight. In Lifeboat 14, 150 yards away, Officer Lowe, in fear of being

swamped, fired four shots into the air warning them not to rush his boat. But he need not have bothered, for they did not have the strength.

When they had safely been transferred from the collapsible, Lowe opened its sea cocks and cut it adrift with three dead on board, their faces covered by lifebelts in a last gesture of dignity. (The collapsible was found on 3 May by the *Olympic*. After the bodies were buried at sea, Gerda Lindell's wedding ring was discovered wedged in the bottom of the boat,

Rossmore Abbott. (Author's collection/*Providence RI Evening Bulletin*)

having slipped off when she let go of August's hand.)

Rosa had little memory of the transfer into Lowe's lifeboat, but Leading Fireman Threlfall reported cradling her in his arms until she was lifted on board the *Carpathia*. There she was given a makeshift bed in the smoking saloon from which she rarely stirred.

Her only comfort was Amy Stanley, whose cabin had been near hers on the *Titanic* and who had known her sons. Talking with Amy about Rossmore and Eugene and their life together made Rosa almost believe that they could still be alive. And while Amy listened she calmly and soothingly worked with a comb to dislodge a tenacious bit of cork that had become tangled in Rosa's long dark hair.

Rosa's husband, Stanton Abbott, a well-known heavyweight boxer and sports promoter in Providence, Rhode Island, had divorced her in 1911. They had been married 18 years and the separation was particularly hard on the boys. Deserted by Stanton, Rosa and her sons were forced into a small apartment where she took in sewing to support them. Thinking that life might be easier if she returned to her brother and mother in St Albans, Hertfordshire, she had left on the *Olympic* in August 1911, never intending to return to America.

All three Abbotts had made a serious attempt to adapt. Rossmore secured a position in a jewellery shop and jokingly wrote home to Providence that he was working in the smallest town in England. Eugene became active in the Salvation Army Corps in St Albans, and Rosa explored the possibility of starting another sewing business.

It was not long before the boys, Americans to the core, became lonely for their friends and familiar surroundings and began asking to return home. Rosa acquiesced and arranged

This beef tea mug with the White Star logo would have been used in all classes and might have contained Lemco to ward off sea-sickness.

passage through the Salvation Army Emigration Department (which had helped 70,000 leave the unemployment of Britain between 1904 and 1912). The nationwide coal strike meant that the Abbotts were transferred from the *Philadelphia* to the *Titanic*. Rossmore wrote to his friends at the Oxford Street School in Providence that he was coming home.

Shattered by his loss, those friends held a memorial service on 23 April at which they sang 'Nearer My God to Thee' and recited the Lord's Prayer. The principal spoke of Rossmore as 'an earnest student of lovable qualities who won distinction by his excellent scholarship by the winning of the Anthony Medal at the school on his graduating day ...' When Rossmore's body was found by the *Mackay-Bennett* the Anthony Medal was in his pocket attached to a watch inscribed 'Oxford St Grammar School'. He was buried at sea, too disfigured to embalm. His brother Eugene was never found.

Rosa slowly recovered from her physical ills and with the compensation for her travails, £150/$750 from the Women's Relief Committee and £50/$250 from the Titanic Relief Fund, left the hospital. In June 1912 she was staying in White Plains, New York, still under a doctor's care. Periodically she visited Major Cowan and his wife from the Salvation Army, who had also looked after the Goldsmiths, and they encouraged her to return again to her family in England who so wanted her there. But Rosa knew that she could never cross that ocean again.

By Christmas 1913 she had moved to Jacksonville, Florida, seeking a climate more favourable to the asthma she had developed from her exposure to the unforgiving North Atlantic. In a letter to Emily Goldsmith dated 1 March 1914 and reprinted in *Echoes in the Night*, she wrote, '... well, dear, I have a

When
travelling
by Sea or Land

take LEMCO with you. There is nothing
so effective as a frequent cup of hot
LEMCO Bouillon and a biscuit for keeping
away the terrible nausea of sea-sickness—
and how delicious it is!

LEMCO is made entirely from pure fresh beef.
It is a splendid strengthener and restorative,
and prevents physical exhaustion by its wonderful
power of stimulating and renewing the weakened
energies.

FOR SPORTSMEN, travellers, explorers, and
all engaged in arduous occupations, LEMCO is
priceless for the variety of uses to which it can
be put, and for its power in supporting the system
against the wear and tear of life.

Thames House - London, E.C.

Lemco

(Author's collection)

surprise for you. I am married [to George
Smith, a London silversmith]. I was not able to
work hard anymore and I had the offer from a
very old friend from London and I accepted him
to care for me and protect me.'

In another letter to Emily she appears to be
making peace with the loss of her sons: 'I have
so many times envied you with Frankie, and me
losing mine, but I trust that they are better off
out of this hard world.' She cautioned Emily,
who was about to remarry, '… have everything
you get in your own name so that if his love
changes, you will be able to keep yourself.' She
went on to say how difficult it was for her
husband to find work and indicated that they
may soon be forced to move. To carry them
through their financial difficulties she was
letting out rooms. She signed her letter 'Rhoda'.

Rosa and her husband disappear from the

Jacksonville City Directory in 1928, and thus
also from our *Titanic* ledger.

Rosa 'Rhoda' Abbott Smith
1877–?

Rossmore Edward Abbott
1896–15 April 1912

Eugene Joseph Abbott
31 March 1898–15 April 1912

Amy Stanley (22)

'Praise the sea, but keep on the land.'
George Herbert

ON THE NIGHT OF 14 April 1912 Amy was
anticipating her arrival at New York Harbour.
Preparing for what she perceived would be a
hectic time, she sat in her cabin writing
postcards home: 'Had a nice trip. Landed safely
in New York. Will write soon.' Very organised,
but slightly premature.

Amy was a plucky girl, the kind you would
want by your side during an emergency.
Ambitious, she desired more than life in Upper
Wolvercote, Oxfordshire, where her father
farmed and owned a general store. Besides,
being the only girl in a family of five teasing
boys, who did nasty things like taking her
bicycle without asking and leaving it out in the
rain to rust, spurred her to move on. In her
early 20s she left for Oxford to become an
apprentice dressmaker and worked in several
fashionable high street shops. Eventually she
went into service in Wallington, Surrey. But
the wider world beckoned and Amy secured a
position with the Dann family in New Haven,
Connecticut. Her friend Grace had already
emigrated and Amy was anxious to join her in
that new adventure.

Isaac Dann and his brothers were wealthy
industrialists, owners of a factory that made

Amy Stanley before she left for America. (The British Library)

Dann Brothers also made the sled used by Commodore Peary in his 1909 trek to the North Pole, an achievement that figured prominently in their advertising. Amy was hired to work as a domestic for Mr and Mrs Dann and their three children, all of whom had reached maturity but were still living under their parents' roof. Amy must have had plenty of work to do, but the only comment she ever made about her employers in later years was that Mrs Dann never put soap and water on her face, using a cold cream instead, a luxury that would have been unthinkable to down-to-earth Amy.

Hence her presence on the *Titanic*. Laying aside her postcard writing and determining that something was wrong, Amy changed from her nightgown to a blue silk dress and had the presence of mind to strap on her cloth bag containing £90/$450. She bundled her fur coat over it all for warmth and, forgoing stockings, jammed her feet into slippers. Being a Third Class passenger with a fur coat was to have interesting consequences for Amy later on.

She helped her cabin mates, governess Elizabeth Dowdell and her five-year-old charge Virginia Emanuel, to dress (right down to Virginia's white kid gloves) and to tie on their lifebelts, then the three of them went up to the Boat Deck. Years later Amy wrote in her diary that as she made her escape she saw passengers kneeling in prayer, rosaries clutched in their hands beseeching, 'Mother of God pray for us sinners now and to the hour of our death'.

Amy's next letter was written from New York City and printed in the *Oxford Times* on 18 May 1912:

'Dear Father and Mother,
I have had a terrible experience, one that I shall never forget as long as I live ... It was about 11.30pm. I got

carriage bodies. They also held a patent for an improved method of bending wood, which was used in the curvilinear furniture popular at the time. It is interesting to note here that the out of bed and put my coat on and went out on deck and asked a steward what was the matter. He told me it was only the engines stopped and ordered all the women back to bed. But I did not go.'

Amy was assisted into Collapsible C by two men whom she had met at meals.

She continues:

'We were rowing for several hours. I seemed to have extra strength to keep up my nerves, for I even made them laugh when I told them we had escaped vaccination, for we were all to have been vaccinated that day ... I was able to fix a rope round the women for them to be pulled up on the *Carpathia* while the men steadied the boat – the women seemed quite stupefied ...'

A cloth bag no doubt similar to the one in which Amy carried her £90.

When she arrived on the deck of the *Carpathia* in her fur coat, those allotting the limited accommodations thought that Amy was upper class and gave her a berth in a cabin, but she was ousted when they discovered their error and her space given to an older woman from First Class. This indignity, coupled with a profound hearing loss from her exposure to the cold, had a lingering effect.

Years later, her son Eugene, looking back on his childhood, believes that she suffered from depression and that her nervousness and strict discipline were the result of her *Titanic* experience. But on the rescue ship she was her stalwart self:

On board the Carpathia Amy used a comb to remove the tangled bits of cork from Rosa Abbott's hair.

'The sight on board was awful, with raving women – barely six women were saved who could say they had not lost a relative. Oh! The widows the *Titanic* has made! I attended to a woman who was picked up on a raft. She has lost two sons on the *Titanic* [the Abbotts]. Their cabin was next to mine.

Don't you think I have been lucky throughout? I remain your loving daughter

Amy'

As the *Carpathia* steamed into New York Harbour, passengers ignored the rain and fog to line the rails calling to each other, 'Get ready to see the lady.' Amy did not know about the Statue of Liberty or its significance to the immigrant, but was impressed at the reverence with which her fellow passengers regarded the welcoming figure of freedom.

Forewarned not to speak to reporters at Pier 54 and feeling dishevelled by the ordeal and lack of hairpins, Amy disembarked with her head shrouded in a piece of fabric that she had ripped from the dangling lining of her blue silk dress. She and her shipmates were hustled through the gauntlet of question-shouting newsmen by New York's police and were taken to a room, given hot coffee and 'delicious food', and questioned about their destination. Then Amy and several others were escorted to the Junior League Hotel for women on 78th Street and the East River – with the newsmen in hot pursuit. The room Amy occupied was a comfortable single with a desk and a chair, but what pleased her most was being able to take a bath and pin up her hair. She stayed there only long enough to get her bearings and a railway ticket to her friend Grace and the Dann family in New Haven. (Amy shared part of her £90 with Grace, whose trunk she was bringing over on the ship.)

Safe in Connecticut she began a correspondence with Rosa Abbott, the Goldsmiths, with whom she had shared that terrible night in Collapsible C, and Sam Collins, who had returned from England and taken a job as a fireman in the Winchester Gun Factory in Connecticut. Several times in later diaries Amy writes of his visits, letters and the 4-inch replica lifeboat he carved for her from the wood of one of *Titanic*'s real lifeboats. But she repeatedly vows that there was nothing between them, which is probably quite true as Fireman Collins had an eye for not one but a bevy of other female *Titanic* survivors.

As Amy became comfortable in America she ventured out more, and one evening at a dance she met her future husband, Eugene Tanner. By this time war was raging in Europe and when the United States joined the fray, Eugene was called for naval duty. Amy moved on from the Danns and in 1918 was living in the Young Women's Christian Association and working in New Haven as a clerk – and waiting for Eugene's safe return. He secured an early discharge, and on 1 November 1918 in Brooklyn, New York, ten days before the Armistice was signed, they were married.

The newlyweds set up a household in Providence, Rhode Island, Eugene's home town, and he went to work for an optical company. The Depression hit them hard, but Amy's tenacity and thrift kept them going and they eked out enough money to install electricity and water in their small home. Amy never worked for others again, holding her family together by raising chickens, growing blackcurrants and blueberries, canning vegetables from her garden and sewing clothing for her children.

The Tanners had two sons, Alfred, born 22 July 1921, and Eugene Junior, born 8 August 1926. Both followed their father into the optical company and Alfred, like his father, served in the Navy during the Second World War. It became a Tanner family tradition when Amy's granddaughter entered the Navy and

This lovely bracelet might have belonged to Amy Stanley, the only Amy on the ship.

rose to the rank of Lieutenant Colonel.

Amy returned to England only once, shortly before she married, and while there she gave a talk to the people in her home town about her experiences on the *Titanic*. She always wanted her story to be told and before her death gave her diary and notes to her daughter-in-law, hoping that they would be compiled and published some day.

Elizabeth Dowdell was born in Union City, New Jersey, and was 31 at the time of the sinking. She had taken Virginia to London to visit her mother, an opera singer named Estelle Emanuele, who was performing there for six months. Elizabeth was quite outspoken about her treatment on the Carpathia, *which she thought was frightful, especially the food, calling it 'hardtack'. When she reached New York, Elizabeth immediately left the pier to take Virginia to the home of her grandparents, Mr and Mrs Samuel Weisel. In the process she missed her own family who presumed that she was dead. Returning home they boarded a trolley only to find that Elizabeth had boarded it as well on her way to find them. Imagine that reunion! Elizabeth became Mrs Fierer and moved to New York City in later years.*

Virginia moved to London as an adult where she changed the Virginia to Vera and the Emanuel to Hanson in a marriage. There is some suggestion that she wrote a book later in her life in which she detailed her Titanic *experiences.*

Amy Zillah Elsie Stanley Tanner
4 June 1889–23 April 1955

Elizabeth Dowdell Fierer
6 September 1880–16 November 1962

Virginia Ethel Emanuel
1907– died as Vera Hanson circa 1972

Louise Heilmann Kink (26)
Louise Gretchen Kink (4)

'Memory is the thing I forget with.'
A child's definition

EMIGRANTS TO THE UNITED STATES between 1892 and 1932 had to survive Ellis Island and the interrogation and medical scrutiny of America's admitting authorities before they could 'breathe free' as promised by the inscription on the Statue of Liberty. It was generally a benign encounter and the majority of immigrants passed through easily to their destinations by train to the far reaches of the continental United States, or by ferry to Lower Manhattan. But from the rejected, stories spread back to the old country, enlarging on the disappointment with every telling. Ellis Island took on the magnitude of the Pearly Gates – being turned back was condemnation to purgatory.

Titanic's surviving Third Class passengers were spared the ordeal of this rite of passage to 'The land of the free and the home of the brave'. United States immigration officials felt that they had suffered enough. To officially welcome them and those of their compatriots whose journey ended in the North Atlantic, a ceremony was held on Ellis Island in June 1991. Louise Kink Pope, Third Class survivor, then 83, unveiled a plaque in their honour, presenting it to the National Park Service. Author John P. Eaton's words grace the plaque: 'Their journey to the land of hope was stayed by death. They sleep in ocean depth, on alien shores, Never to enter the Golden Door. Never

to wake from their dream of freedom.' As these words were being read, a diminutive Louise stood smiling proudly at the crowds gathered there in the 100-degree heat. The Statue of Liberty was visible over her shoulder; a fitting symbol for the girl who was always extremely honoured to have become an American.

The Kink family was one of the few emigrant families to survive the sinking intact. Anton Kink and his wife and daughter, both named Louise, left in Lifeboat 2 from *Titanic*'s port side at 1.45am – but not without difficulty. They were travelling with Anton's younger brother, Vincenz, and his sister, Maria, to Milwaukee from Zurich, Switzerland. The family were assigned different cabins – Louise, little Louise (who liked to be called Lou) and Maria were in a cabin in the stern section of the ship with three other women, and Anton and Vincenz were in the forward section with the men.

Louise Kink Pope on Ellis Island dedicating a plaque to Titanic's *passengers.* (Michael Findlay collection)

Little Louise with her mother and father upon reaching New York. (Author's collection/*Milwaukee Journal*)

When Anton felt the iceberg strike, which he described as an earthquake, he ran with his cabin mates to the forward Third Class promenade in time to see the black berg gliding past. By the time he returned to his cabin, packed and went aft to get the women in his family, the water was sloshing around his ankles and he described the ship as having a decided list to '... the left and forward. The water welled up from the lower deck.'

In the ensuing scramble to escape, Vincenz and Maria were lost, but Anton persevered. Tired of following the crowd, he veered off into the First Class stateroom area, down a corridor and out to a deck where luck provided two lifeboats. He gave an excellent account of the experience in a *Milwaukee Journal* interview on 24 April 1912:

'A sailor took my child and handed her into one of them. My wife was also helped in by the sailors. I was touched upon the shoulder and asked to step back, whereupon my wife and child cried at the top of their voices at my being left behind. I ducked down, broke through those standing about and jumped into the boat as it was lowered.'

Anton thereby escaped the 'Women and children first' death edict.

His presentation of that night seems so methodical and straightforward, his powers of observation and grasp of fact precise. But to little Lou, just a few days past her fourth birthday, it was terrifying and traumatic, so much so that everything in her life up to 14 April 1912 was completely obliterated forever from her memory. Lou's *Titanic* recollections were those told to her by her father or learned in later life when she became involved in *Titanic*-related activities. Her mother, suffering her own emotional reaction, refused to discuss the subject.

In Milwaukee Anton worked in a factory, saving until he had enough set aside to rent a produce farm. This farm was the beginning of Lou's love for the land and a new set of memories – not all happy, unfortunately. It seems that the elder Louise was a difficult woman. Although she looked round and jolly, she was reserved, rigid and demanding. This was in direct contrast to Anton, who may have appeared austere with his slim face, piercing eyes, blade-like nose and formidable moustache, but who was in fact outgoing and charming. These two opposites did not attract and the couple separated in 1919. Ultimately their divorce removed Anton from Lou's life for ever – especially when he moved to South America and remarried.

Lou and her mother remained on the farm and certainly had some good times together, sharing a love of the land. But the older Louise became more set in her ways. She refused to speak English, preferring her native German, and became more hypercritical and smothering of her daughter. When she remarried Lou was finally able to build a life of her own. Leaving school before graduation, she married Harold Pope and had four children. Like her mother's before her, Lou's marriage ended in divorce. But she faced whatever life brought her way with a positive, happy attitude, a sweet smile and boundless energy.

The elder Louise became ill in later years, but Lou would not hear of sending her to a nursing home. She personally took on her mother's care, even though it had a deleterious effect on her own health. But again she rallied, overcoming this as she had overcome tuberculosis, arthritis, and breast cancer.

Despite all this, Lou continued to drive her tractor and to work in a Milwaukee plant nursery. And there were many firsts to keep her young. In 1986 she testified at the United

Louise with the blanket her father wrapped around her and the shoes she wore to leave the ship. (Michael Findlay collection)

States House of Representatives' hearing to explore guidelines for the disposition of the newly discovered *Titanic* wreck. At those hearings she expressed a desire that the ship be untouched. However, this opinion was to alter over the next few years and she became an enthusiastic supporter of artefact exhibitions. She came to believe that the new safety rules brought about by the sinking were life-saving and that *Titanic*'s dead had not been forfeited in vain.

She made her first ocean voyage since 1912 on the *QE2*, travelling to Halifax, Nova Scotia, to place headstones on grave sites of six *Titanic* victims who had been recently identified by Titanic International researchers, Michael Findlay and Brian Meister.

In the end her children and grandchildren

(Michael Findlay collection)

believed that the most important event in her life was her emigration to the United States, and not the vehicle that had taken her only part of the way. Her rallying days at an end, Lou gave in to lung cancer in 1992.

Louise Heilmann Kink Kroepfl
1886–9 October 1979

Louise Gretchen Kink Pope
8 April 1908–25 August 1992

Elin Hakkarainen (24)
Anna Turja (18)
Alice Johnson (26)
Harold Johnson (4)
Eleanor Johnson (18 months)
Laina Heikkinen (26)

'If they were so close to take those pictures, why didn't someone help us?'
Anna Turja

THERE WERE 57 FINNISH passengers in Third Class. They tend to be grouped with the Swedes, but they were as much Eastern European as Scandinavian and deserve a memory of their own. In 1912 Finland was experiencing economic hardship, hunger and the oppressive political thumb of Russia. Loyalties were divided and brother fought brother over allegiance to the Russian masters or to an independent Finland. Regardless of their beliefs, the young men were forcibly conscripted into the Russian Army. Elin Hakkarainen and her husband, Pekka, chose to flee the situation, and the ship they chose was the *Titanic*.

Elin and Pekka had both lived in the United States before they were married, he as a foreman at a steel mill in Monessen, Pennsylvania, for five years, earning $5 a day, and Elin for four years as a domestic in Quincy, Massachusetts. Had they not both returned to Finland and had Elin's sister not known Pekka in Pennsylvania and encouraged him to contact Elin, the two may never have met. They were married in Helsinki on 15 January 1912, three months to the day before their return to America.

Elin's son by her second marriage, Gerald Nummi, worked on a book about his mother's journey to America for many years, but died before its completion. Janet White stepped in to finish it, and the result, *I'm Going To See What Has Happened*, tells Elin's story and those of other Finns on the *Titanic*. Below are highlights from those stories, beginning with Elin's words:

'The fact that I was aboard the *Titanic* on this particular day and time caused me to be a bit of a curiosity during the later years. People would look at me in awe and would never allow me to forget the experience I had gone through. Very often I was questioned to the point of tears.

As Pekka reached to turn out the cabin light, we felt the ship make a sudden turn and heard a scraping sound as if someone had pushed a row of glasses from the shelf to the floor ... My husband jumped out of bed, slipped into his clothes and left the cabin, saying the last words I could ever hear him say, "I'm going to see what has happened." ... After a few moments I grabbed my purse and life jacket and ran out to the passageway. The door at the end of the passageway was locked! I ran to the other end of the passageway and found the door locked also. After a bit of wandering, I discovered another door ... which led to another passageway. A ship's steward appeared with a small group of women saying, "You better come with us. There is another way to get to the upper deck."'

Steward J. E. Hart had already led a group of 30 passengers out of the confusing maze of

Elin Hakkarainen (left) photographed with her friends before her first trip to the United States, circa 1905. (Gerald E. Nummi/Janet A. White collection)

Elin and Pekka Hakkarainen's wedding portrait taken on 15 January 1912. (Gerald E. Nummi/Janet A. White collection)

Third Class to Lifeboat 8 when he came upon a wandering Elin. She joined his second group, made up of many Swedish and Finnish women and children. By this time all of the barriers had been unlocked, and after reaching C Deck via the Third Class aft staircase he and his charges would have had a clear run up a ladder past the Second Class Library, through a door to First Class, up the main First Class stairway to A Deck, then by way of a service ladder to the Boat Deck.

This gold bar pin, which at one time held a stone, may well have been worn by a Third Class woman passenger at the neck of her blouse as was the fashion in 1912.

Once there Elin huddled for warmth against the deck house, which housed the First Class Smoking Room, and looked in vain for Pekka. Lifeboat 15 was about to be lowered to the deck below to pick up other passengers and she was finally forced to get in. As she stepped across the space between the deck and the lifeboat she stumbled and would have plunged to certain death if someone had not caught her arm and dragged her to the safety of the lifeboat. At the stop on A Deck five women, three children and a man with a baby were brought on board, according to Steward Hart's testimony at the American inquiry, packing 70 people into a space designed for 65. All of this activity was conducted in an eerie silence punctuated only by the shouts of the crew for more women and children. Elin continues:

This small heart with a flower design behind glass looks like a bride's gift from her new husband.

'We did reach the water, but could feel the boat rising with the stern before the ropes were released. The screams of the people struggling in the water continued for about a half hour. Suddenly, I realised that my husband was out there, somewhere. I stood up to look at the struggling people in the water. I called, "Pekka, Pekka, I am here, come this way, please come this way." My calls were in vain for I felt sure that he was trapped within the passageway in the ship.'

Elin did not return to her homeland, as was the case with many *Titanic* widows, but gained the confidence to stay on from having lived in the United States before. Moving to Philadelphia she picked up the pieces of her life with the support of the Finnish community and the Lutheran Church. She lived in a boarding house and worked as a dressmaker until moving to Weirton, West Virginia, in 1916 to join friends. It was there that she met Emil Nummi, also Finnish, who worked for the Weirton Steel Company. They married in 1917, in April, the month to remember, and had their only son, Gerald, in 1920. By 1926 Emil had secured a position with the Republic Steel Corporation and the Nummi family moved to Warren, Ohio, where they lived for more than 40 years.

During those years Elin continued to work as a seamstress and tried to avoid the celebrity that came from surviving the *Titanic*. Speaking of it gave her terrible nightmares. But she kept the blanket given her on the *Carpathia*, the necklace she was wearing on the night of the disaster, and her wedding picture with Pekka. In later years she would say of him, 'I knew I would never meet another man so bright and I didn't.'

Elin was an extremely strong lady, exceptionally close to her son, Gerald, who, in a strange twist of fate, died in 1995 on 20 March, the anniversary of her birth. Elin had died of a stroke on 2 January 1957 at the age of 68. Earlier that evening she had been reading Walter Lord's gripping *Titanic* narrative *A Night To Remember*.

* * *

ANNA SOFIA TURJA, 18, was on her way to Ashtabula, Ohio, to join her sister Mary and brother-in-law John Lundi, who had sent the £10/$50 ticket. One of 21 children, Anna had been working since the age of eight as a domestic in Oulainen, Finland. In Ohio she would do the same thing for her sister and brother-in-law until she could get established. In the Nummi/White book her son, Reverend Martin Lundi, speaks of life with a *Titanic* survivor:

'On the morning of April 14th of any given year that I can remember, there was a distinct and unusual silence at breakfast … The mood of the day was set for me when I saw anguish in eyes that filled with tears. Mother would be sitting at the kitchen table and would ask, "Do you remember what day it is today?" "Yes, Mother," I assured her. "I remember." Then she would look down at folded hands and say softly, "But no one can truly understand unless they had been there themselves …" She said the ship "shook and shuddered". But she added she was not afraid because she didn't know what had happened …

Reluctantly, mother dressed warmly, put on her life jacket, and followed her room-mates as they left everything behind, and went to the concert hall where they stopped to listen to the orchestra perform. Still under no sense of panic or danger, the women just sat and listened to the music. Then she said some of the members of the crew came in, stopped the concert, ordered everyone out on deck, then locked up the concert hall doors.'

Anna followed her Finnish friends out to the deck but left them when they went to the Boat Deck, opting to stay on the First Class Promenade where it was warm. While waiting there she saw another ship off on the horizon and was calmed by the assumption that it was coming to their aid. When Lifeboat 11 was lowered to the First Class Promenade area to take on more passengers, Anna readily climbed on board, secure in her belief that the rescue ship was only a short distance away. Packed tightly, No 11 left the starboard side at

Anna Turja ready for her journey. (Reverend Martin Lundi/Nummi-White collection)

1.25am. On board with Anna were Nurse Cleaver with baby Trevor Allison, Edith Russell with her pig 'Maxixe', Elizabeth Nye with her canary (allegedly), Philip Aks in the arms of Argene del Carlo, and Jane Quick with daughters Phyllis and Winnie – a boat of many stories. Anna's friends who had gone to the Boat Deck did not survive.

After a brief sojourn in St Vincent's Hospital, Anna was sent to Ashtabula, Ohio, tagged like a child with her name and destination because she did not understand English. Stepping from the train into the arms of her sister she was overwhelmed by the cheers of a huge crowd gathered there for her arrival, including a handsome Emil Lundi, John's brother. There was double rejoicing because Anna's name had not made the survivors' list and for days she had been presumed dead. In Finland Anna's mother grieved for weeks until a letter from Anna herself arrived to announce her life not her death.

Anna never worked for her sister and brother-in-law because Emil Lundi fell in love with her and proposed marriage, saying he would not allow such a pretty young thing to be a domestic for his brother. Life was a struggle for this branch of the Lundi family; Emil's pay as a school custodian was only £44/$220 a month at the height of his earning power. But Anna was no stranger to hard work and frugality and raised seven children on that modest amount.

In her community she was known as a *Titanic* survivor, but her failure to learn English was a shield against the incessant questioning that had so disturbed Elin Nummi. But when the 1953 movie *Titanic*, with Barbara Stanwyck and Clifton Webb, had an early showing in Ashtabula's Shea Theatre, Anna and her son Martin were in the audience.

'Mother was the guest of honor. It was her first opportunity to view the first movie she had ever seen in her entire life. I went along with her to interpret ... When the movie was over, Mother was silent, and seemed dazed and physically weakened from the experience. One reporter said to me, "Ask your mother if it was realistic." I did. Mother looked up with tears in her eyes, still silently crying for those whose voices have haunted her all her life, and in all innocent ignorance of the magic of Hollywood recreations, said, "If they were so close to take those pictures, why didn't someone help us?"'

After her husband's death in 1952, Anna lived alone, ministering to the sick and participating in church life until she could no longer care for herself and was moved to a convalescent home near family in San Diego, California. She died there in 1982, a woman of 'magnificent faith'.

* * *

LITTLE ELEANOR JOHNSON was on the *Titanic* with her mother, Alice Berg, and four-year-old brother, Harold. Alice had emigrated to St Charles, Illinois, years before in an arranged marriage with a much older Oscar Johnson, but had taken her children back to Finland to visit her ailing father and then on to Sweden for a stay with her husband's family. On the way back to the United States she agreed to chaperone 20-year-old Elin Braf, who was emigrating from Medeltorp, Sweden, to Chicago.

When the iceberg did its damage, Alice and Elin, along with other Third Class passengers, went out on deck and frolicked with the fragments of ice until an officer told them to go back to bed, as the ship was about to get under way. They complied, but were soon roused by their dining steward and told to vacate their cabins.

Eleanor was a toddler at the time, but throughout her life maintained a vague recollection of being held in her mother's arms at a great height surrounded by crying and screaming. Alice, who seldom spoke of the tragedy except to Eleanor, told her that there was a ring of seaman around Lifeboat 15 shouting and gesturing for her to approach. When she reached the edge of the deck, she was afraid to cross the space between the side of the ship and the dangling lifeboat, especially with baby Eleanor in her arms. A man in the boat had encouraged her with, 'Close your eyes and don't look down. Just lean forward and I'll catch you.' Following his instructions she landed safely in the boat.

Elin, with Harold in tow, could not make that same leap of faith. She stood rooted to the deck with fear. Alice shouted, 'Hand Harold down to me, Elin, please, hurry, drop him into the boat.' But Elin remained immobile. In frustration, a seaman finally grabbed the four-year-old and threw him over the side to his mother, leaving Elin behind to perish and Alice to grieve for the loss of the girl who had been placed in her care.

Alice returned with her children to Chicago and eventually had another son, only to lose her husband Oscar shortly thereafter. Still a young woman she remarried, becoming Mrs Carl Peterson. Three more sons and three more daughters followed from that union, making Eleanor and Harold part of a large family, but with a separate and unique relationship of their own.

As an adult Harold became an engineer with the International Harvester Company, married and had a son and a daughter of his own. Eleanor graduated from high school and worked first as a telephone operator, then in a speedometer factory until 1934, when she married Delbert Shuman, a jewellery store owner, and had one son. In 1968 Eleanor lost both Harold and her mother, and in 1981 she lost Delbert. After that she lived alone, occupied with her gardening, knitting and family.

Giving interviews about the *Titanic* was not something a shy Eleanor had done with any regularity over the years, and frankly she could not understand the public's interest in the disaster. But in 1995 she finally agreed to meet a reporter from the *Chicago Tribune*. In response to his question, 'What have you done of a *Titanic* nature over the years?' she responded

Eleanor and Harold Johnson soon after returning to Chicago. (Eleanor Shuman/Michael Findlay collection)

sweetly, 'Mostly refused invitations.'

In 1996 she received an invitation not to be refused – to sail on the RMS Titanic Memorial Cruise to the wreck site. Her son, daughter-in-law and two grandchildren watched as she spoke with passengers, signed autographs and tossed flowers into the sea in commemoration of *Titanic*'s dead. It was a rewarding experience for them to share and it brought peace for Eleanor and understanding to them all.

In March 1998 she was planning to attend a Titanic International event in St Petersburg, Florida, where an exhibition of artefacts was on display at the Florida International Museum.

Eleanor joked that she could not wait and would just love to get her hands on those artefacts. However, not long before the departure date she tripped on a rug in her hallway and ended up, not in Florida, but in hospital with a broken hip. While recuperating she contracted pneumonia, which proved to be too much for her 87-year-old lungs and she passed away on 7 March.

* * *

THE DAY BEFORE LAINA HEIKKINEN was to sail on the *Titanic* she broke out in a rash. Was it a premonition? She always thought so. Rash or not, she had her ticket, it had cost her £4 18s 6d and she was going, come hell or high water. Little did she know it would be both.

Laina reached the ship by the standard Finnish route: from Hanko to Hull, England, on board the *Polaris* and from there to Southampton by train. The route was familiar; she had been to America before, working in New York City as a maid. Lonely there without a family, she had hoped to bring her sister along this time, but her mother forbade it, and Laina made the journey alone.

How Laina got to Portland after the disaster is a testimonial to her adventurous spirit. With the money given her by White Star she first went to Boston, then, on a whim, purchased a ticket on 10 May 1912 to cross the American continent to Oregon. In a Portland boarding house she met her future husband, Jacob Penttila, who had left Finland in 1904 to escape the Russian conscription. After two years of persistent courting, Jacob finally convinced an independent Laina to marry him. The young couple moved to Roselodge, Oregon, where in 1917 their daughter Inez was born.

When Inez was a toddler the Penttilas bought six acres in Clatskanie, Oregon, on a hill overlooking the Columbia River, a property that would remain in the family until 1996. Laina grew vegetables and tended to their few fruit trees, chickens and cow, while Jacob supplemented the family income with carpentry work. At night, their chores completed, Jacob would sit in the fading light serenading Laina and Inez on the kantela, a Finnish folk instrument; their favourite tune was 'Beautiful Ohio'.

Their home had no running water or electricity and was heated by a wood-burning stove, but they were happy, sustained by a close-knit Finnish community with its own stores, churches and social activities. Laina, though strict with Inez and plagued by a nervous condition from her experience on the *Titanic*, enjoyed walking to her friends' homes for coffee and a good chat. Sadly, in later years her legs became paralysed and those visits came to an end. In 1943, having reached only her 57th year of life, Laina passed away.

Nine years later, in 1952, Inez was on board a Swedish freighter returning from the Olympics in Finland when it collided with a whaling boat, opening the bow and igniting a fire in a cargo of turpentine cans. Her immediate thoughts were of her mother's stories and she fully expected to relive them by putting to sea in a rickety lifeboat in the foggy night. Scared to death, she stood watching as the crew fought to bring the flames under control. They succeeded after a three-hour battle and the ship was spared from sharing *Titanic*'s fate. Inez had survived this experience as her mother had survived the *Titanic*, and she repeated to herself one of Laina's favourite sayings: 'You know what the good book would say, "Jumala On Hyva" – "God is Good"'.

With no wardrobes in Third Class, the Finnish girls would have hung their coats on a rack like this.

Eleanor Johnson Shuman
23 September 1910–7 March 1998

Elin Braf
1892–15 April 1912

Laina Heikkinen Penttila
1886–1943

Laina Heikkinen before her wedding. (Inez Perry/
Nummi-White collection)

Elin Dolck Hakkarainen Nummi
20 March 1888–2 January 1957

Pekka Hakkarainen
1 January 1884–15 April 1912

Anna Sofia Turja Lundi
20 June 1893–20 December 1982

Alice Berg Johnson Peterson
21 April 1885–19 December 1968

Harold Johnson
28 January 1908–10 April 1968

Margaret Devaney (19)

*'If her eyes are blue as skys, that's Peggy
    O'Neil.*
*If she's smiling all the while, that's Peggy
    O'Neil.*
If she walks like a shy little rogue,
If she talks with a cute little brogue,
*Sweet personality, full of rascality, that's
    Peggy O'Neil.'*
Song by Harry Pease, G. Nelson/Gilbert
Dodge, written in 1924

BEFORE SHE WAS PEGGY O'NEILL she was
Margaret Devaney, born in Kilmacowen,
County Sligo, Ireland, to a farming family. She,
her parents and seven brothers and sisters lived
in a thatched cottage with dirt floors, no
electricity, and chickens underfoot. They eked
out a living with bits of farming and raised pigs
– one to eat, one to sell. It was a hard,
scrabbling life. Certainly there was bounty, but
not for the masses. Salmon aplenty ran in the
streams near the Devaney farm, but they were
forbidden access to them; the stream could only
be fished with permission of the landowner, in
this case the Crown. But hunger takes chances,
and with a smile Margaret remembered that
there was a wee bit of poaching going on.

She received a basic reading and writing
education, but not in a proper school, as Ireland
did not have teacher training until 1890.
Whoever taught her, however, inspired a
fondness for W. B. Yeats, Ireland's esteemed
poet. He wrote often of the beauty of County

Margaret Devaney as a young woman. (Findlay/ Landsberg collection)

Sligo, calling it 'land of heart's desire'. But beauty does not put food on the table and, like so many others before and after them, the Devaney children left to make their way in America. Two brothers and a sister emigrated before Margaret. One of the brothers, Michael, had a secure position as groom in John D. Rockefeller's stables, and when it became Margaret's turn to continue the chain of migration, he sent the fare.

Yes, it was difficult for 19-year-old Margaret, often called Peggy, to leave behind all that she knew, but this was tempered by the excitement she felt at sailing on the *Titanic*. Often, when Ireland's young people departed for the New World, the family would host an American wake, not knowing if or when they would all be together again. On the evening of Margaret's

wake, her youngest brother, John, presented her with his most prized possession for remembrance, a pocket-knife into which he had had the village smithy fit a new blade. Peggy put it in a safe pocket with her rosary.

Morning dawned and her mother waved goodbye from the door of the cottage, too emotional to accompany yet another child to the train at Ballysodare, the main departure point from County Sligo to the rest of Ireland, and from there the world. So off Margaret went in the horse-drawn 'jaunting-car' with her father and two neighbouring farm girls, Mary Delia Burns and Kate Hagardon, also booked on the *Titanic*. As their train sped from Ballysodare via Dublin to Queenstown, the girls talked of the possibilities life now held. Even so, tears flowed as the last of Ireland disappeared from view and the *Titanic* headed to the open sea accompanied by the strains of 'Erin's Lament' played on the bagpipes by passenger Eugene Daly. (Daly was a 29-year-old Irishman from Athlone, a prominent member of the Gaelic League and the Athlone Pipers' Band; during the voyage he played his pipes for dancing in the Third Class General Room. He survived the sinking by climbing out of the water on to Collapsible B.)

Gregarious Peggy had a wonderful time on board, thrilled with the vessel and enamoured with the appointments, even way down on G Deck where she shared a six-bed cabin with Mary Delia, Kate and other girls of similar dreams and destinations. Fearful of getting lost in the mass of corridors, she made sure her ticket was in her pocket at all times.

She and her friends were assigned to the first seating at the evening meal. On 14 April they lingered over their ragout of beef and potatoes until the stewards shooed them out to set places for the second seating. Grabbing apples from the fruit bowl in the centre of the table, the group went to the General Room to finish their conversation; Peggy went via her cabin in the stern to get John's knife to peel the apples. When the last core was tossed away, she put the knife in the pocket of her sweater for safe keeping. And, as she would say, ''Tis a lucky thing I did.'

It was only a few hours later when the purser rallied everyone to evacuate. Peggy had the presence of mind to layer one garment on another, added the warm sweater she had worn earlier and a dark green knitted cap for good measure. Not knowing what was happening, she and her friends packed their cabin bags and, lugging them behind, started the ascent from G Deck to the lifeboats. They were never given any specific direction or instructions, and four decks into their climb they found their escape route barred by a ladder of about 4 feet topped by a locked gate. Leaving their satchels, Peggy and her friends hitched up their skirts, climbed the ladder and scaled the gate. One of the Sligo girls was miserably seasick and after climbing she lost all energy and slumped to the deck, opting to wait until Peggy returned with some news. The other Sligo girl stayed to look after her.

Peggy got caught up in the crowd surging toward the Boat Deck, led in the direction of the distress flares being set off on the starboard side near the davit where Lifeboat 1 had been. Collapsible C was now in its place and ready for launch. She was hustled into the boat, the final call was made for women and children and Chief Officer Wilde gave the order to lower away. Peggy never had a chance to return to her friends. (Hastily looking around and seeing no other women and children in the vicinity, Bruce Ismay and William Carter took the opportunity to jump into this boat.)

Peggy, who was seated on the side nearest the *Titanic*, had to push the collapsible away from

This floor tile was used in many of the ship's public rooms, especially in Third Class. Margaret might have danced on it during the party in the Third Class General Room on Sunday night.

the sides of the ship as it made its descent, for it was now 1.40am and the list to port was so great that the rub strake or planking running along the side of the collapsible kept catching on the liner's rivets. There was serious concern that either the canvas would rip or the passengers would be tipped out. But there was worse to come. When 'Ismay's Boat', as it was to be dubbed later by the press, reached the water, the oars could not be freed from the oar locks, as they were lashed with stiff, new ropes. Quartermaster Rowe, put in charge by Captain Smith, knew that to remain tied to a sinking ship meant certain death. He urgently called out for a knife. Peggy, feeling in her sweater pocket, found John's 7-inch gift. The ropes were sawed away and the rowing began.

Peggy's most vivid memory of that night was not the fear of being deposited into the sea or being sucked down with the ship, but the anguished screams of the people struggling for their lives in the freezing water. All night long, until she was lifted to the *Carpathia*'s deck, she clutched her rosary and prayed for their souls.

On board the *Carpathia* a crewman tapped her on the shoulder and handed her a small bundle. He whispered, 'Put this under your coat and don't tell anyone.' Somehow he had salvaged the flag from one of *Titanic*'s lifeboats for her as a memento of the experience. What foresight and sense of occasion — or was he just trying to capture the interest of a dark-haired, blue-eyed Irish beauty?

Peggy was not listed on the initial survivors' roster, and her brother Michael had worked himself into a frenzy waiting for the *Carpathia*'s arrival. Commandeering a policeman's horse, he charged through the barricades and searched the pier for her face, but with no luck. Learning that the Queenstown passengers had been taken to St Vincent's Hospital by a Father Grogan, Michael rushed across town to a tearful reunion.

In a 1974 interview, Peggy remembered the years that followed. 'My sister had a nice apartment so I moved in with her. And soon I had a job and was on my way to getting established in the new world', very concise and indicative of her no-nonsense approach to life. She worked for a gynaecologist in both his office and in his home as an au pair for his son. In 1914, on one of the outings with the boy to

Margaret on the beach where she met her husband. With her is the child she looked after until her marriage. (Findlay/Landsberg collection)

a Long Island beach, she met her future husband, John Joseph O'Neill. She was 22 and, not knowing the exact date of her own birth, adopted her new husband's birth date as her own, shaving off a few years in the process. Her children discovered the ruse many years later and one of her daughters thought that she, too, had to find a husband with the same birth date so their marriage could be as compatible as that of her mother and father.

Peggy's parish church was the magnificent St Patrick's Cathedral on Fifth Avenue in New York, and it was there she married John O'Neill, becoming Peggy O'Neill of whose namesake songs are written. Theirs was a simple, comfortable life that revolved around their six children and their church. They rarely took a holiday as John was a second-generation master plumber, self-employed, working long hours to support his family.

From 1820 to 1914 Irish immigrants – 4,500,000 strong – arrived on the shores of the 'New World'. Today there are over 40 million Irish-Americans with names like Gilnagh, Burns, Daly and Murphy who can trace their presence in the United States to courageous emigrants like Margaret Devaney O'Neill.

In the 1950s, with the release of the film *A Night To Remember*, Peggy began to meet other survivors and celebrities from the film world. She joked that author Walter Lord and film producer William MacQuitty both had an eye on her *Titanic* knife and lifeboat flag. But husband John had mounted the flag on a mahogany board for safe keeping, and when it was not at *Titanic* affairs it hung over the entrance to her kitchen. The knife had its own secret place, and the rosary with which she had prayed all night in the lifeboat was given to a niece when she became a nun.

Margaret Devaney O'Neill with author Walter Lord and film producer William MacQuitty, and her flag from one of Titanic's *lifeboats.* (Findlay/Landsberg collection)

In 1952 Peggy returned to Ireland and found Kilmacowen unchanged in the 40 years since she had left, and that lack of progress saddened her. Before returning to America she revisited her old haunts, including Yeats's grave. Etched on his tombstone were lines from a poem he had written about Sligo entitled 'Under Ben Bulben Mountain'. Peggy jotted down the words in her red notebook: 'Cast a cold eye on life, on death. Horseman, pass by.'

It was something she had done well – surviving a shipwreck, adjusting to a new world, producing six wonderful children, and living hale and hearty to a ripe old 82. Her daughter, Helen Landsberg, says that she was a 'great gal'. What better epitaph?

Margaret Devaney O'Neill
3 May 1892–12 June 1974

Leah Aks (18)
Philip Aks (10 months)

'The case of the strawberry birthmark ...'

IN 1953 LEAH AND HER SON Frank, known as Philip, were in New York City registering at a hotel as guests of Twentieth Century Fox, the producers of the movie *Titanic.* Leah suddenly dropped everything and hastened toward a woman crossing the lobby. Calling over her shoulder, she said, 'Phil, come meet Selena Cook. Without her you may have been lost for ever.' It was a joyous reunion and tears came to Phil's eyes whenever he thought of it in later years.

Again and again his mother had told him of April 1912, and over the years her memories had become his. Third Class was not completely booked and Leah felt fortunate to have a cabin for herself and Philip; it made travelling alone with an infant so much easier. Hearing the distress call on Sunday night she had awakened Philip, whom she called Filly, and followed the crowd to the foot of the Third Class aft staircase where throngs stood struggling to make sense of the situation, babbling in a variety of languages and elbowing and pushing each other with their bundles and bags. Leah shrunk back, knowing that she could not press through the crowd.

Leah brought everything she owned on her emigration to America. This cardboard box with its buttons and buckles could possibly have been among her belongings.

Several seamen saw her plight and motioned her out to the open deck area. Making a human ladder with their arms, they half pushed, half lifted her up to Second Class. From there she made her way to the Boat Deck, clutching Filly tightly as they were jostled over and over by the crowd. Once there she waited for her turn in a lifeboat, trusting that all would be well.

Then the unthinkable happened, so fast that Leah did not have time to stop it. Half crazed, a man snatched Filly from her arms and yelling something unintelligible threw her baby, her son, into the sea. Screaming she rushed to the rail searching the darkness for his body, praying that it was a nightmare from which she would soon wake.

From that moment to her boarding the *Carpathia*, Leah's thoughts had been muddled. How she had got in a lifeboat she did not know. She vaguely remembered people burning clothing and waving the flames in the air during the night, and a young girl beside her offering to help find Filly when the rescue boat came. But how could she? He was dead. (The girl was presumably 12-year-old Ruth Becker who had also become separated from her family. Throughout the ordeal she exhibited great maturity and wrote of it later for a children's magazine called *St Nicolas*.)

On the *Carpathia* Leah roamed the deck searching for Filly, but finally, accepting the truth, she curled up on a mattress and retreated into her agony. Selena Cook watched her for two days as she became more disconsolate in her grief and weak from lack of nourishment. On 17 April Selena finally insisted that Leah get some fresh air in the hope that it would stimulate her appetite. Leah only agreed when Selena convinced her that she must keep strong for her husband, Sam. He would need her more than ever now.

Leah sat weeping on the deck, imagining that she heard Filly's cry. Looking up, she saw an Italian lady sitting nearby holding a baby close. Could it be? Racing up to them, Leah grabbed the woman's arm. There was Filly looking at her in joyful recognition! As he reached out for her, the woman clasped him closer and ran off with fear in her eyes.

How awful – two women, one baby. One the tortured rightful mother, the other believing in her hysteria that God meant this baby to be hers since he had dropped the child into her lap. Selena intervened again and the truth was uncovered – literally. Leah confirmed her parentage by undressing Filly and pointing out the strawberry birthmark under his left breast. Not having a change of clothing for the baby, the would-be mother had never seen it. Leah's anguish melted away when she was able to again hold her son. Forever after Philip Aks was known as the 'Titanic Baby'.

There are several versions of this story. In an early interview with the *Norfolk Ledger-Dispatch* on 24 April 1912, Leah claimed that in the crush of rushing to the boats Filly was knocked from her arms. Somehow in the mêlée he had been picked up and put into Lifeboat 11, but of course, at the time, she had no way of knowing that he was safe. She searched the decks until she was thrown into No 13. However they were torn apart, it was the most devastating thing Leah had ever or would ever endure in her lifetime.

The woman who held baby Philip in the lifeboat is presumed to have been Argene del Carlo. She had been separated from her husband, Sebastiano, when he had not been allowed to follow her into the lifeboat. No manner of pleading could persuade the officer in charge that Argene, pregnant, needed Sebastiano by her side. The officer did not understand their Italian and had no patience or time for this one emigrant couple's plea when so many lives were at stake.

As Argene's boat was being lowered, a bundle fell in her lap. For a moment she thought that someone had tossed extra blankets in for the passengers' comfort, but the bundle began to cry. Cuddling the baby close, Argene shared her warmth with Filly through the long night.

Towards morning she began to believe that God had sent this child to her as a replacement for Sebastiano and a brother for the child she carried in her womb.

When Lifeboat 11 arrived at the *Carpathia*, Philip was hoisted up in a bucket towards the throngs of survivors searching every face for that of their own missing loved one. Arriving on deck soon after, Argene grabbed Philip from the arms of the passenger who had taken him from the bucket and claimed him as her own. No one knew any different until Leah heard him – a mother always knows her own baby's cry.

How Leah told Sam of this near loss of their first-born is unknown. But together again, the young family counted their blessings and put down roots in their new community of Norfolk, Virginia. They had never expected anything of this magnitude to happen when they made the decision to move to America and wanted to put it behind them quickly.

Natives of Warsaw, Poland, Leah and Sam

Argene del Carlo (left), the woman who caught the 'Titanic Baby' and held him all night in Lifeboat 11. (Author's collection)

had met and married in London where their son was born. Sam, a tailor, had left for Virginia to find work before Leah and Filly joined him. All the money Sam had earned was used for their journey on the *Titanic*, as Leah's parents had insisted that their daughter travel on an unsinkable ship. Now almost destitute, Sam had to work even harder. Seeing more of a future in the scrap-metal business, he left tailoring behind.

Philip soon had two siblings, a sister whom Leah named Sarah Carpathia in gratitude for the rescue ship, and a brother, Henry, who would become a doctor. Philip, the first-born, never finished high school; instead as a teenager he joined Sam in the scrap-metal business, which he took over many years later when his father retired.

While attending a party in 1929 Philip met and fell madly in love with Marie Miller, a girl from Portsmouth, Virginia, just across the river from Norfolk. He was 19, Marie just 16 and still in high school. But love had its way and after a three-month courtship they secretly eloped to the Carolinas and began what would be 62 years of marriage.

During the Second World War Philip volunteered for the war effort, but the head of the draft board determined that people in the scrap business could serve the war effort best by staying at home to supply the much-needed iron for military vehicles and equipment. So Philip threw himself wholeheartedly into that cause.

Like Marshall Drew and Winnie Troutt, he believed that his extraordinary survival obligated him to a life of helping others. He was gregarious and outgoing with an infectious

Sam, Filly and Leah Aks after being reunited in Norfolk, Virginia. (Michael Findlay collection)

Philip and Leah Aks and Selena Cook at the premier of the 1953 movie Titanic. (Michael Findlay collection)

grin, a deep booming voice tempered by a southern accent, and twinkling eyes. Always ready to participate in the civic and religious affairs of the Norfolk community, he was a 32nd degree Mason, Chancel Commander of the Knights of Pithais, and President of B'rith Sholom, his synagogue.

Leah and her Filly remained close. In the 1930s they appeared together on the radio show *Ripley's Believe It or Not* and, of course, at the premier of the two 1950s *Titanic* films. But *Titanic* was only one thread in the fabric of their lives, not the whole cloth. Although they did make headlines in 1951 around the time of the 39th anniversary of the disaster, when an enterprising reporter from the *Norfolk Virginian Pilot*, looking for a new twist to the oft-told story, discovered that Leah lived only a short distance in Norfolk from another survivor, Celiney Yasbeck, and had done so for over 35

years (something neither of them knew).

Leah died in 1967 and Philip concentrated on his business life. The 'Titanic Baby' was not to emerge again until after his retirement. When the ship was discovered in 1985 his phone rang constantly as the media sought his opinion – which was that he thought it wonderful and hoped that many questions would be answered by the discovery.

Leah Rosen Aks
18 March 1894–22 June 1967

'Frank' Philip Aks
7 June 1911–15 July 1991

Argene del Carlo
6 November 1889–8 October 1970

Selena Rogers Cook
6 April 1890–12 September 1964

Georgette Dean (33)
Bertram Dean (23 months)
Millvina Dean (9 weeks)

'Honestly, I wonder why people are so fascinated.'
Millvina Dean, *People Magazine*, 19 May 1997

TO KNOW MILLVINA DEAN is to love her. At 80-plus she is outgoing, witty, vigorous, indefatigable, charming – in a word, 'delicious'. Yes, she was on the *Titanic* – but no, she doesn't remember. She was a babe in arms travelling with her mother, father and older brother, Bertram, to Wichita, Kansas. Some of her mother's family had already settled there, paving the way and securing a house for the new arrivals to occupy.

In England Bertram Senior had owned a

Ettie with Bertram and Millvina Dean back in England a few years after the disaster. (Millvina Dean/Author's collection)

small public house, but sold it to emigrate to America where he had designs on becoming a tobacconist. He was thrilled to provide his family with passage on the new ship, thinking it 'over the moon', to quote Millvina.

As the ship foundered, 'Ettie' (Georgette's nickname), with Millvina in her arms, settled in the lifeboat, and called out for her husband to pass little Bertram over the railing, but he had wandered away. A hurried search was conducted but the toddler had disappeared and Ettie was forced to leave without him. She took some comfort in knowing that her husband was still on board and would continue to look. It is entirely possible the little boy was found by his father, and equally possible that he was scooped up from the deck by an unidentified saviour and carried to another boat. If he had shouted for his parents he would not have been heard in the confusion and noise of the funnels blowing off steam and the people racing about.

How did it happen that so many children were grabbed willy-nilly and thrown into boats? Some researchers believe it was the frenetic attempt by the seamen loading the boats, knowing that there was an insufficient number, to save as many of the women and children as possible by putting them in any available open seat.

(Baker Charles Joughin was one of those grabbing children by the clothing and tossing them randomly into boats. Afterwards he returned to his cabin and insulated his body by drinking whisky. Flask in hand he returned to the deck, made the perpendicular climb to the stern, rode the ship down to the water like an elevator and stepped off into the sea without getting his hair wet. He was picked up by a lifeboat an hour later.)

Bertram Dean Junior survived, while Bertram Senior did not. Ettie gave up the notion of a life in Kansas and returned with the children to her parents' farm at Netley Marsh near Southampton. During their journey home on the *Adriatic* a newspaper reporter photographed Millvina, captioning it: 'Baby Dean. This bundle of humanity was held by first and second class passengers. They were allowed ten minutes each.' Everyone wanted to touch the tiniest *Titanic* victim. This was Millvina's first brush with celebrity, but it would not be her last.

Things settled down for the Deans when they reached the farm. Ettie received a £40/$200 settlement from the English Red Cross Emergency Relief Fund and a pension of 23 shillings per week for the care of her children. Bertram and Millvina were educated with additional monies set aside by the Titanic Relief Fund, but neither of them was told that it came from their news-making experience, which had also caused the death of their father. Millvina claims that when she did learn about the family tragedy at the age of eight, it was an 'Oh, by the way ...' sort of thing. As she always says, 'I was not brought up with the *Titanic* at all and had no interest in it.'

After eight years the time for mourning was over and Ettie accepted the marriage proposal of the farm's vet, a man named Burden, who had begun to visit more often than the farm animals required. It was a happy marriage for Ettie and a positive experience for Millvina and Bertram. The Dean children were reared in a warm atmosphere surrounded by a Doctor Doolittle menagerie of animals, and this may well have been where Millvina learned to charm the bees out of the trees!

Bertram had more interest in the *Titanic* than his sister. Employed in a Southampton shipyard, it was his good fortune to meet George Beauchamp, a fellow worker who had been employed on the *Titanic* as a fireman. Most of what Bertram learned about the ship was from George. In an interesting twist of fate, Bertram's wife of 60 years, Dorothy, came to

Tea was served to Third Class passengers like the Deans from pots like this.

the marriage with her own *Titanic* credentials. Her father had purchased a music shop in Southampton from the estate of Henry Price Hodges, a Second Class Passenger who perished.

Bert was also possessed of the Dean charm, and although shy and quiet he spoke often of his not so much remembered, as gathered memories, signed his share of autographs and answered his share of questions. He died, mystically, on the 80th anniversary of the sinking, 14 April 1992.

Millvina caught up when she was in the her late 70s. Living in Southampton all of her life she was invited to attend a memorial service for *Titanic*'s crew, mostly residents of that city, and the gates to her past were swung wide. She had worked for the Government during the Second World War, drawing maps, and later served in the purchasing department of an engineering firm in Southampton, nothing that would prepare her for the barrage of attention she received after the wreck was discovered. Her retirement took her in a new direction, leaving her little time for her beloved garden.

Invitations began rolling in to attend conventions, address school groups, appear on talk shows, television and radio. In the beginning, when people asked if she had been on the *Titanic*, she said 'Yes' and the conversation stopped there. That is all she knew. But with her natural joie de vivre she set about learning all she could about her experiences aboard the ship. The rest is history.

In August 1997 she was invited to travel aboard the *QE2* on a transatlantic pilgrimage to America to complete her family's never-taken journey to Wichita, Kansas. When she arrived there the media and the town came out in droves to welcome her. Turning to Bruno Nordmanis, her friend and permanent escort, she said with a Millvina smile that she didn't know she had so many relatives. Those 'relatives' asked what her life would have been like had she not been on the *Titanic*, to which she responded, 'I would have been an American.' America would have been proud to have her, but it is hard to imagine Millvina without her lilting English accent and view of the world.

She continues to receive hundreds of letters inquiring about the ship and her life. With her interest in people she often writes back and asks about them. One of her more curious letters came from a *Titanic* enthusiast begging for a lock of her hair – strange hobby, collecting hair from *Titanic* survivors, but never mind … Kindly, Millvina wrote back telling him that she did not think he really wanted it, as it was very grey. The gentleman persisted and persisted, but she managed not to give in. She finds it difficult to resist requests for autographs, however, and has been known to sit for hours at a time fulfilling demands.

Millvina has had a street named after her, been the guest of honour at the opening of *Titanic* artefact exhibitions, given more interviews than she cares to remember, and has been photographed with hundreds, if not thousands, of *Titanic* enthusiasts. For the life of her she doesn't understand why people are so fascinated, and is only worried that her neighbours may think she is stuck up. No chance of that.

She is happy that people are interested in the history of the ship and are writing plays and movies, but as far as she is concerned she saw *A Night to Remember* and that was enough. Jokingly, she says, 'I never take ice in my drinks.'

Georgette Light Dean Burden
1879–16 September 1975

Bertram Dean
30 June 1886–15 April 1912

Bertram Vere Dean
21 May 1910–14 April 1992

Elizabeth Gladys Millvina Dean
2 February 1912–

Austin Van Billiard (35)
James Van Billiard (10)
Walter Van Billiard (9)

'Although he travelled in steerage, it is believed by the family that Austin Van Billiard was returning home with many thousand dollars' worth of diamonds, mostly uncut.'
Ambler Gazette, 25 April 1912

RUMOURS HAVE PERSISTED over the years that the *Titanic* was carrying a fortune in diamonds. Although not substantiated, the story may have started with James and Walter Van Billiard and their father Austin's swashbuckling love of adventure.

Austin was an American from North Wales, Pennsylvania. His father was chief burgess of the town council and a successful marble and monument merchant. Being the only son, no doubt Austin could have had a comfortable life had he joined his father in the business, but he wanted more of the world than a small corner of Pennsylvania could provide.

In early 1900 Austin, 22 years old and eager, left for Europe knowing that there would be work during the preparations for the Universal Exposition opening in Paris that year on – coincidentally – 15 April. Each participating nation brought the best of its technology to display to the rest of the world. These industrial fairs also encouraged emigration by exposing the hopeful, or the restless like Austin, to the varied economic opportunities outside their own countries. Going to France turned out to be a good choice for Van Billiard

Maude and Austin on their wedding day. (Courtesy of Newton Howard)

business. What an arresting-looking couple they made. Austin was tall and rail-thin with intense eyes and a red imperial moustache. Maude was short and delicate, the top of her head coming barely to Austin's shoulder. But her small size belied a sense of adventure equal to that of her husband. They married on 3 November 1900 and their first child, James William, was born on 20 August 1901.

In 1906 the Van Billiards decided to try mining diamonds in the Congo Free State of Central Africa. Conditions were primitive at best; they lived in tents, cooked over open fires, and like the natives Maude beat their clothing against river rocks to clean them. It was a rough existence, especially for Maude who gave birth to two more children in these circumstances.

James and Walter Van Billiard several years before the family left the Congo for America. (Author's collection)

as he did well working as an electrician for the American and English contingents. His enthusiasm for the venture is evident in this letter home to his father:

'There is yet an awful heap of work to be done on the grounds. There will be spent $27,000,000 to make the fair a success. Strangers are arriving daily from all the continental countries of Europe and all other countries where people read and write. I think the United States and Germany will have the finest display of exhibits, and next will come Russia and England, although for the state building the Italian is the most handsome.'

While in France Austin met Maude Murray, an English girl whose father was in Paris on

The youngest, George, was born in 1912, just before the Van Billiards were scheduled to leave for London (where Maude's parents now lived) on a French vessel. Over the years Austin had written faithfully to his father telling him how lucrative the mines had been. In his last letter from Africa Austin indicated that his ultimate plan was to return to the United States in time for Easter and set up shop as a diamond merchant.

In a forewarning of things to come, the Van Billiards came up against a French law that forbade infants to travel on their ships. Feisty Maude had lived in the African wilds and was not to be deterred by a mere rule of the sea. Her family would leave Africa on that ship – all of them. With characteristic spirit she smuggled her infant on board under her cape while Austin distracted the ship's officer with his posse of three other little Van Billiards.

Home in England Maude became re-acquainted with her parents and civilisation and organised for the move to America, while Austin made a quick trip to Amsterdam to have a few of his stones cut for his American business venture. He returned to London raring to go, but Maude, after the rigours of the last few years, was not well enough to travel. Anxious to keep his promise to his parents of arrival before Easter, Austin decided to go on ahead, taking with him their two eldest children, James and Walter. It was to be a surprise for the elder Van Billiards, as they had never met their grandchildren and James was Grandfather Van Billiard's namesake.

Fable has it that upon boarding the *Titanic* Austin placed his cut diamonds, amounting to £20,000/$100,000, in the purser's safe for protection, keeping only a few of the rougher stones in a waist belt. But where are the cut

Austin Van Billiard and his sons, like many other Third Class male passengers, might have had a pair of heavy work socks such as these among their belongings.

stones? The purser's safe was opened in 1988 and no diamonds were found. Perhaps it was just a tale told by a bragging father that made its way into the press, then became truth by repetition. But maybe there was something to it after all. The *Morristown Daily Register* of 8 May 1912 reported, 'The stock of diamonds Van Billiard had with him did not represent all his possessions, and with the life insurance he carried, he leaves his wife and surviving children in comfortable circumstances.'

Austin did have at least two more stones, not a huge amount but enough to perpetuate the myth, being held in a United States bank as collateral for a loan of £147/$734.28. When the stones were sold for £275/$1,372.18, Maude and the children were given the balance, together with £540/$2,700 from other relief funds and £100/$500 from the Red Cross.

The elder Van Billiards in Pennsylvania only learned that their son and grandsons were on the *Titanic* when Maude cabled them from London – just in time to receive the bodies for burial.

One of the Van Billiard children was found by the *Mackay-Bennett* and identified by the Red Cross as Walter Van Billiard. Among his personal effects were a purse containing a few Danish coins, one ring and two handkerchiefs marked with an 'A'. The Danish coins and the handkerchief tend to indicate that the body might in fact have easily been that of another Third Class boy, but his remains were shipped to Pennsylvania with Austin's as father and son. Contrary to popular reports Austin was alone in the sea and did not have Walter clasped to his chest as was originally reported. Among Austin's effects were a pipe, £3 10s, a gold watch engraved with his father's initials, and a pouch containing 12 diamonds.

The Van Billiard monument. (Michael Findlay collection)

In February 1913 Maude moved to North Wales with her two remaining children. Grief was her biggest cross to bear, not poverty, but she was never as financially comfortable as the townsfolk thought. (In awe they mentioned her television, a 6-by-6-inch wonder, the first in their fair city.) She lived out her years there, saw her other children grow and marry and eventually died in an Episcopal rest home in 1968 at the age of 94. A monument to her husband and two sons who perished in the wreck stands in the Whitemarsh Union Cemetery, but only two (and perhaps only one) of them lie beneath it. James's body was never found.

Austin Van Billiard
9 February 1877–15 April 1912

Maude Van Billiard
13 April 1873–17 January 1968

James Van Billiard
20 August 1901–15 April 1912

Walter Van Billiard
28 February 1903–15 April 1912

Catherine Peter (Joseph) (23)
Michael Peter (Joseph) (4)
Mary Peter (Joseph) (1)

'It was the best of times, it was the worst of times … we had everything before us, we had nothing before us …'
Charles Dickens, *A Tale of Two Cities*

MICHAEL JOSEPH CLEARLY remembered his journey on the *Titanic* until he died in 1991. In fact, he had been dubbed 'Ty' by the nuns at his Catholic grammar school when they learned of his 'miracle' escape from the ship, and that nickname followed him throughout his life. But remembering is one thing, and talking about it to everyone is another.

Michael's parents, Peter and Catherine

Joseph, had come to Detroit, Michigan, from Lebanon well before 1912; in fact, Michael and his sister Mary were both born in the United States. Their father, Peter, had started at the bottom of the economic ladder, as so many newcomers did, taking jobs that Americans and second-generation immigrants were unwilling to do – pushing a peddler's cart, picking up scrap iron, anything and everything to make a go of life in his adopted country. But it was rough going.

In 1911 Peter sent his wife and two children back to Lebanon for a visit. Michael's son Louis, and his grandson Brian, believe that the trip was not a luxury but a necessity precipitated by the hard times the family was experiencing in Detroit. Peter needed more time to get on his financial feet. By April 1912 things must have improved as money was sent for the family to return.

They travelled by freighter from Beirut to Marseilles, then on to Cherbourg where they boarded the ship with others in their party from Lebanon. When Catherine was asked her name, she gave it as she would have done in the old country. Taking her husband's first name as her last, she told the authorities that she was Catherine Peter and her children were Mary and Michael Peter, and that is how they came down to us on the survivors' list.

In the frenzied evacuation Catherine bundled up her two children. Gathering Mary in her arms, she turned to Michael, adjusted the cap on his head and instructed him to hold on to her skirt to keep from getting lost. But that is exactly what happened. They came up via the forward First Class staircase and it was at the landing on the Boat Deck that they most likely became separated. Catherine must have turned to starboard, where she was hustled into Collapsible C, launched at 1.40am, while Michael, undoubtedly and justifiably distracted, was pulled away by the crowd toward the port side. For a four-year-old this

must have been terrifying and bewildering. One minute he was following his mother and the next she had disappeared. He must have wandered around looking for her, calling out in the swirl of people, and finally may have stopped – counting on her to find him because that is what mothers did. But she had left the ship convinced that he had dropped into the water and drowned.

It was his 'guardian angel' that led him to Collapsible D. Launched at 2.05 after waiting as long as possible for any remaining women and children, D was the last lifeboat to leave the ship as the sea water closed in on the bridge. In later years Michael would point to a picture of Collapsible D approaching the *Carpathia* and say, 'See that little boy in the middle there, with the cap on? That's me.' That little boy sat all night in the collapsible with two other parentless children, Michel and Edmond Navratil. Also floating with them among the icebergs were Mrs Henry B. Harris with her broken arm, Mauritz Bjornstrom-Steffanson and Hugh Woolner (both of whom had jumped in as the boat made its descent), Mr and Mrs Frederick Hoyt (Mr Hoyt had been pulled into the boat from the sea), and several Syrian men who had stowed away. When the sun rose, according to Woolner, they

'... saw a great many icebergs of different colours, as the sun struck them. Some looked white, some looked blue, some looked mauve and others looked grey. There was one double-toothed one that looked to be of good size; it must have been about one hundred feet high.'

This was a sight that Michael would remember all of his life – together with his reunion with his mother on the *Carpathia*. Her relief at seeing him was so intense that she fell on him in hysterics, knocking them both to the deck.

On the *Carpathia* the classes were still divided, but less rigidly than on the *Titanic* due

Third Class passengers who may have made the climb to the lifeboats with the Peters (Josephs): (back, l to r) Helga Hirvonen with her daughter, Hildur, and Marguerite Sandstrom on her lap; another unidentified mother and toddler; Mary Nackid holding baby Maria; Antoinette Mallet and son André; William Borak, and Louise Kink. Sitting on the floor are Elias Nicola (Yarred) and George Borak. (Author's collection/New York Evening Journal)

to the cramped quarters resulting from the 705 extra passengers. People sat and slept where they could. Four-year-old Michael from Third Class may very well have seen Vera Quick and her little sister, Phyllis, from Second Class. Perhaps the children even played together. Both families, the Josephs and the Quicks, were going to Detroit and would meet again many years later in a bizarre *Titanic* 'Believe It or Not.'

Home in Detroit, Catherine did not have time to recover from the trauma of almost losing Michael before in the summer of 1913 she gave birth to another boy child who died soon after. And on the heels of that tragedy, Mary died in a fire, never reaching her fourth birthday. Catherine and Peter had now lost two babies and Michael had lost two siblings. Not being able to afford a family plot and not anticipating the need for one so soon in their

young lives, each of the children was buried in a separate section of Mount Olivet Cemetery. In 1915 Catherine, aged 26, gave in to the tuberculosis that had plagued her for years and died, joining them there.

At the age of seven Michael was left alone with his father, who died seven years later of a heart attack. Michael was now 14 and the sole remaining member of the Joseph family. It was a horrible time and not one he chose to discuss or remember in later years. An uncle took him in, but Michael felt the need to strike out on his own. He went to work as a delivery driver for a soft drinks company, where he stayed for 24 years.

During that time he set out to create his own family and interestingly married a woman with the same name as his mother. Together they had four children. His son, Louis, described him as a quiet man who liked nothing better than being surrounded by his family. One of the few relatives to whom he would talk of the *Titanic* was his grandson, Brian, and there the stories of the Quicks and the Josephs converge.

Brian Joseph is the president of a funeral home in suburban Detroit. One day he ran an advertisement for a bookkeeper and Vera Quick's daughter, Jeanette, applied for the position. When Jeanette was ushered into Brian's office for her interview, she could not help but notice a picture of the *Titanic* on the wall behind his desk. Jeanette was taken aback to learn that Brian's grandfather, Michael, was a *Titanic* survivor just like her mother, grandmother and aunt. Overcome with the coincidence of the moment, Jeanette gave Brian a hug and, of course, got the job.

Brian put a similar picture on his grandfather Michael's monument when he died in 1991, and laughs when he says that when he leaves this earth and walks through those Pearly Gates, his grandfather is going to beat the hell out of him for having done so.

Catherine Rizk Joseph
1889–19 June 1915

Michael Joseph
1908–18 May 1991

Mary Joseph
1911–1913/15

Jamilia Nicola (Yarred) (14)
Elias Nicola (Yarred) (12)

'You cannot teach a child to take care of himself unless you will let him try to take care of himself.'
Henry Ward Beecher

JAMILIA YARRED WOKE with a start. She was having that nightmare again. In it Turkish soldiers came into Hakoor, her mountain village, and took her away. Nobody seemed able to stop them. They thought everything belonged to them, the animals, the farm products, even the girls ... When they left for America she wouldn't have to worry any more and then maybe the nightmares would go away.

The area where Jamilia's village stood is today part of Lebanon, but in 1912 it and Syria were combined under Ottoman Turkish rule and generically called Syria. The people in the region were Arabs, but the two countries differed in their religions and their outlook on life. The Lebanese were primarily Christians of one sect or another with political and social

Jamilia Nicola (Yarred). (Courtesy of the Isaac family)

leanings to the West, while the Syrians were mainly Muslim and favoured the eastern way of looking at the world. The Yarreds were Lebanese Maronite Christians.

Lebanese and Syrians alike were suffering under Ottoman rule, the area was being used as a political pawn by Europe and Asia, the economy was in trouble and Syrian and Lebanese men were forced to serve in the Turkish military – all good reasons to emigrate. Jamilia and Elias's mother, two sisters and older brother Isaac had already left the country to settle in Jacksonville, Florida, where the climate was similar to that of their country.

By 1912 the Yarred family had saved enough money for Jamilia, Elias and their father, Nicola, to join the others. Jamilia knew that they were really leaving the day her father sold his mill. He had been grinding wheat in the village for as long as she could remember, and she wondered what he would do in Florida.

On the day of departure Jamilia, Elias and Nicola said goodbye to the village for the last time; they would undoubtedly never return. They and three other families made the 90-mile (130km) trip to Beirut, and boarded a boat to Marseilles, where the trouble began.

The language barrier made them prey to an unscrupulous hotel owner who charged them outrageous daily rates and kept them in his hotel longer than was necessary by misleading them about vessels and sailing schedules. Finally, Nicola was able to extricate them and booked passage on the *Titanic* (on the passenger list of which they were listed under the surname Nicola, in keeping with the tradition of using a father's first name as his children's last). At that time the shipping lines were required to pay the passage of any emigrant who was turned back at Ellis Island for medical reasons, so it became customary practice for agents of the line to do their own preliminary tests on the passengers. Unfortunately, Nicola had an eye infection and was barred from

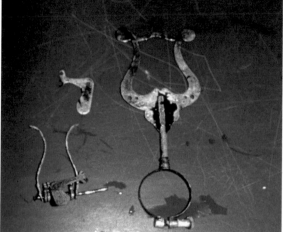

Jamilia sneaked out to hear the music on Sunday night. Perhaps she heard this tune wafting down from First Class, played on instruments the remains of which were recovered from Titanic's *debris field.*

leaving. He gave Jamilia £100/$500 for emergencies, put her in charge of her younger brother and sent the two children off to Cherbourg with other families from their village making the trip. Given the appalling loss of life among the Third Class men, Nicola's eye infection may well have saved his life.

On that Sunday night Elias was in bed asleep and Jamilia had sneaked out to watch the dancing in the Third Class General Room. But soon she, too, went to bed, only to wake a short time later screaming that something was the matter. Elias, tired of her bossing him around, said, 'Go back to bed. You worry too much.' Jamilia was having none of that and dragged him out of bed and into the corridor, which by this time was in pandemonium.

Working their way through the people, Jamilia stopped suddenly. She had forgotten the £100. Turning, she retraced her steps, but was stopped quickly by the water rising in her path. Back again she dragged Elias in his nightclothes out to the deck and up the outside iron ladders from D to C to B and finally to the port side of A Deck near Lifeboat 4. Elias remembers this as an easy climb for him but difficult for Jamilia, who was heavier. Now that he had got the hang of climbing Elias wanted to keep on going and was threatening to climb to the Boat Deck so he could jump down and do it all over again. Jamilia was beside herself with this out-of-control 12-year-old and fast approaching hysteria.

Elias Nicola (Yarred) as a young man in America. (Courtesy of the Isaac family)

Colonel Astor came to the rescue. Many passengers have said that they were saved by John Jacob Astor, or they received a shawl from Madeleine or were given a ribbon by the fair lady to hold up their socks, but in this case an Astor intervention may well have been true. Elias recalled being grabbed by an older man who had just put his wife in Lifeboat 4, and being carried to the very same boat. The man then went back for Jamilia, who stood paralysed. With the aid of crew members Astor placed her in the boat as well.

Dressed only in their nightwear brother and sister both suffered terribly from exposure. The night was one of terror for Jamilia who, traumatised by the ordeal and weakened by the screaming she had done, could not speak for three months. What a relief it must have been when Jamilia and Elias were reunited with their older brother Isaac in New York and taken to their mother in Jacksonville.

Nicola, eye infection under control, joined the family as promised some three months later and they settled in. In an attempt to assimilate, the Yarreds became the Garretts, Jamilia became Amelia and Elias was for ever after known as Louis.

Amelia's childhood ended on the *Titanic*. At 15 she was married to Isaac Isaac (19), a Jacksonville wholesale grocer. Although the marriage was arranged in old world style, it was a good union and the couple had seven children: Sheffield, Fred, Albert, Sophie, Susan, Dorothy and Margaret. Over the years Isaac expanded his business and began to acquire investment property. This income was much needed when after 30 years of marriage he died, leaving Amelia alone with young children and pregnant again. (His death caused her to miscarry.)

She kept busy with her crocheting, cooking and gardening, and poured all of her considerable love and attention into her children and, eventually, her grandchildren.

Jamilia Yarred Isaac with her husband Isaac and their seven children in front of their home in Florida. (Courtesy of the Isaac family)

They all adored their 'Sitti' (Arabic for grandmother) because she had the knack of making each feel special. Amelia held them all close, and four of her seven children continued to live with her in the family home until her death.

Amelia was to experience one tragedy in her life from which she never recovered – the death of her eldest son. In her despair she cried, 'Why didn't I die on the *Titanic?*' Consumed with a grief beyond description she cried herself to death.

Louis Garrett, meanwhile, became a grocer like his father, married and had one son. He did return after all to Lebanon in 1949, this time by aeroplane. As he flew over the wreck site tears welled up in his eyes. When the stewardess asked if there was anything she could do to help, he told her 'No', he was just

remembering the *Titanic*. 'How sad,' she said. 'I remember reading about that.'

Amelia (Jamilia Nicola [Yarred]) Garrett Isaac
1898–8 March 1970

Louis (Elias Nicola [Yarred]) Garrett
1900–30 May 1981

Celiney Yasbeck (15)

'Girl bride torn from husband at pistol point.'
The Detroit News Tribune, 21 April 1912

WHEN CELINEY YASBECK walked into the Third Class passenger department of the White Star Line offices on Manhattan's Lower

Broadway, all heads turned. Her beauty, made even more poignant by the pallor of her skin and the dull look of sorrow in her eyes, heightened the gloom that had settled over those offices since the sinking of the *Titanic*.

She had just been released from the hospital where she had been treated for exposure. In a borrowed, simple black mourning dress, with her glorious dark hair covered in a silken shawl, she spoke in Arabic through an interpreter, D. J. Fayour. Mr Fayour, a banker and old family friend, was looking after Celiney at his home in New York City until she could make sense of what had happened to her. The office workers gathered round to hear her story.

Only 15, Celiney told of being wed to Antoni (Fraza) Yasbeck, aged 27, a scant 50 days earlier. Fraza had enjoyed a successful five years in Wilkes-Barre, Pennsylvania, where he had built up a shoe-selling business with his brothers. When it came time to marry, he sold his share of the business, borrowed £180/$900, took an additional £300/$1,500 from his savings and returned to Hardin, Lebanon, for a bride.

Fraza's friend in Wilkes-Barre, George Moubarek, asked Fraza to bring his wife, Amenia, and their two children back to the United States with him when he returned. Celiney, it turns out, was Amenia's younger sister, so it is highly likely that her marriage to Fraza had been pre-arranged, especially since Celiney's father also lived in Wilkes-Barre. Even so, for her it was a love match to the charming Fraza, whose beautiful singing voice was the talk of their mountain village. Life in America with him was to have been one of great hope and exhilaration.

Opening her clenched hands as she spun her tale, Celiney revealed dyed deep-red nails, her country's tradition for new brides. Sadly, those nails were all that remained of what was to have

This simple gold earring could have been amongst the jewellery Celiney left on the ship.

been her happy new life. Dissolving the language barrier with her hushed universal tones of grief, Celiney told the White Star employees that in Third Class she and her husband had been close enough to the waterline to experience the 'great bump of the ship'. Rushing from their cabin in nightwear, the couple hurried along the corridor to investigate. Through an open door they saw the ship's crew frantically making repairs to the pumps in the boiler room.

Their suspicions of danger confirmed, Fraza and Celiney sprang into action, alerting Celiney's sister and her two sons. Fraza grabbed George by the hand and Celiney took William. With Amenia following they began their climb to safety.

In one 1912 newspaper account, Celiney is interpreted by the reporter to have said that they all ran up on deck. No doubt it was significantly more difficult than that, and it is presumed that they were led in a group with other Lebanese. Their route is difficult to trace, but their confusion and fear might be explained if we attempt to imagine it: via the aft Third Class stairway, their ascent could have taken them up to C Deck, then forward into the freezing air of the open promenade area, up a ladder perhaps, past the Second Class Library and, if access to First Class had been unlocked, they would have continued along a lengthy First Class corridor of luxurious cabins (their doors ludicrously now locked against possible theft), up the magnificent grand staircase for three more decks to, at last, the boats.

Fraza took Celiney's hand to give her strength to endure the weight of her four-year-old nephew, whom she was half carrying, half dragging, and of her own fears as they struggled against the *Titanic*'s significant list to port and the forward dip of her bow. It was disorienting, like a race through a perverse carnival house.

When Celiney and her family at last reached the top deck, an officer directed the women and children into a lifeboat. Shivering in her night dress and crying, Celiney begged her husband not to send her away alone. After all, she reasoned, gesturing wildly about at the empty spaces in the boat, there was plenty of room.

Heeding her pleas, Fraza stepped into the boat and gathered her into his arms. The newlyweds clung together in fear. But immediately Fraza was forced back on to *Titanic*'s deck at the point of an officer's pistol and a screaming Celiney had to be restrained not to follow.

As she told the listening crowd at White Star, 'Of course he obeyed and the last I saw of him he was running toward the other end of the ship. They held me down and said he would go in another boat and join me afterwards. But I never saw him again.'

No one knows in which boat Celiney escaped, but a good case can be made for Collapsible C, lowered away on the starboard side at 1.40am. The Toumas (Thomas) family, also from Lebanon, were in that boat, as was nine-year-old Frank Goldsmith, who remembered the officers near the davit wielding guns to ward off the men panicking and pushing to clamour aboard. So perhaps the 'girl bride' was indeed 'torn from her husband at pistol point'.

Now in the aftermath Celiney asked the White Star Line to provide her with a ticket to Wilkes-Barre to complete the journey that she and Fraza had begun together. She bore the grief of not only the loss of her husband, but of her money, a figure she calculated as £140/$700 and her dowry of jewels worth an additional £200/$1,000.

'It's all gone,' she told a reporter from the *New York Herald*. 'All gone, and I have no husband.'

Better off than some, Celiney had family and friends in Wilkes-Barre to comfort her. Many Syrians, a term used for all emigrants from the area that now comprises both Lebanon and Syria, had come to Pennsylvania at the turn of the century, fleeing the unemployment, famine and forced conscription of their homeland. Celiney's father was among them. But Celiney's wish was to be independent of her father. She held on to the hope that somehow she and Fraza would be reunited. 'I want to be with him,' said the naive girl through her interpreter. 'I hope some ship comes in some city with Fraza on board. He was a good swimmer.'

Celiney waited in New York until all hope was gone, then made her way to Pennsylvania with the help of the Red Cross Relief Fund and

Celiney Yasbeck and Elias Decker on their wedding day. (Courtesy of Robert Decker and family)

other American charities. With the encouragement of the Lebanese community of Wilkes-Barre she met and married Elias Michael Decker in 1915. He, too, was from Hardin, Celiney's village, and they knew of each other. But this marriage, like her first, was arranged. Elias had emigrated in 1914, but his had been a more circuitous route through South America and into Mexico, where his entry into the United Sates was barred until money changed hands at the border.

Celiney, still only 17, was a bride for the second time, but the occasion was celebrated in fine style. The Maronites had just completed a church in Wilkes-Barre and the Decker marriage was the first conducted under its sacred dome. Soon after the nuptials the newlyweds moved to Norfolk where they produced a family of 12 children, the first in 1916 and the last, Robert, in 1935. At the beginning Elias supported his brood by delivering ice – of all things – on a horse-drawn cart. His children have fond memories of helping him lug the heavy, cold, dripping chunks up stairs and into the iceboxes of his clients. In 1939 Elias was able to purchase a gas station, which he ran with his sons until his death in 1949.

Celiney neither wrote nor read English and never learned to drive. But the close-knit community of relatives and friends was always there to support her, especially when her sister Amenia returned home ill with tuberculosis to die. Celiney kept alive the Lebanese traditions, especially on holidays and Sundays when the priests would be invited to dinner to sample her home-made pitta bread, 40-layer baklava and stuffed grape leaves, which she picked from the beach herself.

Picking those leaves from the scuppenak grapes on a Virginia beach was about as close as she ever came to the ocean. The trauma of the *Titanic* experience never left her and she did not speak of it until Walter Lord interviewed her for *A Night to Remember*. It was about then she also met survivor Leah Aks. Unbeknown to either of them they had lived within blocks of each other for 35 years.

Officially there were 154 Syrians on board the Titanic *in Third Class, and 29 were saved: four men, five children and 20 women. These figures are, however, in dispute, as not all embarking at Southampton were listed on the passenger manifest. Recent newspaper accounts suggest that the small Roman Orthodox Village of Kfar Mishki in the lower Bekaa Valley of Eastern Lebanon was devastated by the loss of at least 13 of its inhabitants. They are still seeking restitution.*

Celiney's sons wondered if their mother had seen carafes similar to this one in the Third Class dining room.

In 1993 the French research vessel *Nadir* sailed into Norfolk harbour bringing *Titanic* artefacts to American shores for the first time in 81 years. Captain Frank E. Decker of the Norfolk Police Department, Celiney's eldest son, along with his brother Alvin, were there to represent their mother. They walked through the exhibition of water carafes and plates and stopped to stare at the ship's whistles assembled for the first time since they were placed on *Titanic*'s forward funnel at Harland & Wolff. It was hard for them not to wonder if their mother had eaten from one of those plates during the journey or poured water from the carafe with the White Star logo. And what was she feeling as she heard those whistles in their last distress call as she was being torn from one husband

and pointed to her future with another – their father?

Celiney Alexander Yasbeck Decker
15 July 1896–10 March 1966

Amenia Alexander Moubarek (Borak)
1888–1922

George Moubarek (Borak)
27 November 1904–24 October 1979

William Moubarek (Borak)
15 July 1907–29 August 1975

Women and children last

'Rule of the sea of no avail for large number of the Titanic's passengers.'
New York Tribune, 21 April 1912

TITANIC'S THIRD CLASS suffered enormously on 14–15 April 1912, none more so than the children, with 54 of the 84 little ones under the age of 13 perishing. Those saved were forever left with the shock and horror of being plucked from their sleep by anxious parents only to be thrown without warning into lifeboats, often into the arms of strangers. Deprived of sleep, frozen to the marrow of their bones, hungry and often screaming in fear, they grew up in most cases with only one parent, a widowed mother, certainly depressed, most definitely toiling to make sense of what had happened to her family.

Even more tragic were those families of which no one was left to wonder, to be depressed, to cry. They were swept completely from the face of the earth by a rule of the sea that did not translate to their class. They were lucky if their bodies were retrieved from that sea for burial. Captain Lardner of the search ship *Mackay-Bennett* said movingly of his grim task, 'In one place we saw them scattered over

the surface, looking like a flock of seagulls ... with the white ends of the lifebelt fluttering and flapping up and down with the rise and fall of the waves.'

Some of these Third Class families have been mentioned previously, but the roster of devastation continues.

* * *

ANNA DANBOM and ALFRIDA ANDERSSON, the Brogren sisters, were enjoying every minute on this journey to America surrounded by their husbands and children. Two of Alfrida's children, Ingeborg and Sigrid, had birthdays on 16 April, so she had tucked little presents in her hand baggage for a *Titanic* celebration. But mostly the two families were focusing on life in America.

Anna had lived in the United States before and it was there that she had met her husband, Ernst, a farmer and part-time builder in Stanton, Iowa. Married in Chicago in 1910, the newlyweds went back to Sweden for their honeymoon. It turned into a protracted 18-month stay during which Anna became pregnant and gave birth to their son Gilbert. When Gilbert reached his fourth month the Danboms made arrangements to return to Iowa. By this time Anna had convinced her sister and brother-in-law to emigrate as well.

Alfrida and Anders Andersson, both 39, had been married much longer than the Danboms and had older children: Sigrid (11), Ingeborg (9), Ebba (6), Sigvard (4) and Ellis (2). A family that large would have more opportunities in America's booming economy than in Sweden, where population growth had limited arable land. The Anderssons decided to pursue these opportunities in Winnipeg, Canada, the same city that the Second Class Harts had as their destination.

The seven Anderssons and three Danboms were all obliterated in one wave of the cosmic wand. The only body recovered was that of

The Andersson family. (Claes-Göran Wetterholm Archive, Stockholm)

Ernst Danbom, ironically the one who had made the group's travel arrangements. Among his effects were a solitaire diamond ring, an opal and ruby ring, a gold watch and chain, a jewel case, £53/$266 in paper, and £6/$30 in gold, three tickets and a cheque drawn on an Iowa bank for £264/$1,315.79. On his finger was his wedding ring engraved 'June 6, 1910'. His remains were forwarded to the tiny village in Iowa where his mother, sister and brothers were waiting. This close-knit prairie community turned out en masse for the solemn Lutheran ceremony, conducted in both English and Swedish to honour Ernst's memory and by extension the others who had died with him. Inscribed on his headstone were the words 'Nearer My God To Thee'.

Members of the Danbom family continued to make Iowa their home for many years and were known far and wide as the family who had relatives on the *Titanic*. It was not a fame they appreciated. Eventually one of the nephews, who had been called upon one too many times to tell the family story, wrote an article in which he said, 'I wish the *Titanic* would leave us Danboms alone.'

Ernst Gilbert Danbom
26 October 1877–15 April 1912

Anna Sigrid Danbom
10 March 1884–15 April 1912

Gilbert Sigvard Danbom
16 November 1911–15 April 1912

Alfrida Brogren Andersson
25 December 1872–15 April 1912

Anders Andersson
21 January 1873–15 April 1912

Sigrid Elizabeth Andersson
16 April 1900–15 April 1912

Ingeborg Constancia Andersson
16 April 1902–15 April 1912

Ebba Iris Andersson
14 November 1905–15 April 1912

Sigvard Harald Andersson
21 July 1907–15 April 1912

Ellis Anna Andersson
19 January 1910–15 April 1912

* * *

THE ASPLUNDS were another Swedish family devastated by the tragedy. Like the Danboms, Carl and Selma had lived in America (Massachusetts) for 18 years, and Carl had become a citizen. They were like many other immigrants who, when hard times struck, began to question their initial decision to emigrate. Thinking fondly of Sweden, they sold what they could of their possessions and left with their four children. They remained in Sweden for three years, during which time they had another son, then Carl and Selma sailed again for America, taking with them, like a flock of migrating birds, Filip (13), Clarence (9), Carl and Lillian, five-year-old twins, and little Felix (3).

When the iceberg struck, the Asplunds

Selma Asplund with Lillian and Felix. (Michael Findlay collection)

Lillian and Felix Asplund several years after the disaster. (Claes-Göran Wetterholm Archive, Stockholm)

collected themselves and found a route to A Deck where Lifeboat 4 was still waiting to be loaded through the windows of the enclosed Promenade area. Selma, with Felix in her arms, was put into that boat, which immediately began its creaky descent as the situation was growing more desperate. Looking up she begged someone to save her husband and other children, but only one of the twins, Lillian, was lowered down. Carl Senior was left to stand at the rail with his sons Carl, Clarence and Filip, praying for a miracle. Beside them stood men with the names of Astor, Widener and Ryerson, all now equal as they prepared to die.

Once rescued, Selma continued on to Worcester, Massachusetts, where her two sisters lived, and waited for news of her loved ones' bodies. Only her husband was dragged from the sea and forwarded to her for burial. Selma was inconsolable and grieved every day of her remaining life, refusing ever to discuss the tragedy. For over 50 years she lived with her sorrow until death took her on 15 April 1964, the 52nd anniversary of the disaster.

Felix and Lillian never married, remaining always with their mother. Like Holocaust victims they may have lived with the guilt of survival. Felix had been too small to have personal recollections of that night and was more apt to speak of the incident than his sister Lillian. Now in her 90s, she still honours her mother's wishes and mentions it rarely.

Carl Oscar Asplund
7 May 1871–15 April 1912

Selma Asplund
10 October 1873–15 April 1964

Filip Asplund
12 December 1898–15 April 1912

Clarence Asplund
17 September 1902–15 April 1912

Carl Edgar Asplund
21 October 1906–15 April 1912

Lillian Gertrud Asplund
21 October 1906–

Edvin Felix Asplund
19 March 1909–1 March 1983

* * *

AUGUSTA GOODWIN (43) and her husband Frederick, a 40-year-old electrical engineer, had left Wiltshire, England, for Niagara Falls, New York, where Mr Goodwin's brother, Thomas, had already settled. They and their children Lillian (16), Charles (14), William (11), Jessie (10), Harold (9) and Sidney (18 months), trapped in the bowels of the ship, would not survive.

Walter Lord in *The Night Lives On* heads one of his chapters 'Whatever happened to the Goodwins?' A good question. They spoke English and would certainly have understood

The Goodwin family. (The British Library/*Daily Mirror*)

Sidney Goodwin. (The British Library/*Daily Mirror*)

the danger inherent in the situation. Separated by gender at opposite ends of the vessel, it is easy to speculate that they waited until all family members had assembled before attempting to reach the lifeboats. Once together it is Lord's contention that they waited patiently for the stewards to tell them what to do, unlike the feistier passengers who took it upon themselves to be responsible for their own survival. To quote Mr Lord, 'Frederick and Augusta Goodwin stood with their six children, quietly prepared to meet the end.' All that remains is their final picture from the London *Daily Mirror*.

Many cultures consider elephants as bringers of good luck. This elephant pendant could have been a Third Class passenger's talisman.

Augusta Goodwin
1869–15 April 1912

Frederick Goodwin
1872–15 April 1912

Lillian Goodwin
1896–15 April 1912

Charles Goodwin
1898–15 April 1912

William Goodwin
1901–15 April 1912

Jessie Goodwin
1902–15 April 1912

Harold Goodwin
1903–15 April 1912

Sidney Goodwin
1910–15 April 1912

* * *

FRANCES LEFEBRE and her four children, Mathilde (11), Jeannie (6), Henry (4) and Ida (2) all perished on their way from France to Mystic, Iowa. Her husband Frank had emigrated earlier and was anxiously awaiting their arrival with three other sons and an older married daughter. To add to his distress, he was out of work and had counted on the £160/$800 in cash his wife was bringing with her from France together with household furnishings and £60/$300 worth of clothing.

He petitioned the Red Cross Relief Committee to refund the price of the ticket his wife and children had travelled with – an amount of £35/$172.76 – to help with his immediate living needs. His request was granted, but in checking his story the Red Cross turned up yet another problem for Monsieur Lefebre. It seemed that he had entered the United States illegally, proffering 'false and misleading statements' to the immigration officials on Ellis Island. In August 1912, still grieving the loss of his wife and four youngest children, he and two of his remaining three sons were deported.

Frances Lefebre
1873–15 April 1912

Mathilde Lefebre
1901–15 April 1912

Jeannie Lefebre
1906–15 April 1912

Henry Lefebre
1908–15 April 1912

Ida Lefebre
1910–15 April 1912

* * *

ALMA PÅLSSON (29) left Bjuv, Sweden, on 30 March and went by train to Copenhagen, then by ferry and boat train to Southampton. She and her four children were counting the days until they would be reunited with their husband and father, Nils, whom they had not seen since June 1910. Nils had been a miner in Sweden, but the coal strike of 1909 found him out of work and forced him to emigrate to

Alma and Nils Pålsson with Stina before Nils left for Chicago. (Courtesy of Lars-Inge Glad)

Chicago with two of Alma's brothers. There he became a tram conductor, and by early 1912 had earned the £21 10s 6d/$105 for his family's ticket on the *Titanic*. Travelling with Alma were Torborg (8), Paul (6), Stina (4) and Gösta (2).

In the aft section of the ship Mrs Pålsson may not have felt the collision, but she certainly heard the confusion as the men began to filter back from the bow where water had begun seeping into their quarters. Alone she struggled to dress her children, taking up precious minutes with making sure each of them had on enough layers to protect them from the cold. Then the five of them joined that last wave of passengers surging to the higher decks just before the final plunge. Once there, Carl Jansson and August Wennerström, fellow Swedes, rushed to her aid. Wennerström grabbed one of the smaller children and frantically looked around for an escape. But a torrent of water hurtled up from the bow at that moment and all were swept screaming into the sea. 'Oh, the agony of it!' Colonel Gracie wrote of that moment.

(Wennerström (27) was a Swedish socialist. Having published anti-monarchy pamphlets, he was running from incarceration. He and Carl Jansson made it to Collapsible A. Wennerström died on 25 November 1951 in Culver, Indiana.)

The *Bremen*, a German liner on her way to New York, passed within 4 miles of *Titanic*'s sinking on Saturday 20 April. Her passengers and crew were devastated by the sight of the sea littered with bodies and wreckage. Mrs Johanna Stunke was one of the passengers stalwart enough to remain on deck as a witness to the carnage. The London *Daily Mail* of 25 April quotes her:

'We saw the body of one woman dressed only in her nightdress, and clasping a baby to her breast. Close by was the body of another woman with her arms tightly clasped round a shaggy dog. We saw the bodies of three men in a group, all clinging to a chair. Floating by just beyond them were the bodies of a dozen men, all wearing lifebelts and clinging desperately together as though in their last struggle for life ...'

The *Bremen* wired the coordinates of this tragic tableau to the *Mackay-Bennett*, and on the first day of their funereal sweep of the area they picked up a baby, later presumed to be Gösta Pålsson. But if it were Gösta, what happened to Alma, whose body was not found until days later? Clinical reports describe the baby's remains as: 'Number 4, male, estimated age 2, hair fair, clothing – grey coat with fur on collar and cuffs; brown serge frock; petticoat; flannel garment; pink woollen singlet; brown shoes and stockings. No marks whatever. Probably Third Class.'

The seamen of the *Mackay-Bennett*, saddened and sickened by the sight of the tiny fair-haired nameless baby, sponsored a memorial service for him at St George's Church in Halifax on 4 May 1912. The hearts of Nova Scotians and the world poured out, smothering his miniature white casket under a blanket of flowers. Even the hardened 'boys from the morgue' sent blossoms.

Six *Mackay-Bennett* seamen carried the casket to the horse-drawn hearse, which solemnly conveyed it to Fairview Cemetery for interment. The entire crew erected a stone on which they had engraved: 'Erected to the Memory of an Unknown Child whose remains were recovered after the disaster to the Titanic, April 15th 1912.' The baby's identification as Gösta Pålsson was poignant considering that his grave had quite by chance been placed only a few feet from that of Alma.

Michael Findlay, Titanic International's authority on the passengers, offers another theory on the identity of the 'unknown child'. Margaret Rice, an Irishwoman, was also on board with her sons Albert (10), George (9), Eric (7), Arthur (4) and Eugene (3). She had

Gösta Pålsson. (Courtesy of Lars-Inge Glad)

come first to the United States ten years before settling in New York, where she married William Rice. Rice secured a position as shipping clerk with the Grand Trunk Railroad Company (of which First Class passenger Hays was President; he lost his life but his wife was saved) and the family moved to Montreal, Canada, where it is presumed their four oldest children were born. In 1909 William took a job as a machinist with the Great Northern Railway in Spokane, Washington, and the family moved again. Margaret gave birth to her youngest son, Eugene, there.

Four months after that birth, William was crushed to death beneath the wheels of a locomotive in a bizarre railroad accident. Margaret received £1,300/$6,500 for her loss and the upkeep of her sons and returned to Ireland for the comfort and support of her family. Drawing heavily on her compensation to make ends meet while there, she boarded the *Titanic* with hopes of better economic opportunities in Spokane for her growing sons.

Bertha Mulvihill, another Irish passenger, saw Margaret on deck just before the end with one child in her arms and the others clutching at her skirts in bewilderment. No lifeboats remaining, the Rice family were among the 1,523 who perished. Margaret's body was recovered and buried in Mount Olivet (Halifax), identified as Catholic by her rosary, but unidentified by name. Eventually her identity was secured when a pharmacist in County Athlone, whose name appeared on a vial of pills found in her pocket, confirmed that he had prescribed them for Mrs Rice on 9 April just before she boarded the *Titanic*.

Margaret's body was recovered by the *Mackay-Bennett* on the same day as that of the unknown child. Her son Eugene was the approximate age of Gösta Pålsson and, being of Irish heritage, he too might well have been as described with 'hair, fair'.

Could Findlay be right? Was the unknown child Eugene Rice rather than Gösta Pålsson? Could the original identification have been made as a consolation for the living who wanted to believe that a mother and son could lie eternally together? You decide.

Nils Pålsson was devastated by the loss of his entire family and spent a good deal of money following up news of an orphan child in the hope that it might be one of his own. He filed an insurance claim for £500/$2,500 for the loss of Alma and £300/$1,500 for each of his children, but received only a fraction of that amount. He was still living in Chicago in 1924, but between that date and his death in 1964 there is no information on how he lived with his loss. Alma's mother, a widow, also filed a claim for the loss of her daughter and received

£50/$150 from the British Relief Fund and £75/$375 from the White Star Line.

Alma Cornelia Berglund Pålsson
3 August 1882–15 April 1912

Stina Viola Pålsson
19 June 1903–15 April 1912

Paul Folke Pålsson
14 April 1906–15 April 1912

Torborg Danira Pålsson
19 December 1908–15 April 1912

Gösta Leonard Pålsson
3 January 1910–15 April 1912

Margaret Norton Rice
6 October 1872–15 April 1912

Albert Rice
1902–15 April 1912

George Rice
1903–15 April 1912

Eric Rice
1905–15 April 1912

Arthur Rice
1908–15 April 1912

Eugene Rice
13 October 1909–15 April 1912

* * *

THE ROSTER OF DEATH rolls on with the Sage family. Annie and her husband, John, both 44, and their children Stella (20), George (19), Douglas (18), Frederick (16), Dorothy (13), William (11), Ada (9), Constance (7) and Thomas (4), were moving to Jacksonville, Florida, from Peterborough, England. This was an enterprising group determined to make their way in the world. Stella was a dressmaker, George a barman, Fred a cook and Douglas a baker. John had been a tradesman but sold his shop and went to Canada in 1910 with his

The Sage family. (The British Library/*The Daily Sketch*)

oldest son, George, to work on a farm. In January 1912 they returned and John announced that he had purchased a fruit farm in Florida.

The family was seen on deck near the end when there was still potential for their survival. Stella, the eldest girl, had in fact entered a lifeboat and sat waiting for the rest of her family to find seats. When that did not happen she stepped out again to her death with the ten other Sages – all their potential lost to the sea. Only William's body was found, identified by the writing on the ticket in his pocket: 'Will Sage, berth 126'.

He was buried at sea with the other bodies

It was so cold on that Sunday night that many passengers resorted to hot water bottles for warmth.

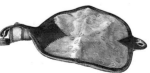

too disfigured to embalm. Hearing of this practice, victims' families were up in arms, and emotions ran high. Not only had White Star killed their loved ones with a belief in the infallibility of its ship, but with sea burials it was depriving them of bidding their dead a fitting farewell. After much criticism, the company stopped the procedure and ordered all bodies to be brought to Halifax to be claimed or buried there.

In William Sage's case, no one waited on a distant shore to claim his remains. In his case it was perhaps fitting that he be committed to the North Atlantic where the other ten members of his family had found their final resting place.

John Sage
1867–15 April 1912

Annie Sage
1868–15 April 1912

Stella Sage
1891–15 April 1912

George Sage
1892–15 April 1912

Douglas Sage
1894–15 April 1912

Frederick Sage
1895–15 April 1912

Dorothy Sage
1899–15 April 1912

William Sage
1901–15 April 1912

Ada Sage
1903–15 April 1912

Constance Sage
1905–15 April 1912

Thomas Sage
1908–15 April 1912

* * *

THE UPPER PENINSULA of Michigan was the destination for a number of the *Titanic's* emigrant passengers. Workers were recruited from all over Europe to work there in the copper mines, the Skoog family from Hallekis, Sweden, among them. They had first come to Michigan at the end of the 19th century, and William went to work in the Pewabic Mine in Iron Mountain, becoming a naturalised citizen in 1905. Between 1900 and 1910 the Skoogs had four children: Thorsten, Mabel, Harald and Margit. Their future looked excellent.

Anna and William gave their children chores to do, believing that responsibility built character. At the age of seven, Thorsten, the oldest child, was chosen to carry his father's dinner pail over the hills from their home to the mine for the midday meal. Thorsten enjoyed this duty as his father often rewarded him with a left-over cookie or a bite of his mother's pasties, which he particularly loved when she filled them with wild game.

Thorsten was fascinated by trains and on his way to the mine he usually stopped by the railroad yard to see the engines. On a lucky day the shunting engine would be heading towards the mine and he could hitch a ride. The first Saturday in November was freezing and the ground was covered with a layer of crunchy new snow. Thorsten's toes under the thin leather of his shoes ached from the cold and when he saw the engine pulling out of the yard he took off at a gallop to catch it. As the Chicago & North

The Skoog family: Thorsten, William, Harald and Mabel, with mother Anna standing at the back. The youngest Skoog, Margit, is missing, indicating that the photograph was taken in 1910 before her birth. (Author's collection/Hazel Dault)

Western locomotive moved forward on the flagman's signal, Thorsten leapt in the air, reaching out for his customary hitching spot. In that instant the train jolted and Thorsten was thrown to the track, his face buried in the sharp gravel and his legs pinned between the excruciating weight of the engine's wheels and the metal rail.

The yard workers rushed him to the hospital but it was too late to save his left leg and the toes on his right foot, which were amputated. The railroad made a settlement, as they had in the Rice case, and with it William and Anna bought a house in a section of Iron Mountain with fewer hills so Thorsten would have an easier time learning to walk on crutches, which were now a permanent part of his existence.

Yearning for Sweden, in November 1911 the Skoogs sold their home and furnishings – except their piano – and left for the old country. It was, however, a short-lived visit and four months later friends in Iron Mountain received a letter from them: 'Dear Friends, We plan to return to America next month. We were fortunate to seek passage on the new and beautiful luxury liner *Titanic* … our spirits soar. How wonderful it will be to see all of you again.'

Travelling with them was Ellen Pettersson (18) and a relative, Jenny Lovisa Henriksson (28), from Stockholm.

The Skoogs' bodies were never found. Climbing to safety on a listing ship amid throngs of anxious, shoving passengers in their last-minute dash to safety would have been impossible for a family with a child on crutches. The only body from this group to be found was Jenny's, although it remained unidentified until 1991 when Titanic International researchers, poring over the grim details of the bodies and their effects, noticed that body number 3 had a 'J. H.' sewn into her

This dictionary would have been a great help for any of Titanic's *families struggling with English as a second language.*

chemise. Jenny now rests beneath a headstone inscribed with her name.

What was left of the family estate, including the piano, was liquidated and the money sent to William's mother and father in Sweden. But they would never accept any compensation from the White Star Line, claiming that their son's life was worth far more than any paltry amount the company could offer.

Anna Skoog
13 November 1868–15 April 1912

William Skoog
6 April 1872–15 April 1912

Karl Thorsten Skoog
13 July 1900–15 April 1912

Mabel Skoog
22 July 1902–15 April 1912

Harald Skoog
22 August 1906–15 April 1912

Margit Elizabeth Skoog
14 April 1910–15 April 1912

Jenny Lovisa Henriksson
21 December 1883–15 April 1912

Ellen Pettersson
19 July 1893–15 April 1912

* * *

THESE ARE BY NO MEANS all of the families devastated by this journey into oblivion. Let it be said that any family that lived through this nightmare or was diminished by the tragedy is one too many.

Theories on the causes of the disaster will one day be replaced by scientific knowledge. Already, metallurgic analyses have identified manufacturing flaws in the rivets and steel, which may have resulted in the ship's inability to withstand the collision. With continued technological advances our understanding of the reasons why the *Titanic* sank may well be complete.

Sadly, the same cannot be said of the passengers; our knowledge of their lives will never be complete. Many survivors could not speak of their trauma, others were too young to remember what happened, and so many perished that their lives and their experiences on 15 April 1912 can never be reconstructed. Even though other stories remain to be told, there will always be faces missing from the family album called *Titanic: Women and Children First*.

APPENDIX ONE

SURVIVAL RATE
BY CLASS

A CHART SHOWING the number of women and children by class who were saved or perished

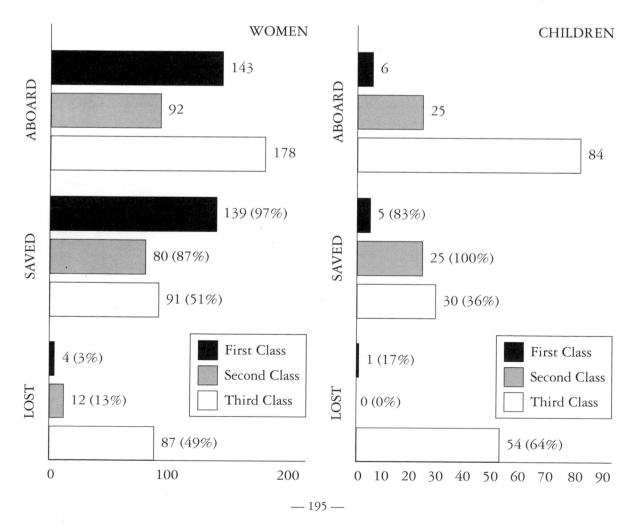

WOMEN

ABOARD	
First Class	143
Second Class	92
Third Class	178

SAVED	
First Class	139 (97%)
Second Class	80 (87%)
Third Class	91 (51%)

LOST	
First Class	4 (3%)
Second Class	12 (13%)
Third Class	87 (49%)

First Class
Second Class
Third Class

0   100   200

CHILDREN

ABOARD	
First Class	6
Second Class	25
Third Class	84

SAVED	
First Class	5 (83%)
Second Class	25 (100%)
Third Class	30 (36%)

LOST	
First Class	1 (17%)
Second Class	0 (0%)
Third Class	54 (64%)

First Class
Second Class
Third Class

0 10 20 30 40 50 60 70 80 90

APPENDIX TWO

TITANIC PASSENGER LIST, 10 APRIL 1912

by Michael A. Findlay

I WOULD LIKE TO THANK the following people who assisted in this great effort to put together the most up-to-date and accurate passenger list from the *Titanic*:

Mr Carles Bonet i Corbalan from Spain, for his friendship and for the wonderful material he supplied on the Spanish passengers, in particular his discovery of Mr and Mrs Peñasco.

Mr Robert L. Bracken from New Jersey, USA, for all the help, encouragement, support and friendship that was so much appreciated, and also for his encyclopedic knowledge that he kindly shared and which resulted in this work. His particular area of expertise on the Syrian and Irish passengers is truly remarkable.

Mr Herman DeWulf from Belgium for all his work on the Belgians.

Mr John P. Eaton from New York, USA, colleague and friend, who never failed to pass along any *Titanic* passenger-related material that came his way. There was never a time when I couldn't call with a question with which Jack couldn't be of some assistance. His knowledge and expertise on the *Titanic* as a whole cannot be mirrored.

Mr Peter Engberg from Sweden for all his

work on the many Scandinavians and for sharing his knowledge and interest in chasing up who went in each boat.

Mr Charles A. Haas from New Jersey, USA, whose friendship and expertise I value.

Mr Alan Hustak from Montreal, Quebec, Canada, for all the truly fascinating work he shared on the Canadians who were aboard.

Mr Per Kristian Sebak from Norway for all his work on the Norwegians.

Mr Brian Ticehurst from the United Kingdom and of the British Titanic Society for all his work on the British passengers.

Mr Claes-Göran Wetterholm from Sweden for all his truly remarkable work on the Scandinavians.

Mr Geoffrey Whitfield from the United Kingdom and of the British Titanic Society for all his work on the British passengers.

It would be impossible to thank all of the many hundreds of descendants of the passengers of the *Titanic* who contributed to the accuracy of this list but I would like to express my thanks to those who showed great interest in this project and offered their assistance:

Titanic survivors: Mr Frank P. Aks, Mrs Ruth Becker Blanchard, Mr Alden G. Caldwell, Mr

Bertram V. Dean, Miss Millvina Dean, Mr Marshall Drew, Mrs Edith Brown Haisman, Miss Eva Hart, Mrs Nan Harper Pont, Mrs Louise Kink Pope, Mrs Marjorie Newell Robb, Mrs Eleanor Johnson Shuman, and Mrs Winifred Quick Van Tongerloo.

Descendants: Mr Peter Blank, Mr Ralph Blank, Mr Henry Siegel Cavendish, Mr Thomas P.

Crolius, Mr Thayer Cumings, Mr Arthur Dodge, Miss Nell Greenfield, Mr James J. Heslin, Mrs Gretchen L. H. Hyde, Mrs Helen O'Neill Landsberg, Mr Michel Navratil, Mr Gerald Nummi, Mrs Hollie Silverthorne, Mrs Margaret Easton Starbuck, and Mr Nicholas Wade

In the following list, names in **bold** denote those who were rescued.

First Class Passengers

Name	Age	1912 residence(s)	Lifeboat No
Allen, Miss Elisabeth Walton	29	St Louis, Missouri	2
Allison, Mr Hudson Joshua Creighton	30	Montreal, Quebec	
Allison, Mrs Hudson Joshua Creighton (nee Bessie Waldo Daniels)	25	Montreal, Quebec	
and Maid (Miss Sarah Daniels)		Montreal, Quebec	8
Allison, Miss Helen Loraine	2	Montreal, Quebec	
Allison, Master Hudson Trevor	11m	Montreal, Quebec	11
and Nurse (Miss Alice Mary Cleaver)		Montreal, Quebec	11
Anderson, Mr Harry	47	New York, New York	3
Andrews, Miss Kornelia Theodosia	63	Hudson, New York	10
Andrews, Mr Thomas	39	Belfast, Ireland	
Appleton, Mrs Edward Dale (nee Charlotte Lamson)	53	Bayside, Queens, New York	2
Artagaveytia, Mr Ramon	71	Buenos Aires, Argentina	
Astor, Col John Jacob	47	New York, New York	
and Manservant (Victor Robbins)		New York, New York	
Astor, Mrs John Jacob (nee Madeleine Talmadge Force)	19	New York, New York	4
and Maid (Miss Rosalie Bidois)		New York, New York	4
Aubart, Mrs N. (Leontine Pauline)		Paris, France	9
and Maid (Miss Emma Sagesser)		Paris, France	9
Barkworth, Mr Algernon Henry	48	Hessle, England	B
Baumann, Mr John D.		New York, New York	
Baxter, Mrs James (nee Helene De Lanaudiere-Chaput)	50	Montreal, Quebec	6
Baxter, Mr Quigg Edmond	24	Montreal, Quebec	
Beattie, Mr Thomson	36	Winnipeg, Manitoba	
Beckwith, Mr Richard Leonard	37	New York, New York	5
Beckwith, Mrs Richard Leonard (nee Sallie Monypeny)	45	New York, New York	5
Behr, Mr Karl Howell	26	New York, New York	5
Birnbaum, Mr Jacob	25	Antwerp, Belgium	
Bishop, Mr Dickinson H.	25	Dowagiac, Michigan	7
Bishop, Mrs Dickinson H. (nee Helen Margaret Walton)	19	Dowagiac, Michigan	7
Blackwell, Mr Stephen Weart	45	Trenton, New Jersey	
Blank, Mr Henry	39	Glen Ridge, New Jersey	7
Bonnell, Miss Caroline	29	Youngstown, Ohio	8
Bonnell, Miss Elizabeth (Lily)	61	Birkdale, England	8
Borebank, Mr John James		Winnipeg, Manitoba	
Bowen, Miss Grace Scott	45	Cooperstown, New York	4

Name	Age	1912 residence(s)	Lifeboat No
Bowerman, Miss Elsie E.	22	St Leonards, England	6
Brady, Mr John Bertram		Pomery, Washington	
Brandeis, Mr Emil	48	Omaha, Nebraska	
Brayton (Bradley), Mr George		Los Angeles, California	15
Brown, Mrs James Joseph (nee Margaret Tobin)	44	Denver, Colorado	6
Brown, Mrs John Murray (nee Caroline Lane Lamson)	59	Acton, Massachusetts	D
Bucknell, Mrs William Robert (nee Emma Eliza Ward)	60	Philadelphia, Pennsylvania	8
and Maid (Miss Albina Bazzani)		Philadelphia, Pennsylvania	8
Butt, Major Archibald Willingham	45	Washington, DC	
Calderhead, Mr Edward Pennington	42	New York, New York	5
Candee, Mrs Edward (nee Helen Churchill Hungerford)	53	Washington, DC	6
Cardeza, Mrs James Warburton Martinez (nee Charlotte Wardle Drake)	58	Germantown, Pennsylvania	3
and Maid (Miss Anna Ward)	35	Germantown, Pennsylvania	3
Cardeza, Mr Thomas Drake Martinez	36	Germantown, Pennsylvania	3
and Manservant (Gustave Lesneur)		Germantown, Pennsylvania	3
Carlson, Mr Frans Olof	33		
Carrau, Mr Francisco M.	31	Montevideo, Uruguay	
Carrau, Mr Jose Pedro	17	Montevideo, Uruguay	
Carter, Mr William Ernest	36	Bryn Mawr, Pennsylvania	C
Carter, Mrs William Ernest (nee Lucile Polk)	36	Bryn Mawr, Pennsylvania	4
and Maid (Miss Augusta Serepeca)		Bryn Mawr, Pennsylvania	4
Carter, Miss Lucile Polk	14	Bryn Mawr, Pennsylvania	4
Carter, Master William Thornton 2nd	11	Bryn Mawr, Pennsylvania	4
and Manservant (Alexander Cairns)		Bryn Mawr, Pennsylvania	
Case, Mr Howard Brown	48	Ascot, England	
Cassebeer, Mrs Henry Arthur Jr (nee Genevieve Fosdick)		New York, New York	5
Cavendish, Mr Tyrell William	36	Staffordshire, England	
Cavendish, Mrs Tyrell William (nee Julia Florence Siegel)	25	Staffordshire, England	6
and Maid (Miss Nellie Barber)		Staffordshire, England	6

Name	Age	1912 residence(s)	Lifeboat No	Name	Age	1912 residence(s)	Lifeboat No
Chaffee, Mr Herbert Fuller	47	Amenia, North Dakota		Flegenheim, Mrs Alfred		New York/Berlin,	7
Chaffee, Mrs Herbert Fuller	48	Amenia, North Dakota		(Antoinette)		Germany	
(nee Carrie Toogood)				Flynn, Mr John Irwin	36	Brooklyn, New York	5
Chambers, Mr Norman	27	New York, New York/	5	Foreman, Mr Benjamin Laventall	30	New York, New York	
Campbell		Ithaca, New York		Fortune, Mr Mark	64	Winnipeg, Manitoba	
Chambers, Mrs Norman	31	New York, New York/	5	Fortune, Mrs Mark (nee Mary	60	Winnipeg, Manitoba	10
Campbell (nee Bertha Griggs)		Ithaca, New York		McDougald)			
Cherry, Miss Gladys	30	London, England	8	Fortune, Miss Alice Elizabeth	24	Winnipeg, Manitoba	10
Chevre, Mr Paul Romaine	45	Paris, France	7	Fortune, Miss Ethel Flora	28	Winnipeg, Manitoba	10
Chibnall, Mrs Arthur (nee Edith		St Leonards, England	6	Fortune, Miss Mabel	23	Winnipeg, Manitoba	10
Martha Bowerman Barber)				Fortune, Mr Charles Alexander	19	Winnipeg, Manitoba	
Chisholm, Mr Roderick Robert		Belfast, Ireland		Franklin, Mr Thomas Parnham		London, England	
Clark, Mr Walter Miller	28	Los Angeles, California		Frauenthal, Dr Henry William	50	New York, New York	5
Clark, Mrs Walter Miller (nee	26	Los Angeles, California	4	Frauenthal, Mrs Henry William		New York, New York	5
Virginia McDowell)				(nee Clara Heinsheimer)			
Clifford, Mr George Quincy	40	Stoughton, Massachusetts		Frauenthal, Mr Isaac Gerald	43	New York, New York	5
Colley, Mr Edward Pomeroy	37	Victoria, British		Frolicher, Miss Hedwig	22	Zurich, Switzerland	5
		Columbia		Marguerite			
Compton, Mrs Alexander Taylor				Frolicher-Stehli, Mr Maxmillian	60	Zurich, Switzerland	5
(nee Mary Eliza Ingersoll)	64	Lakewood, New Jersey	14	Josef			
Compton, Miss Sara Rebecca	39	Lakewood, New Jersey	14	Frolicher-Stehli, Mrs Maxmillian	48	Zurich, Switzerland	5
Compton, Mr Alexander Taylor Jr	37	Lakewood, New Jersey		Josef (nee Margrit Emerentia			
Cornell, Mrs Robert Clifford	55	New York, New York	2	Stehli)			
(nee Malvina Helen Lamson)				Futrelle, Mr Jacques	37	Scituate, Massachusetts	
Crafton, Mr John Bertram	59	Roachdale, Indiana		Futrelle, Mrs Jacques (nee Lily	35	Scituate, Massachusetts	9
Crosby, Capt Edward Gifford	70	Milwaukee, Wisconsin		May Peel)			
Crosby, Mrs Edward Gifford	69	Milwaukee, Wisconsin	5	Gee, Mr Arthur H.	47	St Annes on Sea,	
(nee Catherine Elizabeth						Lancashire, England	
Halstead)				Gibson, Miss Dorothy	22	New York, New York	7
Crosby, Miss Harriet R.	36	Milwaukee, Wisconsin	5	Gibson, Mrs Leonard (nee	45	New York, New York	7
Cumings, Mr John Bradley	39	New York, New York		Pauline C. Boeson)			
Cumings, Mrs John Bradley	38	New York, New York	4	Goldenberg, Mr Samuel L.		Nice, France/New York,	5
(nee Florence Briggs Thayer)						New York	
Daly, Mr Peter Denis		Lima, Peru	A	Goldenberg, Mrs Samuel L. (nee		Nice, France/New York,	5
Daniel, Mr Robert Williams	27	Philadelphia,		Edwiga 'Ella' Grabowska)		New York	
		Pennsylvania		Goldschmidt, Mr George B.	71	New York, New York	
Davidson, Mr Thornton	31	Montreal, Quebec		Gordon, Sir Cosmo Edmund	49	London, England	1
Davidson, Mrs Thornton (nee	28	Montreal, Quebec	3	Duff			
Orian Hays)				Gordon, Lady Duff (nee Lucile	48	London, England	1
de Villiers, Mrs B. (Miss Berthe	24	Brussels, Belgium	6	Wallace Sutherland)			
Antonine Mayne)				and Maid (Miss Laura Mabel		London, England	1
Dick, Mr Albert Adrian	31	Calgary, Alberta	3	Francatelli)			
Dick, Mrs Albert Adrian (nee	17	Calgary, Alberta	3	Gracie, Colonel Archibald IV	54	Washington, DC	B
Vera Gillespie)				Graham, Mr George Edward	38	Winnipeg, Manitoba	
Dodge, Dr Washington		San Francisco, California	13	Graham, Mrs William	58	Greenwich, Connecticut	3
Dodge, Mrs Washington (nee		San Francisco, California	5/7	Thompson (nee Edith			
Ruth Vidaver)				Junkins)			
Dodge, Master Washington	4	San Francisco, California	5/7	Graham, Miss Margaret	19	Greenwich, Connecticut	3
Douglas, Mr Walter Donald	50	Minneapolis, Minnesota		Greenfield, Mrs Leo David (nee	45	New York, New York	7
Douglas, Mrs Walter Donald	48	Minneapolis, Minnesota	2	Blanche Strouse)			
(nee Mahala Dutton)				Greenfield, Mr William Bertram	23	New York, New York	7
and Maid (Miss Bertha LeRoy)		Minneapolis, Minnesota	2	Guggenheim, Mr Benjamin	46	New York, New York	
Douglas, Mrs Frederick Charles	27	Montreal, Quebec	6	and Manservant (Victor Giglio)		New York, New York	
(nee Mary-Helene 'Suzette'				Harder, Mr George Achilles	25	Brooklyn, New York	5
Baxter)				Harder, Mrs George Achilles	21	Brooklyn, New York	5
Dulles, Mr William Crothers	39	Philadelphia,		(nee Dorothy Annan)			
		Pennsylvania		Harper, Mr Henry Sleeper	48	New York, New York	3
Earnshaw, Mrs Boulton (nee	23	Mt Airy, Philadelphia,	7	and Manservant (Hamad		Cairo, Egypt/New York	3
Olive Potter)		Pennsylvania		Hassab)			
Endres, Miss Caroline Louise	39	New York, New York	4	Harper, Mrs Henry Sleeper (nee	49	New York, New York	3
Eustis, Miss Elizabeth Mussey	53	Brookline, Massachussetts	4	Myra Haxtun)			
Evans, Miss Edith Corse	36	New York, New York		Harris, Mr Henry Burkhardt	45	New York, New York	

Name	Age	1912 residence(s)	Lifeboat No	Name	Age	1912 residence(s)	Lifeboat No
Harris, Mrs Henry Burkhardt (nee Irene 'Renee' Wallach)	35	New York, New York	D	Marvin, Mrs Daniel Warner (nee Mary Graham Carmichael Farquharson)	17	New York, New York	
Harrison, Mr William Henry		Wallasey, Cheshire, England		McCaffry, Mr Thomas Francis	46	Vancouver, British Columbia	
Haven (Homer), Mr Harry		Indianapolis, Indiana	15	McCarthy, Mr Timothy J.	54	Dorchester, Massachusetts	
Hawksford, Mr Walter James		Kingston, Surrey, England		McGough, Mr James Robert	36	Philadelphia, Pennsylvania	7
Hays, Mr Charles Melville	55	Montreal, Quebec		Meyer, Mr Edgar Joseph	28	New York, New York	
Hays, Mrs Charles Melville (nee Clara Jennings Gregg)	52	Montreal, Quebec	3	Meyer, Mrs Edgar Joseph (nee Leila Saks)	25	New York, New York	6
and Maid (Miss Anne Perreault)	33	Montreal, Quebec	3	Millet, Mr Francis Davis	65		
Hays, Miss Margaret Bechstein	24	New York, New York	7	Minahan, Dr William Edward	44	Fon du lac, Wisconsin	
Head, Mr Christopher	42	Middlesex, England		Minahan, Mrs William Edward (nee Lillian E. Thorpe)	37	Fon du lac, Wisconsin	14/D
Hilliard, Mr Herbert Henry		Brighton, Massachusetts		Minahan, Miss Daisy E.	33	Green Bay, Wisconsin	14/D
Hipkins, Mr William Edward		Birmingham, England		Mock, Mr Philip E.		New York, New York	11
Hippach, Mrs Louis Albert (nee Ida Sophia Fischer)	44	Chicago, Illinois	4	Molson, Mr Harry Markland	55	Montreal, Quebec	
Hippach, Miss Jean Gertrude	17	Chicago, Illinois	4	Moore, Mr Clarence Bloomfield and Manservant (Charles H. Harrington)	47	Washington, DC	
Hogeboom, Mrs John C. (nee Anna Andrews)	50	Hudson, New York	10	Natsch, Mr Charles	36	Brooklyn, New York	
Holverson, Mr Alexander Oskar	42	New York, New York		Newell, Mr Arthur Webster	58	Lexington, Massachusetts	
Holverson, Mrs Alexander Oskar (nee Mary Aline Towner)	35	New York, New York		Newell, Miss Madeleine	31	Lexington, Massachusetts	6
Hoyt, Mr Frederick Maxfield	38	New York, New York/ Stamford, Connecticut	D	Newell, Miss Marjorie	23	Lexington, Massachusetts	6
				Newsom, Miss Helen Monypeny	19	New York, New York	5
Hoyt, Mrs Frederick Maxfield (nee Jane Ann Forby)	32	New York, New York/ Stamford, Connecticut	D	Nicholson, Mr Arthur Ernest	64	Isle of Wight, England	
Hoyt, Mr William Fisher		New York, New York		Ostby, Mr Engelhart Cornelius	64	Providence, Rhode Island	
Isham, Miss Ann Eliza	50	Chicago, Illinois		Ostby, Miss Helen Raghnild	22	Providence, Rhode Island	5
Ismay, Mr Joseph Bruce and Manservant (John Richard Fry)	49	Liverpool, England	C	Ovies y Rodriguez, Mr Servando			
				Parr, Mr William Henry Marsh	29		
Jones, Mr Charles Cresson	46	Bennington, Vermont		Partner, Mr Austin		Surbiton Hill, Surrey, England	
Julian, Mr Henry Forbes	51	Torquay, Devon, England		Payne, Mr Vivian Arthur Ponsonby	22	Montreal, Quebec	
Kent, Mr Edward Austin	58	Buffalo, New York		Pears, Mr Thomas	29	Isleworth, England	
Kenyon, Mr Frederick R.	41	Pittsburgh, Pennsylvania/ Noank, Connecticut		Pears, Mrs Thomas (nee Edith Wearne)	22	Isleworth, England	8
Kenyon, Mrs Frederick R. (nee Marion Stauffer)		Pittsburgh, Pennsylvania/ Noank, Connecticut	8	Peñasco y Castellana, Mr Victor	24	Madrid, Spain	
Kimball, Mr Edwin Nelson Jr	42	Boston, Massachusetts	5	Peñasco y Castellana, Mrs Victor (nee Maria Josefa Perez de Soto y Vallejo)	22	Madrid, Spain	8
Kimball, Mrs Edwin Nelson Jr (nee Gertrude Parsons)	45	Boston, Massachusetts	5	and Maid (Miss Fermina Oliva y Ocana)	39	Madrid, Spain	8
Klaber, Mr Herman				Peuchen, Major Arthur Godfrey	52	Toronto, Ontario	6
Leader, Dr Alice Farnham		New York, New York	8	Porter, Mr Walter Chamberlain	46	Worcester, Massachusetts	
Lewy, Mr Erwin G.		Chicago, Illinois		Potter, Mrs Thomas, Jr (nee Lily Alexiena Wilson)	56	Mt Airy, Philadelphia, Pennsylvania	7
Lindeberg-Lind, Mr Erik Gustaf (booked as Mr Edward Lingrey)	42	Stockholm, Sweden		Reuchlin, Jonkheer John George		Rotterdam, Netherlands	
Lindstrom, Mrs Carl Johan (nee Sigrid Posse)	55	Stockholm, Sweden	6	Rheims, Mr George Lucien		Paris, France/New York	A
Lines, Mrs Ernest H. (nee Elizabeth Lindsey James)	50	Paris, France	9	Robert, Mrs Edward Scott (nee Elisabeth Walton McMillan)		St Louis, Missouri	2
Lines, Miss Mary Conover	16	Paris, France	9	and Maid (Miss Emilie Kreuchen)		St Louis, Missouri	2
Long, Mr Milton Clyde	29	Springfield, Massachusetts		Roebling, Mr Washington Augustus II	31	Trenton, New Jersey	
Longley, Miss Gretchen Fiske	21	Hudson, New York	10	Romaine, Mr Charles Hallis		New York, New York	15
Loring, Mr Joseph Holland	30	New York, New York		Rood, Mr Hugh R.		Seattle, Washington	
Madill, Miss Georgette Alexandra	15	St Louis, Missouri	2	Rosenbaum (Russell), Miss Edith Louise	33	Paris, France	11
Maguire, Mr John Edward	30	Brockton, Massachusetts					
Marechal, Mr Pierre		Paris, France	7	Ross, Mr John Hugo		Winnipeg, Manitoba	
Marvin, Mr Daniel Warner	18	New York, New York		Rosenshine, Mr George	46	New York, New York	

Name	Age	1912 residence(s)	Lifeboat No
Rothes, Countess of (Noëlle Lucy Martha-Dyer-Edwards)	27	London, England	8
and Maid (Miss Ruberta Maioni)	16		8
Rothschild, Mr Martin	46	New York, New York	
Rothschild, Mrs Martin (nee Elizabeth L. Barrett)	54	New York, New York	6
Rowe, Mr Alfred			
Ryerson, Mr Arthur Larned	61	Cooperstown, New York	
Ryerson, Mrs Arthur Larned (nee Emily Maria Borie)	48	Cooperstown, New York	4
and Maid (Miss Victorine Chandanson)		Cooperstown, New York	4
Ryerson, Miss Emily Borie	18	Cooperstown, New York	4
Ryerson, Miss Suzette Parker	21	Cooperstown, New York	4
Ryerson, Master John (Jack) Borie	13	Cooperstown, New York	4
Saalfeld, Mr Adolph		Manchester, England	
Salomon, Mr Abraham L.		New York, New York	1
Schabert, Mrs Paul (nee Emma Mock)		New York, New York	11
Seward, Mr Frederic Kimber	34	New York, New York	7
Shutes, Miss Elizabeth W.	40	New York, New York	3
Silverthorne, Mr Spencer Victor	36	St Louis, Missouri	5
Silvey, Mr William Baird	50	Duluth, Minnesota	
Silvey, Mrs William Baird (nee Alice Munger)	39	Duluth, Minnesota	
Simonius-Blumer, Col Alfons	56	Basel, Switzerland	3
Sloper, Mr William Thomson	28	New Britain, Connecticut	7
Smart, Mr John Montgomery		New York, New York	
Smith, Mr James Clinch	56	St James, Long Island, New York	
Smith, Mr Lucian Philip	24	Huntington, West Virginia	
Smith, Mrs Lucian Philip (nee Mary Eloise Hughes)	18	Huntington, West Virginia	6
Smith, Mr Richard William		Streatham, Surrey, England	
Snyder, Mr John Pillsbury	24	Minneapolis, Minnesota	7
Snyder, Mrs John Pillsbury (nee Nelle Stevenson)	23	Minneapolis, Minnesota	7
Spedden, Mr Frederic Oakley	45	Tuxedo Park, New York	3
Spedden, Mrs Frederic Oakley (nee Margaretta Corning Stone)	40	Tuxedo Park, New York	3
and Maid (Miss Helen Alice Wilson)		Tuxedo Park, New York	3
Spedden, Master Robert Douglas	6	Tuxedo Park, New York	3
and Nurse (Miss Elizabeth M. Burns)		Tuxedo Park, New York	3
Spencer, Mr William Augustus	57	Paris, France	
Spencer, Mrs William Augustus (nee Marie Eugenie)		Paris, France	
and Maid (Miss Elise Lurette)		Paris, France	
Staehlin, Dr Max	32	Basel, Switzerland	3
Stead, Mr William Thomas	62	Middlesex, England	
Stengel, Mr Charles Emil Henry	54	Newark, New Jersey	1
Stengel, Mrs Charles Emil Henry (nee Annie May Morris)	43	Newark, New Jersey	5
Stephenson, Mrs Walter Bertram (nee Martha Eustis)	52	Haverford, Pennsylvania	4
Stewart, Mr Albert A.	54	Paris, France/New York	
Stone, Mrs George Nelson (nee Martha Evelyn)		Cincinnati, Ohio	6
and Maid (Miss Amelia Icard)		Cincinnati, Ohio	6
Straus, Mr Isidor	67	New York, New York	
and Manservant (John Farthing)		New York, New York	
Straus, Mrs Isidor (nee Ida Blun)	63	New York, New York	
and Maid (Miss Ellen Bird)		New York, New York	8
Sutton, Mr Frederick	61	Haddonfield, New Jersey	
Swift, Mrs Frederick Joel (nee Margaret Welles Barron)	48	Brooklyn, New York	8
Taussig, Mr Emil	53	New York, New York	
Taussig, Mrs Emil (nee Tillie Mandelbaum)		New York, New York	8
Taussig, Miss Ruth	18	New York, New York	8
Taylor, Mr Elmer Zebley	48	London, England/ East Orange, NJ	5
Taylor, Mrs Elmer Zebley (nee Juliet Cummins Wright)		London, England/ East Orange, NJ	5
Thayer, Mr John Borland	49	Haverford, Pennsylvania	
Thayer, Mrs John Borland (nee Marian Longstreth Morris)	39	Haverford, Pennsylvania	4
and Maid (Miss Margaret Fleming)		Haverford, Pennsylvania	4
Thayer, Mr John (Jack) Borland Jr	17	Haverford, Pennsylvania	B
Thorne, Mrs Gertrude Maybelle		New York, New York	
Tucker, Mr Gilbert Milligan Jr	31	Albany, New York	7
Uruchurtu, Mr Manuel E.		Mexico City, Mexico	
Van Derhoef, Mr Wyckoff	61	Brooklyn, New York	
von Drachstedt, Baron (Alfred Nourney)	20	Cologne, Germany	7
Walker, Mr William Anderson	47	East Orange, New Jersey	
Warren, Mr Frank Manley	63	Portland, Oregon	
Warren, Mrs Frank Manley (nee Anna Sophia Atkinson)	60	Portland, Oregon	5
Weir, Col John		New York, New York	
White, Mrs John Stuart (nee Ella Holmes)	55	New York, New York	8
and Maid (Miss Nellie M. Bessette)		New York, New York	8
and Manservant (Sante Reghini)		Brooklyn, New York	
White, Mr Percival Wayland	54	Brunswick, Maine	
White, Mr Richard Frasar	21	Brunswick, Maine	
Wick, Col George Dennick	57	Youngstown, Ohio	
Wick, Mrs George Dennick (nee Mary Hitchcock)	45	Youngstown, Ohio	8
Wick, Miss Mary Natalie	31	Youngstown, Ohio	8
Widener, Mr George Dunton	50	Elkins Park, Pennsylvania	
and Manservant (Edward H. Keeping)		Elkins Park, Pennsylvania	
Widener, Mrs George Dunton (nee Eleanor Elkins)	50	Elkins Park, Pennsylvania	4
and Maid (Miss Emily Geiger)		Elkins Park, Pennsylvania	4
Widener, Mr Harry Elkins	27	Elkins Park, Pennsylvania	
Willard, Miss Constance	20	Duluth, Minnesota	
Williams, Mr Charles Duane	51	Geneva, Switzerland	
Williams, Mr Fletcher Lambert		London, England	
Williams, Mr Richard Norris II	21	Geneva, Switzerland	A
Woolner, Mr Hugh		London, England	D
Wright, Mr George		Halifax, Nova Scotia	
Young, Miss Marie Grice	36	New York, New York	8

Name	Age	1912 residence(s)	Lifeboat No

Second Class Passengers

Name	Age	1912 residence(s)	Lifeboat No
Abelson, Mr Samson	30	Russia to New York, New York	
Abelson, Mrs Samson (Anna)	28	Russia to New York, New York	
Aldworth, Mr Charles Augustus	30	London, England, to Bryn Mawr, Pennsylvania	
Andrew, Mr Edgar Samuel	18	Buenos Aires, Argentina, to Trenton, New Jersey	
Andrew, Mr Frank	25	Redruth, Cornwall, England, to Houghton, Michigan	
Angle, Mr William A.	34	Warwick, England	
Angle, Mrs William A. (nee Florence Agnes Hughes)	36	Warwick, England	
Ashby, Mr John	57	West Hoboken, New Jersey	
Bailey, Mr Percy Andrew	18	Penzance, Cornwall, England, to Akron, Ohio	
Bainbrigge, Mr Charles R.	23	Guernsey, Channel Islands	
Balls, Mrs Ada Anna (nee Hall)	36	London, England, to Jacksonville, Florida	14
Banfield, Mr Frederick James	28	Plymouth, England, to Hancock, Michigan	
Bateman, Rev Robert James	51	Jacksonville, Florida	
Beane, Mr Edward	32	Norwich, England, to New York	
Beane, Mrs Edward (nee Ethel Clarke)	19	Norwich, England, to New York	
Beauchamp, Mr Henry James	28	London, England	
Becker, Mrs Allen Oliver (nee Nellie E. Baumgardner)	36	India to Benton Harbor, Michigan	11
Becker, Miss Marion Louise	4	India to Benton Harbor, Michigan	11
Becker, Master Richard F.	1	India to Benton Harbor, Michigan	11
Becker, Miss Ruth Elizabeth	12	India to Benton Harbor, Michigan	13
Beesley, Mr Lawrence	34	London, England	13
Bentham, Miss Lillian W.	19	Rochester, New York	
Berriman, Mr William J.	23	St Ives, Cornwall, England, to Calumet, Michigan	
Botsford, Mr William Hull	25	Elmira, New York/ Orange, New Jersey	
Bowenur, Mr Solomon	42	London, England	
Bracken, Mr James H.	27	Lake Arthur, Chavez County, New Mexico	
Brown, Miss Amelia (Mildred)	24	London, England, to Montreal, Quebec	11
Brown, Mr Thomas William Solomon	60	Cape Town, South Africa, to Seattle, Washington	
Brown, Mrs Thomas William Solomon (nee Elizabeth Catherine Ford)	40	Cape Town, South Africa, to Seattle, Washington	14
Brown, Miss Edith Eileen	15	Cape Town, South Africa, to Seattle, Washington	14
Bryhl, Miss Dagmar	20	Skara, Sweden, to Rockford, Illinois	12
Bryhl, Mr Kurt Arnold Gottfried	25	Skara, Sweden, to Rockford, Illinois	
Buss, Miss Kate	36	Sittingbourne, England, to San Diego, California	9
Butler, Mr Reginald Fenton	25	Southsea, Hampshire, England	
Byles, Rev Thomas Rousell Davids	42	London, England	
Bystrom, Mrs Karolina	42	New York, New York	
Caldwell, Mr Albert Francis	26	Bangkok, returning to Roseville, Illinois	13
Caldwell, Mrs Albert Francis (nee Sylvia Mae Harbaugh)	26	Bangkok, returning to Roseville, Illinois	13
Caldwell, Master Alden Gates	10m	Bangkok, returning to Roseville, Illinois	13
Cameron, Miss Clear Annie	31	London, England, to Mamaroneck, New York	14
Campbell, Mr William	21	Belfast, Ireland	
Carbines, Mr William	19	St Ives, Cornwall, England, to Houghton, Michigan	
Carter, Rev Ernest Courtenay	54	London, England	
Carter, Mrs Ernest Courtenay (nee Lillian Hughes)	44	London, England	
Chapman, Mr Charles H.	52	Bronx, New York	
Chapman, Mr John Henry	35	St Neots, Cornwall, England, to Spokane, Washington	
Chapman, Mrs John Henry (nee Sarah Elizabeth Lawry)	28	St Neots, Cornwall, England, to Spokane, Washington	
Christy, Mrs Alice Frances		London, England	
Christy, Miss Juli R.		London, England	
Clarke, Mr Charles Valentine	29	England to San Francisco, California	
Clarke, Mrs Charles Valentine (nee Ada Maria Winfield)	28	England to San Francisco, California	14
Coleridge, Mr Reginald Charles	29	Hartford, Huntingdonshire, England	
Collander, Mr Erik	27	Helsinki, Finland	
Collett, Mr Sidney C. Stuart	24	London, England, to New York	9
Collyer, Mr Harvey	31	Bishopstoke, Hampshire, England	
Collyer, Mrs Harvey (nee Charlotte Annie Tate)	31	Bishopstoke, Hampshire, England	14
Collyer, Miss Marjorie Lottie	8	Bishopstoke, Hampshire, England	14
Cook, Mrs Arthur H. (nee Selena Rogers)	22	England, returning to Pennsylvania	14
Corbett, Mrs Walter Harris (nee Irene Colvin)	30	Provo, Utah	
Corey, Mrs Percy C. (nee Mary Phyllis Elizabeth Miller)		Pittsburgh, Pennnsylvania	
Cotterill, Mr Harry	20	Penzance, Cornwall, England, to Akron, Ohio	
Cunningham, Mr Alfred Fleming	21	Belfast, Ireland	
Davies, Mr Charles Henry	18	Lyndhurst, Hampshire, England	

Name	Age	1912 residence(s)	Lifeboat No	Name	Age	1912 residence(s)	Lifeboat No
Davis, Mrs Agnes Mary (nee Friggens)	49	St Ives, Cornwall, England, to Houghton, Michigan	14	Gale, Mr Shadrach	38	Harrobarrow, England, to Clear Creek, Colorado	
Davis, Master John Morgan	8	St Ives, Cornwall, England, to Houghton, Michigan	14	**Garside, Miss Ethel**	34	Brooklyn, New York	
				Gaskell, Mr Alfred	16	Liverpool, England, to Montreal, Quebec	
Davis, Miss Mary	28	London, England, to Staten Island, New York	13	Gavey, Mr Lawrence	26	Guernsey, Channel Islands, to Elizabeth, New Jersey	
Deacon, Mr Percy William	17	Lyndhurst, Hampshire, England		Gilbert, Mr William	45	Cornwall, England	
de Brito, Mr Jose Joaquim		Portugal to Sao Paolo, Brazil		Giles, Mr Edgar	24	Port Leven, Cornwall, England, to Camden, New Jersey	
del Carlo, Mr Sebastiano	29	Lucca, Italy, returning to Chicago, Illinois		Giles, Mr Frederick Edward	21	Port Leven, Cornwall, England, to Camden, New Jersey	
del Carlo, Mrs Sebastiano (nee Argene Genovesi)	22	Lucca, Italy, to Chicago, Illinois		Giles, Mr Ralph	22	West Kensington, London, England	
Denbuoy, Mr Herbert	25	Guernsey, Channel Islands, to Elizabeth, New Jersey		Gill, Mr John William		Clevedon, England	
				Gillespie, Mr William Henry	34	Vancouver, British Columbia	
Dibden, Mr William	18	Lyndhurst, Hampshire, England		Givard, Mr Hans Christensen	30		
				Greenberg, Mr Samuel		Bronx, New York	
Doling, Mrs Ada Julia	32	Southampton, England		Hale, Mr Reginald	30	Auburn, New York	
Doling, Miss Elsie	18	Southampton, England		**Hamalainen, Mrs William (Anna)**	23	Detroit, Michigan	4
Douton, Mr William Joseph	54	Holley, New York		**Hamalainen, Master Viljo (William)**	1	Detroit, Michigan	4
Drew, Mr James Vivian	42	Cornwall, England, returning to Greenport, New York		Harbeck, Mr William H.	44	Toledo, Ohio	
Drew, Mrs James Vivian (nee Lulu Thorne Christian)	34	Cornwall, England, returning to Greenport, New York		Harper, Rev John	28	Denmark Hill, Surrey, England, to Chicago, Illinois	
Drew, Master Marshall Brines	8	Cornwall, England, returning to Greenport, New York		**Harper, Miss Annie Jessie (Nina)**	6	Denmark Hill, Surrey, England, to Chicago, Illinois	11
Duran y More, Miss Asuncion		Barcelona, Spain, to Havana, Cuba	12	**Harris, Mr George**	30	London, England	
				Harris, Mr Walter		Walthamstow, Essex, England	
Duran y More, Miss Florentina		Barcelona, Spain, to Havana, Cuba		Hart, Mr Benjamin	48	Essex, England, to Winnipeg, Manitoba	
Eitemiller, Mr George Floyd	23	London, England, to Detroit, Michigan		**Hart, Mrs Benjamin (nee Esther Louisa Bloomfield)**	49	Essex, England, to Winnipeg, Manitoba	14
Enander, Mr Ingvar	21	Goteborg, Sweden, to Rockford, Illinois		**Hart, Miss Eva Miriam**	7	Essex, England, to Winnipeg, Manitoba	14
Fahlstrom, Mr Arne Jonas	18	Oslo, Norway, to Bayonne, New Jersey		Herman, Mr Samuel	49	Yeovil, Somerset, England, to Bernardsville, New Jersey	
Faunthorpe, Mr Harry		Liverpool, England, to Philadelphia, Pennsylvania		**Herman, Mrs Samuel (nee Jane Laver)**	48	Yeovil, Somerset, England, to Bernardsville, New Jersey	9
Faunthorpe, Mrs Harry (Mrs Elizabeth Anne Wilkinson)		Liverpool, England, to Philadelphia, Pennsylvania		**Herman, Miss Alice**	24	Yeovil, Somerset, England, to Bernardsville, New Jersey	9
Fillbrook, Mr Charles J.	18	Truro, Cornwall, England, to Houghton, Michigan		**Herman, Miss Kate**	24	Yeovil, Somerset, England, to Bernardsville, New Jersey	9
Fox, Mr Stanley Hubert	38	Rochester, New York		**Hewlett, Mrs Frederick Rufford (nee Mary D. Kingcome)**		India to Rapid City, South Dakota	13
Frost, Mr Anthony W.	37	Belfast, Ireland					
Funk, Miss Annie Clemmer	38	India, returning to Bally, Pennsylvania		Hickman, Mr Leonard Mark	24	London, England, to Neepawa, Manitoba	
Fynney, Mr Joseph J.	35	Liverpool, England, to Montreal, Quebec		Hickman, Mr Lewis	32	London, England, to Neepawa, Manitoba	
Gale, Mr Harry	35	Harrobarrow, England, to Clear Creek, Colorado		Hickman, Mr Stanley George	21	London, England, to Neepawa, Manitoba	

Name	Age	1912 residence(s)	Lifeboat No	Name	Age	1912 residence(s)	Lifeboat No
Hiltunen, Miss Martta	24	Kontiolahti, Finland, to Detroit, Michigan		**Keane, Miss Hanora A. (Nora)**		Harrisburg, Pennsylvania	
Hocking, Mrs Elizabeth (nee Needs)	53	Penzance, Cornwall, England, to Akron, Ohio		**Kelly, Mrs Florence (Fannie)**	45	London, England, to New York	
Hocking, Mr George Sidney	23	Penzance, Cornwall, England, to Akron, Ohio		Kirkland, Rev Charles Leonard	57	Old Town, Maine	
				Knight, Mr Robert			
Hocking, Miss Ellen (Nellie)	20	Penzance, Cornwall, England, to Akron, Ohio		Kvillner, Mr Johan Henrik Johnanesson	31	Sweden to Arlington, New Jersey	
				Lahtinen, Rev William	30	Minneapolis, Minnesota	
Hocking, Mr Samuel James Metcalfe		Devonport, Plymouth, England		Lahtinen, Mrs William (nee Anna Sylvan)	26	Minneapolis, Minnesota	
Hodges, Mr Henry Price	52	Southampton, England		Lamb, Mr John Joseph		Providence, Rhode Island	
Hoffman, Mr (in reality Navratil, Michel)	32	Nice, France		**Lamore, Mrs Amelia (Milley)**	34	Chicago, Illinois	14
				Laroche, Mr Joseph Lemercier	26	Paris, France, to Haiti	
Hoffman, Master (Navratil, Master Edmond Roger)	2	Nice, France	D	**Laroche, Mrs Joseph Lemercier (nee Juliet Marie Louise Lafargue)**	22	Paris, France, to Haiti	
Hoffman, Master (Navratil, Master Michel Marcel)	3	Nice, France	D	**Laroche, Miss Louise**	1	Paris, France, to Haiti	
				Laroche, Miss Simonne Marie Anne	3	Paris, France, to Haiti	
Hold, Mr Stephen	42	Cornwall, England, returning to Sacramento, California		**Lehmann, Miss Berthe**		Berne, Switzerland, to Central City, Iowa	14
				Leitch, Miss Jessie W.		London, England, to Chicago, Illinois	11
Hold, Mrs Stephen (nee Annie Margaret Gregory)	36	Cornwall, England, returning to Sacramento, California		Levy, Mr Rene Jacques	36	Montreal, Quebec	
				Leyson, Mr Robert William Norman	25	South Kensington, London, England	
Hood, Mr Ambrose Jr	21	New Forest, England		Lingane, Mr John			
Hosono, Mr Masabumi	41	Tokyo, Japan	10	Louch, Mr Charles Alexander	50	Weston-super-Mare, England	
Howard, Mr Benjamin	63	Swindon, England, to Idaho		**Louch, Mrs Charles Alexander (nee Alice Adelaide Slow)**	42	Weston-super-Mare, England	14
Howard, Mrs Benjamin (nee Ellen Truelove Arman)	60	Swindon, England, to Idaho		Mack, Mrs Mary	57	Southampton, England, to New York, New York	
Hunt, Mr George Henry	33	Ashstead, England, returning to Philadelphia, Pennsylvania		Malachard, Mr Noel		Paris, France	
				Mallet, Mr Albert		Paris, France, to Montreal, Quebec	
Ilett, Miss Bertha	17	Jersey, Channel Islands, to New York		**Mallet, Mrs Albert (nee Antoinette)**		Paris, France, to Montreal, Quebec	
Jacobsohn, Mr Sydney Samuel	42	London, England		**Mallet, Master Andre**	2	Paris, France, to Montreal, Quebec	
Jacobsohn, Mrs Sydney Samuel (nee Amy Frances Cohen)	24	London, England		Mangiavacchi, Mr Serafino Emilio		New York, New York	
Jarvis, Mr John Denzil	47	Stoneygate, Leicester, England		Marshall, Mr Henry (in reality Morley, Henry Samuel)	38	Worcester, England	
Jefferys, Mr Clifford Thomas	24	Guernsey, Channel Islands, to Elizabeth, New Jersey		**Marshall, Mrs Henry (Phillips, Miss Kate Louise)**	19	Worcester, England	
Jefferys, Mr Ernest Wilfred	22	Guernsey, Channel Islands to Elizabeth, New Jersey		Matthews, Mr William John	30	St Austell, Cornwall, England	
Jenkin, Mr Stephen Curnow	32	St Ives, Cornwall, returning to Houghton, Michigan		Maybery, Mr Frank Hubert	37	Weston-super-Mare, England, to Moose Jaw, Saskatchewan	
				McCrae, Mr Arthur Gordon	33	Sydney, Australia	
Jerwan, Mrs Amin S. (nee Marie Marthe Thuillard)	23	New York, New York	11	McCrie, Mr James Matthew		Sarnia, Ontario	
Kantor, Mr Sinai	34	Moscow, Russia, to Bronx, New York		McKane, Mr Peter David	46	Rochester, New York	
Kantor, Mrs Sinai (nee Miriam Sternin)		Moscow, Russia, to Bronx, New York		**Mellenger, Mrs Claude L. W. (nee Elizabeth Anne Maidment)**	41	England to Bennington, Vermont	14
Karnes, Mrs J. Frank (nee Claire Bennett)	22	Pittsburgh, Pennsylvania		**Mellenger, Miss Madeleine Violet**	13	England to Bennington, Vermont	14
				Mellor, Mr William John	19	Chelsea, London, England	B
Keane, Mr Daniel		Limerick, Ireland		Meyer, Mr August	30	Harrow-on-the-Hill, Middlesex, England	

Name	Age	1912 residence(s)	Lifeboat No
Milling, Mr Jacob Christian	48	Copenhagen, Denmark	
Mitchell, Mr Henry Michael	71	Guernsey, Channel Islands, to Montclair, New Jersey	
Montvila, Rev Juozas (Joseph)	27	Lithuania to Worcester, Massachusetts	
Moraweck, Dr Ernest	53	Frankfort, Kentucky	
Mudd, Mr Thomas Charles	16	Halesworth, Suffolk, England	
Myles, Mr Thomas Francis	64	Cambridge, Massachusetts	
Nasser (Nassrallah), Mr Nicholas		New York, New York	
Nasser (Nasrallah), Mrs Nicholas (nee Adele)	15	New York, New York	
Nesson, Mr Israel	26	Boston, Massachusetts	
Nicholls, Mr Joseph Charles	19	St Ives, Cornwall, England, to Houghton, Michigan	
Norman, Mr Robert Douglas	28	Glasgow, Scotland	
Nye, Mrs Edward Ernest (nee Elizabeth Ramell)	29	Folkestone, England, to New York, New York	11
Otter, Mr Richard	39	Middleburg Heights, Ohio	
Oxenham, Mr Percy Thomas	22	Ponders End, England, to North Bergen, New Jersey	
Padro y Manent, Mr Julian		Barcelona, Spain, to Havana, Cuba	
Pain, Dr Alfred	24	Hamilton, Ontario	
Pallas y Castillo, Mr Emilio		Barcelona, Spain, to Havana, Cuba	
Parker, Mr Clifford Richard		Guernsey, Channel Islands	
Parkes, Mr Frank	18	Belfast, Ireland	
Parrish, Mrs Lutie (nee Davis)		Woodford County, Kentucky	12
Pengelly, Mr Frederick William	20	Gunnislake, England, to Butte, Montana	
Pernot, Mr Rene		Paris, France	
Peruschitz, Rev Joseph M.			
Phillips, Mr Robert	42	Ilfracombe, Devon, England, to New Brighton, Pennsylvania	
Phillips, Miss Alice Caroline	21	Ilfracombe, Devon, England, to New Brighton, Pennsylvania	12
Pinsky, Miss Rosa	33	Russia	
Ponesell, Mr Martin	34	Denmark to New York, New York	
Portaluppi, Mr Emilio		Milford, New Hampshire	
Pulbaun, Mr Frans		Paris, France	
Quick, Mrs Frederick C. (nee Jane Richards)	33	Cornwall, England, to Detroit, Michigan	11
Quick, Miss Phyllis May	2	Cornwall, England, to Detroit, Michigan	11
Quick, Miss Vera Winifred	8	Cornwall, England, to Detroit, Michigan	11
Reeves, Mr David	36	Brighton, England	
Renouf, Mr Peter Henry	34	Elizabeth, New Jersey	
Renouf, Mrs Peter Henry (nee Lily Elizabeth Jefferys)	30	Elizabeth, New Jersey	
Reynaldo, Mrs Encarnacion			
Richard, Mr Emile	23	Paris, France, to Montreal, Quebec	
Richards, Mrs James Sibley (nee Emily Hocking)	24	Penzance, Cornwall, England, to Akron, Ohio	
Richards, Master Sibley George	10m	Penzance, Cornwall, England, to Akron, Ohio	
Richards, Master William Rowe	3	Penzance, Cornwall, England, to Akron, Ohio	
Ridsdale, Miss Lucy	50	Milwaukee, Wisconsin	
Rogers, Mr Harry	18	Tavistock, Devon, England, to Wilkes-Barre, Pennsylvania	
Rugg, Miss Emily	21	Guernsey, Channel Islands, to Wilmington, Delaware	
Sedgwick, Mr Charles Frederick Waddington		Liverpool, England	
Sharp, Mr Percival James		Hornsey, England	
Shelley, Mrs William (nee Imanita Hall)	25	Deer Lodge, Montana	
Silven, Miss Lyyli Karolina	18	Finland to Minneapolis, Minnesota	
Sincock, Miss Maude	20	St Ives, Cornwall, England, to Hancock, Minnesota	11
Siukkonen, Miss Anna	30	Finland to Washington, DC	
Sjostedt, Mr Ernst Adolf	59	Sault St Marie, Ontario	
Slayter, Miss Hilda Mary	30	Halifax, Nova Scotia	13
Slemen, Mr Richard James	35	Cornwall, England	
Smith (Schmidt), Mr Augustus	22	Newark, New Jersey	
Smith, Miss Marion			
Sobey, Mr Hayden Samuel James	25	Cornwall, England, to Houghton, Michigan	
Stanton, Mr Samuel Ward	41	New York, New York	
Stokes, Mr Philip Joseph	25	Kent, England, to Detroit, Michigan	
Swane, Mr George	26	England to Montreal, Quebec	
Sweet, Mr George Frederick	16	Yeovil, Somerset, England, to Bernardsville, New Jersey	
Toomey, Miss Ellen	50	Indianapolis, Indiana	
Troupiansky, Mr Mosen Aaron	22		
Trout, Mrs William H. (Jessie L.)	28	Columbus, Ohio	
Troutt, Miss Edwina Celia	27	Bath, England, to Auburndale, Massachusetts	
Turpin, Mr William John	29	Plymouth, England, to Salt Lake City, Utah	
Turpin, Mrs William John (nee Dorothy Ann Wonnacott)	27	Plymouth, England, to Salt Lake City, Utah	
Veale, Mr James	38	Barre, Vermont	
Walcroft, Miss Nellie	35	Mamaroneck, New York	14
Ware, Mr John James	30	Bristol, England	
Ware, Mrs John James (nee Florence Louise Long)	28	Bristol, England	

Name	Age	1912 residence(s)	Lifeboat No
Ware, Mr William Jeffrey	23	Gunnislake, Devon, England	
Watt, Mrs James (nee Bessie Inglis Milne)	40	Aberdeen, Scotland, to Portland, Oregon	9
Watt, Miss Bertha	12	Aberdeen, Scotland, to Portland, Oregon	9
Webber, Miss Susan	37	Bude, Devon, England, to Hartford, Connecticut	10
Weisz, Mr Leopold	28	Bromsgrove, England, to Montreal, Quebec	
Weisz, Mrs Leopold (nee Mathilde Francoise Pede)	32	Bromsgrove, England, to Montreal, Quebec	
Wells, Mrs Arthur Henry (nee Addie Dart Trevaskis)	29	Cornwall, England, to Akron, Ohio	14
Wells, Miss Joan	4	Cornwall, England, to Akron, Ohio	14
Wells, Master Ralph Lester	2	Cornwall, England, to Akron, Ohio	14
West, Mr Edwy Arthur	36	Bournemouth, England, to Florida	
West, Mrs Edwy Arthur (nee Ada Mary Worth)	33	Bournemouth, England, to Florida	
West, Miss Barbara J.		Bournemouth, England, to Florida	
West, Miss Constance Miriam		Bournemouth, England, to Florida	
Wheadon, Mr Edward H.			
Wheeler, Mr Edwin (Fred)			
Wilhelms, Mr Charles	32	London, England	9
Williams, Mr Charles Eugene		Chicago, Illinois	14
Wright, Miss Marion	26	Yeovil, Somerset, England, to Cottage Grove, Oregon	9
Yrois, Miss Henriette		Paris, France	

The Titanic's Bandsmen (travelling in Second Class)

Brailey, Mr Theodore Ronald	London, England
Bricoux, Mr Roger Marie	London, England
Clarke, Mr John Frederick Preston	Liverpool, England
Hartley, Mr Wallace Henry (Bandmaster)	Colne, Lancashire, England
Hume, Mr John Law (Jock)	Dumfries, Scotland
Krins, Mr George Alexander	Liege, Belgium
Taylor, Mr Percy Cornelius	Clapham, London, England
Woodward, Mr John Wesley	Headington, Oxford, England

Third Class Passengers: British subjects embarked at Southampton

Name	Age	1912 residence(s)	Lifeboat No
Abbing, Mr Anthony	42	Cincinnati, Ohio	
Abbott, Mrs Stanton (nee Rosa Hunt)	35	England, returning to East Providence, Rhode Island	A
Abbott, Mr Eugene Joseph	14	England returning to East Providence, Rhode Island	
Abbott, Mr Rossmore Edward	16	England returning to East Providence, Rhode Island	
Adams, Mr John (in reality May, Mr Richard)	26	Bournemouth, England	
Aks, Mrs Sam (nee Leah Rosen)	18	London, England, to Norfolk, Virginia	13
Aks, Master Philip	10m	London, England, to Norfolk, Virginia	11
Alexander, Mr William	23	Great Yarmouth, Norfolk, England, to Albion, New York	
Allen, Mr William Henry	35	Lower Clapton, Middlesex, England	
Allum, Mr Owen George	17	Windsor, England, to New York, New York	
Badman, Miss Emily Louise	18	Clevedon, England, to Skaneateles, New York	
Barton, Mr David John	22	Wicken, England, to New York	
Beavan, Mr William Thomas	18	Gillingham, Kent, England, to Russell, Illinois	
Bing, Mr Lee	32	Hong Kong to New York, New York	
Bowen, Mr David	26	Treherbert, Cardiff, Wales	
Braund, Mr Lewis Richard	29	Bridgerule, Devon, England	
Braund, Mr Owen Harris	22	Bridgerule, Devon, England	
Brocklebank, Mr William Alfred	35	Broomfield, Chelmsford, England	
Cann, Mr Ernest Charles	21	Penwithick, Cornwall, England	
Carver, Mr Albert John	28	St Denys, Southampton, England	
Celotti, Mr Francesco	24	London, England	
Chip, Mr Chong	32	Hong Kong to New York, New York	
Christmann, Mr Emil	29	London, England	
Cohen, Mr Gurshun (Gus)	19	London, England, to Brooklyn, New York	
Cook, Mr Jacob	43	Russia	
Corn, Mr Harry	30	London, England	
Coutts, Mrs William (nee Minnie Trainer)	36	Salisbury, England, to Brooklyn, New York	2
Coutts, Master Neville Leslie	3	Salisbury, England, to Brooklyn, New York	2
Coutts, Master William Loch	9	Salisbury, England, to Brooklyn, New York	2
Coxon, Mr Daniel	39	Merrill, Wisconsin	
Crease, Mr Ernest James	19	Bristol, England, to Cleveland, Ohio	
Cribb, Mr John Hatfield	44	Bournemouth, England, to Newark, New Jersey	
Cribb, Miss Laura Mary	17	Bournemouth, England, to Newark, New Jersey	
Dahl, Mr Karl (Charles) Edward	45	Adelaide, Australia	15

Name	Age	1912 residence(s)	Lifeboat No	Name	Age	1912 residence(s)	Lifeboat No
Davies, Mr Alfred J.	24	West Bromwich, England, to Pontiac, Michigan		Gilinsky, Mr Eliezer (Leslie)	22		
Davies, Mr Evan	21	Glais, Swansea, South Wales		Goldsmith, Mr Frank John	33	Strood, Kent, England, to Detroit, Michigan	
Davies, Mr John Samuel	22	West Bromwich, England, to Pontiac, Michigan		**Goldsmith, Mrs Frank John (nee Emily Alice Brown)**	31	Strood, Kent, England, to Detroit, Michigan	C
Davies, Mr Joseph	17	West Bromwich, England, to Pontiac, Michigan		**Goldsmith, Master Frank John William**	9	Strood, Kent, England, to Detroit, Michigan	C
Davison, Mr Thomas Henry		Liverpool, England, to Bedford, Ohio		Goldsmith, Mr Nathan	41	Bryn Mawr, Pennsylvania	
Davison, Mrs Thomas Henry (nee Mary E. Finck)		Liverpool, England, to Bedford, Ohio		Goodwin, Mr Charles Frederick	40	Wiltshire, England, to Niagara Falls, New York	
Dean, Mr Bertram Frank	25	Devon, England, to Wichita, Kansas		Goodwin, Mrs Charles Frederick (nee Augusta Tyler)	43	Wiltshire, England, to Niagara Falls, New York	
Dean, Mrs Bertram Frank (nee Eva Georgetta Light)	33	Devon, England, to Wichita, Kansas		Goodwin, Mr Charles Edward	14	Wiltshire, England, to Niagara Falls, New York	
Dean, Master Bertram Vere	1	Devon, England, to Wichita, Kansas		Goodwin, Miss Jessie Allis	10	Wiltshire, England, to Niagara Falls, New York	
Dean, Miss Elizabeth Gladys Millvina	2m	Devon, England, to Wichita, Kansas		Goodwin, Master Harold Victor	9	Wiltshire, England, to Niagara Falls, New York	
Dennis, Mr Samuel	23	Holsworthy, Devon, England		Goodwin, Miss Lillian Amy	16	Wiltshire, England, to Niagara Falls, New York	
Dennis, Mr William	26	Holsworthy, Devon, England		Goodwin, Master Sidney Leonard	2	Wiltshire, England, to Niagara Falls, New York	
Dorkings, Mr Edward Arthur	19	England to Oglesby, Illinois	B	Goodwin, Master William Frederick	11	Wiltshire, England, to Niagara Falls, New York	
Dowdell, Miss Elizabeth	31	Union Hill, New Jersey	13	Green, Mr George Henry	40	Dorking, Surrey, England	
Drapkin, Miss Jenie	23	London, England, to New York, New York		Guest, Mr Robert	23	London, England	
Duquemin, Mr Joseph	24	England to Albion, New York	D	Harknett, Miss Phoebe Alice	21	London, England	
Elsbury, Mr William James	48	Gurnee, Lake County, Illinois		Harmer, Mr Abraham (in reality Livshin, Mr David)	25	Manchester, England	
Emanuel, Miss Virginia Ethel	5	London, England, to New York, New York	13	**Hee, Mr Ling**	24	Hong Kong to New York, New York	
Everett, Mr Thomas James	36	Bristol, England, heading to Troy, New York		**Howard, Miss May Elizabeth**		Southampton, England, to Albion, New York	C
Foo, Mr Chung	32	Hong Kong to New York, New York		**Hyman, Mr Abraham**	34	England to Springfield, Massachusetts	
Ford, Mr Arthur	22	Bridgwater, Somerset, England, to Elmira, New York		Johnson, Mr Alfred	49	Southampton, England	
Ford, Mrs Edward (nee Margaret Ann Watson)	48	Rotherfield, Sussex, England, to Essex County, Massachusetts		Johnson, Mr William Cahoone Jr	19	Hawthorne, New Jersey	
Ford, Miss Dollina Margaret (Daisy)	21	Rotherfield, Sussex, England, to Essex County, Massachusetts		Johnston, Mr Andrew Emslie	35	Thornton Heath, Surrey, England	
Ford, Mr Ernest Watson	18	Rotherfield, Sussex, England, to Essex County, Massachusetts		Johnston, Mrs Andrew Emslie (nee Eliza 'Lily' Watson)	34	Thornton Heath, Surrey, England	
Ford, Miss Robina Maggie (Ruby)	9	Rotherfield, Sussex, England, to Essex County, Massachusetts		Johnston, Miss Catherine Nellie (Carrie)	7	Thornton Heath, Surrey, England	
Ford, Mr William Neal	16	Rotherfield, Sussex, England, to Essex County, Massachusetts		Johnston, Master William Arthur (Willie)	9	Thornton Heath, Surrey, England	
				Keefe, Mr Arthur	39	Rahway, New Jersey	
				Kelly, Mr James	44	London, England	
Franklin, Mr Charles (in reality Fardon, Mr Charles)	38	Southampton, England		**Lam, Mr Ali**	38	Hong Kong to New York, New York	
Garfirth, Mr John	22	Wollaston, Northamptonshire, England		Lam, Mr Len	23	Hong Kong to New York, New York	
				Lang, Mr Fang	26	Hong Kong to New York, New York	
				Leonard, Mr Lionel		Southampton, England	

Name	Age	1912 residence(s)	Lifeboat No	Name	Age	1912 residence(s)	Lifeboat No
Lester, Mr James	39	West Bromwich, England, to Pontiac, Michigan		Petersen, Mr Marius	24		
Ling, Mr Lee	28	Hong Kong to New York, New York		Reed, Mr James George	19	Penarth, Cardiff, South Wales	
Lithman, Mr Simon	20	Edinburgh, Scotland		Reynolds, Mr Harold J.	21	Lewisham, London, England	
Lobb, Mr William Arthur	30	St Austell, England, returning to Scranton, Pennsylvania		Risien, Mr Samuel Beard	68	Groesbeck, Texas	
				Risien, Mrs Samuel Beard (Emma)	58	Groesbeck, Texas	
Lobb, Mrs William Arthur (nee Cordelia Stanlick)	26	St Austell, England, returning to Scranton, Pennsylvania		Robins, Mr Alexander A.	49	Yonkers, New York	
				Robins, Mrs Alexander A. (nee Grace Charity Lawry)	47	Yonkers, New York	
Lockyer, Mr Edward Thomas	21	London, England, to Ontario, New York		Rogers, Mr William John	29	Glais, Swansea, South Wales	
Lovell, Mr John Hall	20	Holsworthy, Devon, England		Roth, Miss Sarah A.	26	London, England, to New York, New York	
MacKay, Mr George William	30	London, England		Rouse, Mr Richard Henry	50	Sittingbourne, England, to Cleveland, Ohio	
Maisner, Mr Simon	34	London, England		Rush, Mr Alfred George John	16	Kent, England, to Detroit, Michigan	
McNamee, Mr Neal	24	Ruskey, Co Donegal, Ireland/Salisbury, England		Sadowitz, Mr Harry	17	London, England, heading to Providence, Rhode Island	
McNamee, Mrs Neal (nee Eileen O'Leary)	19	Ruskey, Co Donegal, Ireland/Salisbury, England		Sage, Mr John George	44	Peterborough, England, to Jacksonville, Florida	
Meanwell, Mrs Marion (nee Ogden)	63			Sage, Mrs John George (nee Annie Bullen)	44	Peterborough, England, to Jacksonville, Florida	
Meek, Mrs Howard Martin (nee Annie Louise Rowley)	31	Penarth, Cardiff, South Wales		Sage, Miss Ada	9	Peterborough, England, to Jacksonville, Florida	
Meo, Mr Alfonso	48	Bournemouth, England		Sage, Miss Constance Gladys	7	Peterborough, England, to Jacksonville, Florida	
Miles, Mr Frank	23	Greenwich, England		Sage, Miss Dorothy Edith (Dolly)	13	Peterborough, England, to Jacksonville, Florida	
Moore, Mrs Bella	27	Russia to New York, New York		Sage, Mr Douglas Bullen	18	Peterborough, England, to Jacksonville, Florida	
Moore, Master Meyer	6	Russia to New York, New York		Sage, Mr Frederick	16	Peterborough, England, to Jacksonville, Florida	
Moore, Mr Leonard Charles	19	Kingston, England, returning to Hoboken, New Jersey		Sage, Mr George John	19	Peterborough, England, to Jacksonville, Florida	
Morley, Mr William	34	Petworth, Sussex, England		Sage, Miss Stella Anna	20	Peterborough, England, to Jacksonville, Florida	
Moutal, Mr Rahamin Haim	28	London, England		Sage, Master Thomas Henry	4	Peterborough, England, to Jacksonville, Florida	
Murdlin, Mr Joseph	22	London, England		Sage, Master William Henry	11	Peterborough, England, to Jacksonville, Florida	
Nancarrow, Mr William Henry	34	St Austell, Cornwall, England, to Yonkers, New York		Saeter, Mr Simon Sivertsen	44	Buvika, Norway	
Niklasson, Mr Samuel	28	Orust, Sweden		Saundercock, Mr William Henry	20	Penwithick, Cornwall, England	
Nosworthy, Mr Richard Cater	20	Newton Abbot, Devon, England, to Canada		Sawyer, Mr Frederick Charles	23	Basingstoke, Hampshire, England, to Halley, Michigan	
Patchett, Mr George	19	Wollaston, Northamptonshire, England		Shellard, Mr Frederick Blainey	55	Troy, New York	
Peacock, Mrs Benjamin (nee Edith Treasteall Nile)	26	Cornwall, England, heading to Elizabeth, New Jersey		Shorney, Mr Charles Joseph	22	Brighton, England, to New York, New York	
Peacock, Master Alfred Edward	9m	Cornwall, England, heading to Elizabeth, New Jersey		Simmons, Mr John	39		
				Sirota, Mr Maurice	20	London, England	
Peacock, Miss Treasteall	3	Cornwall, England, heading to Elizabeth, New Jersey		Slocovski, Mr Selman Francis	31		
				Somerton, Mr Francis William	31	Great Field, Cheltenham, England	
Pearce, Mr Ernest	32	Southampton, England		Spector, Mr Woolf	23	London, England	
Peduzzi, Mr Joseph	24	London, England		Spinner, Mr Henry John	32	Worcester, England	
Perkin, Mr John Henry	22	Holsworthy, Devon, England		Stanley, Miss Amy Elsie	22	England to New Haven, Connecticut	C

Name	Age	1912 residence(s)	Lifeboat No	Name	Age	1912 residence(s)	Lifeboat No
Stanley, Mr Ernest Roland	21	Bristol, England, to Cleveland, Ohio		Ahlin, Mrs Johanna Persdotter	40	Sweden to Akeley, Minnesota	
Storey, Mr Thomas	51	Liverpool, England		Aijo-Nirva, Mr Isak	41	Finland to Sudbury, Ontario	
Sunderland, Mr Victor Francis	19	London, England, to Cleveland, Ohio	B	Alhomaki, Mr Ilmari Rudolf	20	Salo, Finland, to Astoria, Oregon	
Sutehall, Mr Henry Jr	26	Kenmore, New York		Andersen, Mr Albert Karvin	32	Bergen, Norway, to New York, New York	
Theobald, Mr Thomas Leonard	34	Kent, England, to Detroit, Michigan		Andersson, Mr Anders Johan	39	Sweden to Winnipeg, Manitoba	
Thomson, Mr Alexander Morrison	36	Scotland		Andersson, Mrs Anders Johan (nee Alfrida K. Brogren)	39	Sweden to Winnipeg, Manitoba	
Thorneycroft, Mr Percival	36	England to Clinton, New York		Andersson, Miss Ebba Iris	6	Sweden to Winnipeg, Manitoba	
Thorneycroft, Mrs Percival (nee Florence Kate White)	32	England to Clinton, New York		Andersson, Miss Ellis Anna Maria	2	Sweden to Winnipeg, Manitoba	
Toerber, Mr Ernest William	41	Kensington, London, England		Andersson, Miss Ingeborg Constancia	9	Sweden to Winnipeg, Manitoba	
Tomlin, Mr Ernest Portage	22	Notting Hill, London, England		Andersson, Miss Sigrid Elizabeth	11	Sweden to Winnipeg, Manitoba	
Tornquist, Mr William Henry	25	Stockholm, Sweden, to New York, New York	A	Andersson, Master Sigvard Harald Elias	4	Sweden to Winnipeg, Manitoba	
Trembisky (Pickard), Mr Berk	32	London, England		**Andersson, Miss Erna Alexandra**	17	Finland to New York, New York	
Van Billiard, Mr Austin Blyler	35	Cape Town, South Africa, to North Wales, Pennsylvania		Andersson, Miss Ida Augusta Margareta	38	Vadsbro, Sweden, to Ministee, Michigan	
Van Billiard, Master James William	10	Cape Town, South Africa, to North Wales, Pennsylvania		Andersson, Mr Johan Samuel	26	Hartford, Connecticut	
				Andreasson, Mr Paul Edvin	20	Sweden to Chicago, Illinois	
Van Billiard, Master Walter John	9	Cape Town, South Africa, to North Wales, Pennsylvania		Angheloff, Mr Minko	26	Bulgaria to Chicago, Illinois	
Ware, Mr Frederick William	38	Blackheath, London, England		Arnold, Mr Josef	25	Altdorf, Switzerland	
Warren, Mr Charles William	30	Portsmouth, Devon, England		Arnold, Mrs Josef (nee Josephine Frank)	18	Altdorf, Switzerland	
Webber, Mr James	62	San Francisco, California/ South Africa		Aronsson, Mr Ernst Axel Algot	24	Sweden to Joliet, Illinois	
Widegren, Mr Charles Peter	51	Jamaica, Queens Co, New York		Asplund, Mr Carl Oscar Wilhelm	40	Sweden, returning to Worcester, Massachusetts	
Wilkes, Mrs Ellen (nee Needs)	45	Cornwall, England, to Akron, Ohio		**Asplund, Mrs Carl Oscar (nee Selma Augusta Johansson)**	38	Sweden, returning to Worcester, Massachusetts	4
Willer, Mr Aaron	37	Chicago, Illinois					
Willey, Mr Edward	18	Drayton, England, to Schenectady, New York		Asplund, Master Carl Edgar	5	Sweden, returning to Worcester, Massachusetts	
Williams, Mr Howard Hugh (Harry)	28	Guernsey, Channel Islands		Asplund, Master Clarence Gustaf Hugo	9	Sweden, returning to Worcester, Massachusetts	
Williams, Mr Leslie		Tonypandy, Wales		**Asplund, Master Edvin Rojj Felix**	3	Sweden, returning to Worcester, Massachusetts	4
Windelov, Mr Einar	21			Asplund, Master Filip Oscar	13	Sweden, returning to Worcester, Massachusetts	
Wiseman, Mr Phillippe	54	Quebec City, Quebec		**Asplund, Miss Lillian Gertrud**	5	Sweden, returning to Worcester, Massachusetts	4

Third Class Passengers: non-British subjects embarked at Southampton

Name	Age	1912 residence(s)	Lifeboat No	Name	Age	1912 residence(s)	Lifeboat No
Abelseth, Miss Karen Marie Kristiane	16	Orskog, Norway, to Los Angeles, California		**Asplund, Mr John Charles**	23	Oskarshamn, Sweden, to Minneapolis	
Abelseth, Mr Olaus Jorgensen	25	Perkins County, South Dakota	A	Assam, Mr Ali	23		
Abrahamsson, Mr August	20	Taalintehdas, Finland, to Hoboken, New Jersey	15	Augustsson, Mr Albert	23	Krakoryd, Sweden, to Bloomington, Illinois	
Adahl, Mr Mauritz Nils Martin	30	Asarum, Sweden, to Brooklyn, New York					

Name	Age	1912 residence(s)	Lifeboat No	Name	Age	1912 residence(s)	Lifeboat No
Backstrom, Mr Karl Alfred	32	Ruotsinpyhtaa, Finland, to New York		Delalic, Mr Regyo	25	Batic, Bosnia, to Harrisburg, Pennsylvania	
Backstrom, Mrs Karl Alfred (nee Marie Mathilde Gustafsson)	33	Ruotsinpyhtaa, Finland, to New York		**De Messemaecker, Mr William Joseph**	36	Belgium, returning to Tampico, Montana	
Balkic, Mr Kerim	26	Batic, Bosnia, to Harrisburg, Pennsylvania		**De Messemeacker, Mrs William Joseph (nee Anna)**	36	Belgium, returning to Tampico, Montana	
Bengtsson, Mr John Viktor	26	Krakkudden, Sweden, to Illinois		**De Mulder, Mr Theodore**	30	Aspelare, Belgium, to Detroit, Michigan	
Berglund, Mr Karl Ivar Sven	22	Tranvik, Finland, to New York		De Pelsmaeker, Mr Alphonse	17	Heldergem, Belgium, to Gladstone, Michigan	
Birkeland, Mr Hans Martin Monsen	21	Habbestad, Bremnes, Norway, to New York, New York		Dibo, Mr Elias			
				Dika, Mr Mirko	17	Ogulin, Croatia, to Vancouver, British Columbia	
Bjorklund, Mr Ernst Herbert	18	Stockholm, Sweden, to New York		Dimic, Mr Jovan	42	Ostroica, Croatia, to Red Lodge, Montana	
Bostandyeff, Mr Guentcho	26	Bulgaria to Chicago, Illinois		Dintcheff, Mr Valtcho	43		
Braf, Miss Elin Ester Maria	20	Medeltorp, Sweden, to Chicago, Illinois		Dyker, Mr Adolf Fredrik	23	West Haven, Connecticut	
Brobeck, Mr Karl Rudolf	22	Sweden to Worcester, Massachusetts		**Dyker, Mrs Adolf Fredrik (nee Anna Elizabeth Judith Andersson)**	22	West Haven, Connecticut	
Cacic, Mr Grego	18	Kula, Croatia, to Chicago, Illinois		Ecimovic, Mr Jeso	17	Lipova Glavica, Croatia, to Hammond, Indiana	
Cacic, Mr Luka	38	Kula, Croatia, to Chicago, Illinois		Edvardsson, Mr Gustaf Hjalmar	18	Tofta, Sweden, to Joilet, Illinois	
Cacic, Miss Manda	21	Kula, Croatia, to Chicago, Illinois		Eklund, Mr Hans Linus	16	Karberg, Sweden, to Jerome Junction, Arizona	
Cacic, Miss Marija	30	Kula, Croatia, to Chicago, Illinois		Ekstrom, Mr Johan	45	Effington Rut, South Dakota	
Calic, Mr Peter	17	Breznik, Croatia, to Sault St Marie, Michigan		**Finoli, Mr Luigi**	36	Italy to Philadelphia, Pennsylvania	
Carlsson, Mr Carl Robert	24	Goteborg, Sweden, to Huntley, Illinois		Fischer, Mr Eberhard Telander			
Carlsson, Mr Julius	33			Goncalves, Mr Manuel Estanslas	38	Portugal	
Carlsson, Mr August Sigfrid	28	Dagsas, Sweden, to Fower, Minnesota		Gronnestad, Mr Daniel Danielsen	32	Foresvik, Bokn, Rogaland, Norway, to Portland, Oregon	
Coelho, Mr Domingos Fernandes	20	Portugal		Gustafsson, Mr Alfred Ossian	20	Chicago, Illinois	
Coleff, Mr Fotio	24	Bulgaria to Chicago, Illinois		Gustafsson, Mr Anders Vilhelm	37	Ruotsinphytaa, Finland, to New York	
Coleff, Mr Peyo	36	Bulgaria to Chicago, Illinois		Gustafsson, Mr Johan Birger	28	Ruotsinphytaa, Finland, to New York	
Cor, Mr Bartol	35	Ogulin, Croatia, to Great Falls, Montana		Gustafsson, Mr Karl Gideon	19	Myren, Sweden, to New York, New York	
Cor, Mr Ivan	27	Ogulin, Croatia, to Great Falls, Montana		Haas, Miss Aloisia	24	Altdorf, Switzerland	
Cor, Mr Ludovik	19	Ogulin, Croatia, to St Louis, Missouri		Hagland, Mr Ingvald Olai Olsen	28	Hagland, Skaare, Hordaland, Norway to Belmar, New Jersey	
Dahlberg, Miss Gerda Ulrika	22	Norrlot, Sweden, to Chicago, Illinois		Hagland, Mr Konrad Mathias Reiersen	19	Hagland, Skaare, Hordaland, Norway, to Belmar, New Jersey	
Dakic, Mr Branko	19						
Danbom, Mr Ernst Gilbert	34	Sweden, returning to Stanton, Iowa		Hakkarainen, Mr Pekka Pietari	28	Helsinki, Finland, to Monessen, Pennsylvania	
Danbom, Mrs Ernest Gilbert (nee Anna Sigrid Maria Brogren)	28	Sweden, returning to Stanton, Iowa		**Hakkarainen, Mrs Pekka Pietari (nee Elin Dolk)**	24	Helsinki, Finland, to Monessen, Pennsylvania	15
Danbom, Master Gilbert Sigvard Emanuel	4m	Sweden, returning to Stanton, Iowa					
Danoff, Mr Yoto	27	Bulgaria to Chicago, Illinois		Hampe, Mr Leo Jerome	19	Westrozebeke, Belgium	
Dantchoff, Mr Khristo	25	Bulgaria to Chicago, Illinois		Hansen, Mr Henrik Juul	26	Denmark to Racine, Wisconsin	

Name	Age	1912 residence(s)	Lifeboat No	Name	Age	1912 residence(s)	Lifeboat No
Hansen, Mr Henry Damsgaard	21	Denmark to Racine, Wisconsin		**Johnson, Mrs Oscar W. (nee Alice Berg)**	26	St Charles, Illinois	15
Hansen, Mr Peter Claus	41	Racine, Wisconsin		**Johnson, Miss Eleanor Ileen**	1	St Charles, Illinois	15
Hansen, Mrs Peter Claus (nee Jennie L. Howard)	45	Racine, Wisconsin		**Johnson, Master Harold Theodor**	4	St Charles, Illinois	15
Hedman, Mr Oscar	27	Sioux Falls, South Dakota		Jonkoff, Mr Lazor			
				Jonsson, Mr Carl	32	Huntley, Illinois	
Heikkinen, Miss Laina	26	Helsinki, Finland, to New York		Jonsson, Mr Nils Hilding	27		
Heininen, Miss Wendla Maria	23	Laitila, Finland, to New York		Jussila, Miss Aina Maria	21	Paavola, Finland, to New York	
Hellstrom, Miss Hilda Maria	22	Sweden to Evanston, Illinois	13	**Jussila, Mr Erik**	32	Helsinki, Finland, to Monessen, Pennsylvania	
Hendekovic, Mr Ignaz	28	Vagovina, Croatia, to Harrisburg, Pennsylvania		Jussila, Miss Katriina	20	Paavola, Finland, to New York	
Henriksson, Miss Jenny Lovisa	28	Stockholm, Sweden, to Iron Mountain, Michigan		Kallio, Mr Nikolai Erland	17	Finland to Sudbury, Ontario	
Hirvonen, Mrs Alexander (nee Helga E.)		Taalintehdas, Finland, to Monessen, Pennsylvania		Kalvig, Mr Johannes K. Halverson	21	Flokatveit, Etne, Norway, to Story City, Iowa	
Hirvonen, Miss Hildur E.	2	Taalintehdas, Finland, to Monessen, Pennsylvania		Karajic, Mr Milan	30	Kravarsko, Croatia, to Youngstown, Ohio	
				Karlsson, Mr Einar Gervasius	21	Oskarshamn, Sweden, to Brooklyn	13
Holm, Mr John Fredrik Alexander	43	Karlshamn, Sweden, to New York		Karlsson, Mr Julius Konrad Eugen	33	Goteborg, Sweden	
Holten, Mr Johan Martin	28	Kristiansund, Norway, to New York		Karlsson, Mr Nils August	22	Sweden to Palmer, Massachusetts	
Honkanen, Miss Eluna	27	Finland to New York, New York		Kekic, Mr Tido	38		
				Kink, Mr Anton	29	Zurich, Switzerland, to Milwaukee, Wisconsin	2
Humblen, Mr Adolf Mathias Nikolai Olsen	42	Borgund, Norway, to Milwaukee, Wisconsin		**Kink, Mrs Anton (nee Louise Heilmann)**	26	Zurich, Switzerland, to Milwaukee, Wisconsin	2
Ilieff, Mr Ylio				**Kink, Miss Louise Gretchen**	4	Zurich, Switzerland, to Milwaukee, Wisconsin	2
Ilmakangas, Miss Ida Livija	27	New York, New York		Kink, Miss Maria	22	Zurich, Switzerland, to Milwaukee, Wisconsin	
Ilmakangas, Miss Pieta Sofia	25	Paavola, Finland, to New York, New York		Kink, Mr Vincenz	27	Zurich, Switzerland, to Milwaukee, Wisconsin	
Ivanoff, Mr Kolio		Bulgaria		Klasen, Mrs Hulda Kristina	36	Grimshult, Sweden, to Los Angeles, California	
Jansson, Mr Carl Olof	21	Orebro, Sweden, to Swedeburg, Nebraska	A	Klasen, Miss Gertrud Emilia	1	Grimshult, Sweden, to Los Angeles, California	
Jardin, Mr Jose Netto	21						
Jensen, Miss Carla Christine	19	Denmark to Portland, Oregon		Klasen, Mr Klas Albin	18	Grimshult, Sweden, to Los Angeles, California	
Jensen, Mr Hans Peder	20			Kraeff, Mr Theodor			
Jensen, Mr Niels Peder	48	Denmark to Portland, Oregon		Laitinen, Miss Kristina Sofia	37	Helsingfors, Finland, to New York	
Jensen, Mr Svend Lauritz	17	Denmark to Portland, Oregon		Laleff, Mr Kristo	23	Bulgaria to Chicago, Illinois	
Johannessen-Bratthammer, Mr Bernt	29	Eike, Avaldsnes, Norway, to New York, New York	13	**Landergren, Miss Aurora Adelia**	22	Karlshamn, Sweden, to New York, New York	13
Johanson, Mr Jakob Alfred	34	Uusikaarlepyy, Finland, to Vancouver, British Columbia		Larsson, Mr August Viktor	29	Stamford, Connecticut	
				Larsson, Mr Bengt Edvin	29	Stockholm, Sweden, to Hartford, Connecticut	
Johansson, Mr Erik	22	Frostensmala, Sweden		Larsson-Rondberg, Mr Edvard	22	Sweden to Missoula, Montana	
Johansson, Mr Gustaff Joel	33	Bockebo, Sweden, to Cheyenne, North Dakota		Lefebre, Mrs Frank (Frances)	39	France to Mystic, Iowa	
Johansson, Mr Karl Johan	31	Duluth, Minnesota		Lefebre, Master Henry	4	France to Mystic, Iowa	
Johansson, Mr Nils	29	Chicago, Illinois		Lefebre, Miss Ida	2	France to Mystic, Iowa	
Johansson, Mr Oskar L.	26			Lefebre, Miss Jeannie	6	France to Mystic, Iowa	
Johnson, Mr Malcolm Joackim	33	Minneapolis, Minnesota		Lefebre, Miss Mathilde	11	France to Mystic, Iowa	

Name	Age	1912 residence(s)	Lifeboat No	Name	Age	1912 residence(s)	Lifeboat No
Leinonen, Mr Antti Gustaf	32	Finland to New York, New York		Nieminen, Miss Manta Josefina	29	Abo, Finland, to Aberdeen, Washington	
Lievens, Mr Rene	24	Heldergem, Belgium					
Lindahl, Miss Agda V.	25	Stockholm, Sweden, to Saranac Lake, New York		Niklasson, Mr Samuel	28	Orust, Sweden	
				Nilsson, Mr August Ferdinand	21	Sweden to St Paul, Minnesota	
Lindblom, Miss Augusta Charlotta	45	Stockholm, Sweden, to Stratford, Connecticut		**Nilsson, Miss Berta Oliva**	18	Ransbysater, Sweden, to Missoula, Montana	
Lindell, Mr Edvard Bengtsson	36	Helsingborg, Sweden, to Hartford, Connecticut		**Nilsson, Miss Helmina Josefina**	26	Ramkvilla, Sweden, to Joliet, Illinois	13
Lindell, Mrs Edvard Bengtsson (Elin Gerda)	30	Helsingborg, Sweden, to Hartford, Connecticut		Niskanen, Mr Johan	39	Boston, Massachusetts	
Linhart, Mr Wenzel				**Nysten, Miss Anna**	22	Sweden to Passaic, New Jersey	
Lindqvist, Mr Eino William	20	Dals, Finland, to Monessen, Pennsylvania		Nysveen, Mr Johannes H.	61	Nysvea, Oyer, Oppland, Norway, to Hillsboro, North Dakota	
Lulich, Mr Nicola	27	Konjskobrdo, Croatia, to Chicago, Illinois		Odahl, Mr Nils Martin	23	Orsjo, Sweden, to Peoria, Illinois	
Lundahl, Mr Johan	51	Fyrnan, Sweden, to Spokane, Washington		**Ohman, Miss Velin**	22	Mariestad, Sweden, to Chicago, Illinois	
Lundin, Miss Olga Elida	23	Meriden, Connecticut		Olsen, Mr Karl Siegwart Andreas	42	Norway, returning to Brooklyn, New York	
Lundstrom, Mr Thure Edvin	32	Gislof, Sweden, to Los Angeles, California		**Olsen, Master Arthur Carl**	9	Trondheim, Norway, to Brooklyn, New York	13
Lyntakoff, Mr Stanko	44	Bulgaria to Coon Rapids, Iowa		Olsen, Mr Henry Margido	28	Bergen, Norway, to New York, New York	
Madsen, Mr Frithiof Arne	22	Trondheim, Norway, to Brooklyn, New York	13	Olsen, Mr Ole M.	27	Broderick, Saskatchewan, Canada	
Maenpaa, Mr Matti Alexanteri	22	Finland to Sudbury, Ontario		Olsson, Miss Elida	31	Sweden to St Paul, Minnesota	
Makinen, Mr Kalle Edvard	29	Ikalis, Finland, to Glassport, Pennsylvania		Olsson, Mr Nils Johan	28	Eslov, Sweden	
				Olsson, Mr Oscar Johansson	32		B
Marinko, Mr Dmitri	23			Olsvigen, Mr Thor Andersen	20	Vikersund, Norway, to Cameron, Wisconsin	
Markim, Mr Joachim							
Markoff, Mr Marin	35	Bulgaria to Chicago, Illinois		Oreskovic, Miss Jeka	23	Brdovec, Croatia, to Chicago, Illinois	
Matinoff, Mr Nicola				Oreskovic, Mr Luka	20	Brdovec, Croatia, to Chicago, Illinois	
Melkebuk, Mr Philemon							
Midtsjo, Mr Karl Albert	21	Midtsjo, Ski, Akershus, Norway, to Chicago, Illinois		Oreskovic, Miss Marija	20	Brdovec, Croatia, to Chicago, Illinois	
Mihoff, Mr Stoytcho	28	Bulgaria		Osen, Mr Olof Elon	16	Sweden to Ethan, North Dakota	
Mineff, Mr Ivan	24	Bulgaria to Coon Rapids, Iowa		**Osman, Miss Maria**	31	Austria to Steubenville, Ohio	
Minkoff, Mr Lazar	21	Bulgaria to Coon Rapids, Iowa		Pålsson, Mrs Nils (nee Alma) Cornelia Berglund	29	Bjuv, Sweden, to Chicago, Illinois	
Mirkoff, Mr Mito	23	Bulgaria		Pålsson, Master Gösta Leonard	2	Bjuv, Sweden, to Chicago, Illinois	
Moen, Mr Sigurd Hansen	25	Bergen, Norway, to Minneapolis, Minnesota		Pålsson, Master Paul Folke	6	Bjuv, Sweden, to Chicago, Illinois	
Moss, Mr Albert Johan	29	Bergen, Norway, to New York, New York	B	Pålsson, Miss Stina Viola	8	Bjuv, Sweden, to Chicago, Illinois	
Myhrman, Mr Per Fabian Oliver Malkolm	18	Kristinehamn, Sweden, to Chicago, Illinois		Pålsson, Miss Torborg Danira	3	Bjuv, Sweden, to Chicago, Illinois	
				Panula, Mrs John (Maria Emilia)	41	Coal Center, Pennsylvania	
Naidenoff, Mr Penko	22	Bulgaria to Chicago, Illinois		Panula, Mr Ernesti Arvid	16	Coal Center, Pennsylvania	
				Panula, Mr Jaakko Arnold	14	Coal Center, Pennsylvania	
Nankoff, Mr Minko	32	Bulgaria to Chicago, Illinois		Panula, Master Juha Niilo	7	Coal Center, Pennsylvania	
				Panula, Master Urho Abraham	2	Coal Center, Pennsylvania	
Nenkoff, Mr Christo	22	Bulagria to Chicago, Illinois		Panula, Master William	1	Coal Center, Pennsylvania	
				Pasic, Mr Jakob	21		

Name	Age	1912 residence(s)	Lifeboat No	Name	Age	1912 residence(s)	Lifeboat No
Pavlovic, Mr Stefan	32	Austria to Harrisburg, Pennsylvania		Sjoblom, Miss Anna Sofia	18	Finland to Olympia, Washington	
Pecruic, Mr Mate	17	Bukovac, Croatia, to Chicago, Illinois		Skoog, Mr William	40	Sweden, returning to Iron Mountain, Michigan	
Pecruic, Mr Tome	24	Bukovac, Croatia, to Chicago, Illinois		Skoog, Mrs William (nee Anna Bernhardina Karlsson)	43	Sweden, returning to Iron Mountain, Michigan	
Pedersen, Mr Olaf	28	Sandefjord, Norway, to Seattle, Washington		Skoog, Master Harald	5	Sweden, returning to Iron Mountain, Michigan	
Pekoniemi, Mr Edvard	21	Finland		Skoog, Master Karl Thorston	11	Sweden, returning to Iron Mountain, Michigan	
Peltomaki, Mr Nikolai Johannes	25	Finland to New York, New York		Skoog, Miss Mabel	9	Sweden, returning to Iron Mountain, Michigan	
Persson, Mr Ernst Ulrik	25	Stockholm, Sweden, to Indianapolis, Indiana		Skoog, Miss Margrit	2	Sweden, returning to Iron Mountain, Michigan	
Petersen, Mr Marius	24	Denmark		Slabenoff, Mr Petco	42	Bulgaria	
Petranec, Miss Matilda	31	Vagovina, Croatia, to Harrisburg, Pennsylvania		Smiljanovic, Mr Mile	37		
				Soholt, Mr Peter Andreas Lauritz Andersen	19	Orskog, Norway, to Minneapolis, Minnesota	
Petroff, Mr Nedeca	19	Bulgaria to Chicago, Illinois					
Petroff, Mr Pentcho	29	Bulgaria to Chicago, Illinois		Solvang, Mrs Lena Jacobsen	63	Skaare, Hordaland, Norway, to Centerville, South Dakota	
Pettersson, Miss Ellen Natalia	18	Stockholm, Sweden, to Iron Mountain, Michigan		Staneff, Mr Ivan	23	Bulgaria to Chicago, Illinois	
Pettersson, Mr Johan Emil	25	Vastermo, Sweden, to Chicago, Illinois		Stankovic, Mr Jovan			
Plotcharsky, Mr Vasil	27			Stoyehoff, Mr Ilia	19	Bulgaria	
Radeff, Mr Alexander	27	Bulgaria to Chicago, Illinois		Strandberg, Miss Ida Sofia	22	Abo, Finland, to New York, New York	
Riihiivuori, Miss Sanni	21	Finland to Coal Center, Pennsylvania		**Stranden, Mr Juho**	31	Kides, Finland, to Duluth, Minnesota	
Rintamaki, Mr Matti		Pantane, Finland, to Sudbury, Ontario		Strilic, Mr Ivan	27	Vucevo, Croatia, to Chicago, Illinois	
Rommetvedt, Mr Knut Paust	21	Sola, Norway, heading to New York, New York		Strom, Mrs Wilhelm (nee Elna Matilda Persson)	29	Indian Harbor, Indiana	
Rosblom, Mrs Viktor (Helena Wilhelmina)	41	Raumo, Finland, to Astoria, Oregon		Strom, Miss Selma Matilda	2	Indian Harbor, Indiana	
Rosblom, Miss Salli Helena	2	Raumo, Finland, to Astoria, Oregon		**Sundman, Mr Johan Julian**	44	Munsala, Finland, to Cheyenne, Wyoming	
Rosblom, Mr Viktor Rickard	18	Raumo, Finland, to Astoria, Oregon		Svensson, Mr Johan	74	Reftele, Sweden, to Effington Rut, South Dakota	
Salander, Mr Karl Johan	24	Tjarby, Sweden, to Red Wing, Minnesota		**Svensson, Mr Johan Cervin**	14	Knared, Sweden, to Beresford, South Dakota	13
Salkjelsvik, Miss Anna Kristine	21	Skodje, Norway, to Proctor, Minnesota		Svensson, Mr Olof	24	Osby, Sweden	
Salonen, Mr Johan Werner	39	Aberdeen, Washington		**Tenglin, Mr Gunnar Isidor**	25	Stockholm, Sweden, to Burlington, Iowa	A
Sandstrom, Mrs Hjalmar (nee Agnes Charlotta Bengtsson)	24	Motala, Sweden, to San Francisco, California	13	Tikkanen, Mr Juho	32	Finland to New York, New York	
Sandstrom, Miss Beatrice Irene	1	Motala, Sweden, to San Francisco, California	13	Todoroff, Mr Lalio	23	Bulgaria to Chicago, Illinois	
Sandstrom, Miss Margurite Rut	4	Motala, Sweden, to San Francisco, California	13	Turcin, Mr Stefan	36	Kravarsko, Croatia, to Youngstown, Ohio	
Sap, Mr Jules	25	Zwevezele, Belgium, to Detroit, Michigan		**Turja, Miss Anna Sofia**	18	Sweden to Ashtabula, Ohio	
Scheerlinckx, Mr Jean	29	Haaltert, Belgium, to Detroit, Michigan		**Turkula, Mrs Hedvig**	65	Finland to Hibbing, Montana	
Sdycoff, Mr Todor	42	Bulgaria to Chicago, Illinois		Uzelac, Mr Jovo	17	Breznik, Croatia, to Sault St Marie, Michigan	
Sivic, Mr Husein	40	Batic, Bosnia, to Harrisburg, Pennsylvania		Vandercruyssen, Mr Victor	47	Zwevezele, Belgium, to Detroit, Michigan	
Sivola, Mr Antti William	21	Mountain Home, Idaho		Van den Steen, Mr Leo	28	Heldergem, Belgium	

Name	Age	1912 residence(s)	Lifeboat No
Vanderplancke, Miss Augusta	18	Zwevezele, Belgium, to Detroit, Michigan	
Vanderplancke, Mr Jules	31	Zwevezele, Belgium, to Detroit, Michigan	
Vanderplancke, Mrs Jules (nee Emilie Vandermoortele)	31	Zwevezele, Belgium, to Detroit, Michigan	
Vanderplancke, Mr Leo	15	Zwevezele, Belgium, to Detroit, Michigan	
Van de Velde, Mr Johannes Joseph	36	Denderhoutem, Belgium	
Van Impe, Mr Jean Baptiste	36	Bergstraat, Kerksken, Belgium	
Van Impe, Mrs Jean Baptiste (nee Rosalie Govaerts)	30	Bergstraat, Kerksken, Belgium	
Van Impe, Miss Catherine	10	Bergstraat, Kerksken, Belgium	
Van Melkebeke, Mr Philemon	23	Haaltert, Belgium, to Detroit, Michigan	
Vendel, Mr Olof Edvin	20	Sweden to St Paul, Minnesota	
Vestrom, Miss Hulda Amanda Adolfina	14	Salmunds, Sweden, to Los Angeles, California	
Vonk, Mr Jenko	22	Austria to New York, New York	
Waelens, Mr Achille	22	Ruiselede, Belgium, to Stanton, Ohio	
Wennerstrom, Mr August Edvard	27	Malmo, Sweden, to New York, New York	A
Wiklund, Mr Jacob Alfred	18	Nicolaistad, Finland, to Montreal, Quebec	
Wiklund, Mr Karl Johan	21	Nicolaistad, Finland, to Montreal, Quebec	
Wirz, Mr Albert	26	Zurich, Switzerland, to Beloit, Wisconsin	
Wittevrongel, Mr Camilius Aloysius	36	Westrozebeke, Belgium	
Zimmerman, Mr Leo	29		

Third Class Passengers: Syrian, Greek, Turkish and Armenian subjects embarked at Cherbourg

Name	Age	1912 residence(s)	Lifeboat No
Abraham, Mrs Joseph (nee Sophie Easu)	18	Greensburg, Pennsylvania	
Ali, Mr William	25	Argentina	
Asim, Mr Adola	35		
Assaf, Mr Gerios		Kafarmiskey, Lebanon, to Ottawa, Ontario	
Assaf, Mrs Mariana Khalil	45	Kafarmiskey, Lebanon, to Ottawa, Ontario	C
Assam, Mr Ali	23		
Attala, Miss Malaka	17		
Attala, Mr Solomon			
Baclini, Mrs Solomon (nee Latifa Qurban)	20	Syria, heading to Brooklyn, New York	C
Baclini, Miss Eugenie	4	Syria, heading to Brooklyn, New York	C
Baclini, Miss Helene	11m	Syria, heading to Brooklyn, New York	C

Name	Age	1912 residence(s)	Lifeboat No
Baclini, Miss Maria	5	Syria, heading to Brooklyn, New York	C
Badt, Mr Mohamed	40		
Banoura, Miss Ayoub	15	Syria, heading to Youngstown, Ohio	C
Barbara, Mrs Catherine	45	Kafarmiskey, Lebanon, to Ottawa, Ontario	
Barbara, Miss Saude	18	Kafarmiskey, Lebanon, to Ottawa, Ontario	
Betros, Mr Tannous			
Boulos, Mr Hanna		Kafarmiskey, Lebanon, to Ottawa, Ontario	
Boulos, Mrs Joseph (Sultana)	36	Syria, heading to Kent, Ontario	
Boulos, Master Akar	6	Syria, heading to Kent, Ontario	
Boulos, Miss Laura	9	Syria, heading to Kent, Ontario	
Brahim, Mr Youssef	30		
Caram (Kareem), Mr Joseph		Kafarmiskey, Lebanon, to Ottawa, Ontario	
Caram (Kareem), Mrs Joseph (Maria Elias)		Kafarmiskey, Lebanon, to Ottawa, Ontario	
Cassem, Mr Nassef Belmenly		Lebanon, heading to Fredericksburg, Virginia	
Catavelas, Mr Vassilios	18	Greece, heading to Milwaukee, Wisconsin	
Chehab, Emir Farres		Beirut, Lebanon	
Chronopoulos, Mr Apostolos		Greece	
Chronopoulos, Mr Demetrios		Greece	
Daher, Mr Tannous			
Dibo, Mr Elias			
Drazenovic, Mr Josef	33	Hrastelnica, Croatia, to Niagara Falls, New York	
Elias, Mr Joseph		Kafarmiskey, Lebanon, to Ottawa, Ontario	
George, Mrs Shanini (Jenny)	40	Lebanon, returning to Youngstown, Ohio	C
Gheorgheff, Mr Stanio		Bulgaria, heading to Butte, Montana	
Hanna, Mr Mansour		Kafarmiskey, Lebanon, to Ottawa, Ontario	
Hassan, Master Houssein G. M.	11	Lebanon, heading to Fredericksburg, Virginia	
Karun, Mr Franz	37	Galesburg, Illinois	
Karun, Miss Anna Mary	3	Galesburg, Illinois	
Kassem, Mr Fared			
Khalil, Mr Betros	25	Hardin, Lebanon, to Wilkes-Barre, Pennsylvania	
Khalil, Mrs Betros (Zahie)	20	Hardin, Lebanon, to Wilkes-Barre, Pennsylvania	
Khalil, Mr Solomon	27	Kafarmiskey, Lebanon, to Ottawa, Ontario	
Kiamie, Miss Adele Najib	15	Lebanon, returning to Brooklyn, New York	C
Kraeff, Mr Theodor		Bulgaria	

Name	Age	1912 residence(s)	Lifeboat No	Name	Age	1912 residence(s)	Lifeboat No
Krekorian, Mr Neshan	25	Lebanon, heading to Brantford, Ontario	10	Seman, Master Betros	9	Hardin, Lebanon, to Wilkes-Barre, Pennsylvania	
Lahowd, Mr Sarkis	30	Turkey		Shedid (Sitik), Mr Daher	19	Turkey, returning to Kulpmont, Pennsylvania	
Leeni, Mr Fahim		Beirut, Lebanon, heading to Dayton, Ohio		Sirayanian, Mr Arsun		Turkey, heading to Brantford, Ontario	
Lemberopolous, Mr Peter L.	30	Greece, heading to Stamford, Connecticut		Stankovic, Mr Jovan	33	Sisak, Croatia	
Mamee, Mr Hanna				**Thomas, Mrs Alexander (Thelma)**	16	Hardin, Lebanon, to Wilkes-Barre, Pennsylvania	C
Mardirosian, Mr Sarkis	25	Turkey					
Markun, Mr Johann	33	Bela, Croatia, heading to New York, New York		**Thomas, Master Assed Alexander**	5m	Hardin, Lebanon, to Wilkes-Barre, Pennsylvania	D
Masselmany, Mrs Fatima	17	Lebanon, heading to Dearborn, Michigan	C	Thomas, Mr Charles		Hardin, Lebanon, returning to Wilkes-Barre, Pennsylvania	
Moubarek (Borak), Mr Hanna (John)		Hardin, Lebanon, to Wilkes-Barre, Pennsylvania		Thomas, Mr John			
				Thomas, Mr John Jr	15		
Moubarek (Borak), Mrs George (nee Amenia Alexander)	24	Hardin, Lebanon, to Wilkes-Barre, Pennsylvania	C	Thomas, Mr Tannous			
				Torfa, Mr Assad	20		
				Toufik, Mr Nahil			
Moubarek (Borak), Master George	7	Hardin, Lebanon, to Wilkes-Barre, Pennsylvania	C	**Touma (Thomas), Mrs Darwin (nee Anna Razi)**	27	Tibnin, Syria, to Dowagiac, Michigan	C
Moubarek (Borak), Master William	4	Hardin, Lebanon, to Wilkes-Barre, Pennsylvania	C	**Touma (Thomas), Master George**	7	Tibnin, Syria, to Dowagiac, Michigan	C
Moussa, Mrs Mantoura Boulos		Lebanon to Troy, New York	C	**Touma (Thomas), Miss Hanna**	9	Tibnin, Syria, to Dowagiac, Michigan	C
Naked (Nackid), Mr Said	20	Lebanon, heading to Waterbury, Connecticut	C	**Vartanian, Mr David**		Turkey to Brantford, Ontario	A
				Wazli, Mr Yousif			
Naked (Nackid), Mrs Said (nee Mary Mowad)	19	Lebanon, heading to Waterbury, Connecticut	C	Willer, Mr Aaron		Chicago, Illinois	
				Yalsevac, Mr Ivan	29	Topolovac, Croatia, to Galesburg, Illinois	
Naked (Nackid), Miss Mary	1	Lebanon, heading to Waterbury, Connecticut	C	Yasbeck, Mr Antoni	27	Lebanon, returning to Wilkes-Barre, Pennsylvania	
Nasr, Mr Mustafa				**Yasbeck, Mrs Antoni (Celiney)**	15	Lebanon, returning to Wilkes-Barre, Pennsylvania	
Nassr, Mr Saad Jean							
Nicola (Yarred), Master Elias	12	Hakoor, Lebanon, to Jacksonville, Florida		Youssef, Mr Gerios			
Nicola (Yarred), Miss Jamilia	14	Hakoor, Lebanon, to Jacksonville, Florida		Youssef, Mr Gerios			
				Zabour, Miss Hileni	16		
Novel, Mr Mansour		Kafarmiskey, Lebanon, to Sherbrooke, Quebec		Zabour, Miss Tamini			
				Zakarian, Mr Artun		Turkey to Brantford, Ontario	
Paulner, Mr Uscher							
Peter (Joseph), Mrs Catherine	23	Detroit, Michigan	C	Zakarian, Mr Maprieder		Turkey to Brantford, Ontario	
Peter (Joseph), Miss Mary	1	Detroit, Michigan	C				
Peter (Joseph), Master Michael J.	4	Detroit, Michigan	D				
Rafoul, Mr Baccos							
Razi, Mr Rachid							
Saad, Mr Amin							
Samaan, Mr Elias		Hardin, Lebanon, to Wilkes-Barre, Pennsylvania					

Third Class Passengers: Irish subjects embarked at Queenstown, Ireland

Name	Age	1912 residence(s)	Lifeboat No
Samaan, Mr Hanna		Hardin, Lebanon, to Wilkes-Barre, Pennsylvania	
Barry, Miss Julia	27	New York, New York	
Bourke, Mr John	28	Co Mayo to Chicago, Illinois	
Bourke, Mrs John (Katherine)	32	Co Mayo to Chicago, Illinois	
Samaan, Mr Youssef		Hardin, Lebanon, to Wilkes-Barre, Pennsylvania	
Bourke, Miss Mary		Ireland to Chicago, Illinois	

Name	Age	1912 residence(s)	Lifeboat No	Name	Age	1912 residence(s)	Lifeboat No
Bradley, Miss Bridget Delia	18	Kingwilliamstown, Co Cork, to Glens Falls, New York	13	Hagardon, Miss Kate	17	Co Sligo to New York, New York	
Buckley, Mr Daniel	21	Kingwilliamstown, Co Cork to New York, New York		Hart, Mr Henry	28	Ireland to Boston, Massachusetts	
Buckley, Miss Katherine	20	Cork City, Co Cork, to Roxbury, Massachusetts		**Healy, Miss Nora**		Co Galway, Ireland, to New York, New York	
Burke, Mr Jeremiah	19	Co Cork to Charlestown, Massachusetts		Hegarty, Miss Nora	18	Co Cork, Ireland, to Charlestown, Massachusetts	
Burns, Miss Mary Delia	18	Co Sligo to New York, New York		Hemming, Miss Nora	21		
Canavan, Miss Mary	21			Henery, Miss Delia	23		
Canavan, Mr Patrick	21	Co Mayo to Philadelphia, Pennsylvania		Horgan, Mr John	41		
				Jermyn, Miss Annie	22	Co Cork to East Lynn, Massachusetts	
Carr, Miss Helen	16	Co Longford to New York, New York		Keane, Mr Andrew	20	Ireland to Auburndale, Massachusetts	
Carr, Miss Jeannie	37	Co Sligo to Hartford, Connecticut		**Kelly, Miss Annie Kate**		Co Mayo to Chicago, Illinois	
Colbert, Mr Patrick	24	Co Limerick to Sherbrooke, Quebec		Kelly, Mr James			
Conlin, Mr Thomas Henry	31	Ireland, returning to Philadelphia, Pennsylvania		**Kelly, Miss Mary**	21	Co Westmeath to New York, New York	D
Connaghton, Mr Michael	31	Ireland, heading to Brooklyn, New York		**Kennedy, Mr John**	24	Co Limerick to New York, New York	
Connolly, Miss Kate				Kiernan, Mr John	25	Ireland, returning to Jersey City, New Jersey	
Connolly, Miss Kate	21			Kiernan, Mr Philip	19	Co Longford to Jersey City, New Jersey	
Connors, Mr Patrick				Kilgannon, Mr Thomas J.	21	Co Galway to New York, New York	
Daly, Mr Eugene	31	Co Athlone to New York, New York	B	Lane, Mr Patrick		Co Limerick to New York, New York	
Daly, Miss Marcella	30	Co Athlone to New York, New York		Lemon, Mr Denis	21		
Devaney, Miss Margaret	19	Kilmacowen, Co Sligo, to New York, New York	C	Lemon, Mrs Denis (Mary)	20		
Dewan, Mr Frank				Linehan, Mr Michael	21		
Donohue, Miss Bridget	21	Co Mayo		**Madigan, Miss Margaret**	25	Co Limerick to New York, New York	
Dooley, Mr Patrick	32	Ireland to New York, New York		Mahon, Miss Bridget Delia	20	Co Mayo to ?	
Doyle, Miss Elizabeth	24	Ireland to New York, New York		Mangan, Miss Mary	32	Co Mayo to Chicago, Illinois	
Driscoll, Miss Bridget		Ballydehob, Co Cork, to New York, New York		**Mannion, Miss Margaret**	24	Ireland to New York, New York	
Farrell, Mr James		Aughnacliff, Co Longford, to New York, New York		**McCarthy, Miss Katie**	24	Co Tipperary, Ireland to Guttenberg, New Jersey	
Flynn, Mr James	28	Co Mayo		**McCormack, Mr Thomas J.**	19	Co Longford, returning to Bayonne, New Jersey	
Flynn, Mr John		Ireland to New York, New York		**McCoy, Miss Agnes**	28	Co Longford to Brooklyn, New York	
Foley, Mr Joseph		Ireland to Chicago, Illinois		**McCoy, Miss Alice**	22	Co Longford to Brooklyn, New York	
Foley, Mr William				**McCoy, Mr Bernard**	21	Co Longford to Brooklyn, New York	
Fox, Mr Patrick		Ireland to New York, New York		**McDermott, Miss Bridget Delia**	31	Co Mayo to New York, New York	
Gallagher, Mr Martin	25	Ireland, returning to Rye, New York		McElroy, Mr Michael			
Gilnagh, Miss Katie	16	Co Longford, Ireland, to New York, New York		**McGovern, Miss Mary**	22	Co Cavan to New York, New York	
Glynn, Miss Mary Agatha		Co Clare, Ireland, to Washington, DC		**McGowan, Miss Annie**	16	Co Mayo to Chicago, Illinois	
				McGowan, Miss Katherine	36	Co Mayo, returning to Chicago, Illinois	

Name	Age	1912 residence(s)	Lifeboat No	Name	Age	1912 residence(s)	Lifeboat No
McMahon, Mr Martin	20	Co Clare to New York, New York		O'Keefe, Mr Patrick	22	Co Waterford to New York, New York	B
McNeil, Miss Bridget				O'Leary, Miss Nora	17	Kingwilliamstown, Co Cork, to New York, New York	
Mechan, Mr John	22	Ireland, heading to Paterson, New Jersey					
Mocklare, Miss Helen Mary	23	Co Galway to New York, New York		O'Sullivan, Miss Bridget	22		
				Peters, Miss Katie	26		
Moran, Miss Bertha	28	Ireland, returning to Bronx, New York		Rice, Mrs William (nee Margaret Norton)	39	Co Athlone, returning to Spokane, Washington	
Moran, Mr Daniel J.	27	Ireland, returning to Bronx, New York		Rice, Master Albert	10	Co Athlone, returning to Spokane, Washington	
Moran, Mr James	22			Rice, Master Arthur	4	Co Athlone, returning to Spokane, Washington	
Morrow, Mr Thomas Rowan	30	Ireland, heading to Gleichen, Alberta		Rice, Master George	9	Co Athlone, returning to Spokane, Washington	
Mullins, Miss Katie	19	Co Longford to New York, New York		Rice, Master Eric	7	Co Athlone, returning to Spokane, Washington	
Mulvihill, Miss Bertha E.		Ireland, returning to Providence, Rhode Island		Rice, Master Eugene	2	Co Athlone, returning to Spokane, Washington	
Murphy, Miss Katherine		Co Longford to New York, New York		Riordan, Miss Hannah	20	Kingwilliamstown, Co Cork, to New York, New York	
Murphy, Miss Margaret Jane		Co Longford to New York, New York		Ryan, Mr Edward		Co Limerick to Troy, New York	14
Murphy, Miss Nora	28	Ireland to New York, New York		Ryan, Mr Patrick		Askeaton, Co Limerick, to Bronx, New York	
Naughton, Miss Hannah	21	Co Cork to New York		Sadlier, Mr Matthew	20	Ireland to Lakewood, New Jersey	
Nemaugh, Mr Robert	26	Ireland to Chicago, Illinois		Scanlon, Mr James		Ireland to New York, New York	
O'Brien, Mr Denis	21			Shaughnesay, Mr Patrick		Ireland to New York, New York	
O'Brien, Mr Thomas	26	Co Limerick to New York, New York		Shine, Miss Ellen	20	Co Cork to New York, New York	
O'Brien, Mrs Thomas (nee Hannah Godfrey)	26	Co Limerick to New York, New York		Smyth, Miss Julia	20	Co Cavan to New York, New York	
O'Connell, Mr Patrick D.	17			Tobin, Mr Roger		Co Tipperary to New York, New York	
O'Connor, Mr Maurice		Co Limerick to New York, New York					
O'Connor, Mr Patrick	24						
O'Dwyer, Miss Nellie	23	Co Limerick to New York, New York.					

ACKNOWLEDGEMENTS

W HERE TO BEGIN? A book such as this rests on the cooperation of so many people. Initially it began to take shape with the creative input of my daughter, Samantha Geller, who had a full-blown design concept in her head and who was instrumental in securing and supervising the wonderful paintings provided by Jason Manley. Much of the passenger information and historical data was contributed by Michael Findlay of Titanic International Inc, whose unbelievable generosity is overwhelming.

So many other researchers also took the calls, answered the questions and sent the photos, and I list them not in any particular order, but with grateful thanks for making my job so much easier: Historians John P. Eaton and Charles A. Haas for their encouragement and wise counsel (just how many times can one person ask the pound-to-dollar ratio in 1912?); Philip Croucher; Robert Bracken; Carles Bonet i Corbalan; Alan Hustak; Janet White; Olivier Mendez; Stan Hamper; Claes-Göran Wetterholm; Hazel Dault; Nina Johnson; Kay Hadley; Frederick Rueckert; Newton Howard; and the staffs of the libraries, historical societies, government agencies, newspapers, service organisations, museums and archives whom I plagued in the United States, Canada and Great Britain.

To the folks who went out of their way: Alison Roelich, Pastor Robert Gerhart, Drew Likens, Debra Given, Reverend John Willard, Dr Charleton Shaw, Graham Young, Deborah Mazur, Ed Voves, Retha Godfrey, Nicky Gilman, Dr Ronald Denny, William MacQuitty, Walter Lord, Dik Barton, Korkye and Joe Sternburgh, Susan Mitchem, I. Bay, Matthew Hankins, Ray Armour, Matt Tulloch, Adrian Walmsley, Dennis Richman, Suzanne Feldman and Dora Cooke.

To RMS Titanic Inc and George Tulloch in particular for his friendship, generosity and happy voice on the telephone. To Dr Stéphane Pennec of LP3 Conservation, again for friendship, but also for his interest in the project and stunning artefact photographs.

Speaking of photographs, William Hull was a master at improving all those bad shots I took, and Dr Lois Berman was equally masterful in sorting through my grammar and upside-down sentences.

Of course, my heart and profound thanks goes out to the survivors, always inundated with requests for information, who were most gracious when I came knocking: Millvina Dean, Louise Laroche, Eleanor Johnson Shuman, Louise Kink Pope, Edith Brown Haisman, and Ellen Phillips Walker. And to their family members and friends who also willingly probed their pasts and provided their photos: Marie Aks, Sophie Isaac, Mona Isaac, Phyllis Ryerse, Brian and Louis Joseph, Jeanette Happel, Cathy Gay, Elizabeth McLain, Helen Landsberg, Eugene, Dorothy and Jessica Tanner, Lars-Inge Glad, Derick Shonfeld, Isabelle Woolcott, The Earl of Rothes, Caroll Sharin-Binotto, Robert Decker, Barbara St Armand Kurt, Jane Nummi, Inez Perry, Vera Jones and Reverend Martin Lundi.

Lastly, thanks and love to my family, friends and Daisy for their patience throughout — and to the Lady of the Jet Bead and the Child of the Marble.

SELECTED BIBLIOGRAPHY

Biel, Stephen *Down With The Old Canoe* (W. W. Norton, 1996)

Bryceson, Dave *The Titanic Disaster As Reported in the British National Press April–July 1912* (Patrick Stephens Limited/W. W. Norton, 1997)

Davie, Michael *Titanic: The Death and Life of a Legend* (Alfred A. Knopf, 1987)

Drager, Carey L. 'They Never Forgot: Michigan Survivors of the Titanic', *Michigan History Magazine* (Michigan Department of State, March/April 1997)

Duff Gordon, Lady Lucy *Discretions and Indiscretions* (Jarrolds Publishers Limited, 1932)

Eaton, John P. & Haas, Charles A. *Titanic: Destination Disaster* (Patrick Stephens Limited/W. W. Norton, 1987)
Titanic: Triumph and Tragedy (Patrick Stephens Limited, 1986/W. W. Norton, 1994)

Goldsmith, Frank J. W. *Echoes in the Night: Memories of a Titanic Survivor* (Titanic Historical Society, 1991)

Hart, Eva, MBE JP *Shadow of Titanic* (Greenwich University Press, 1994)

Hart, Moss *Act One* (Random House, 1959)

Hyslop, Donald, Forsyth, Alastair & Jemima, Sheila *Titanic Voices* (Southampton City Council, 1994)

Lord, Walter *A Night To Remember* (Henry Holt, 1955)

Lynch, Donald & Marschall, Ken *Titanic: An Illustrated History* (Hyperion, 1992)

MacQuitty, William *A Life To Remember* (Quartet Books, 1991)

Marshall, Logan (ed) *Sinking of the Titanic and Great Sea Disasters* (L. T. Myers, 1912)

Morris, Leslie A. *Harry Elkins Widener and A. S. W. Rosenbach: Of Books and Friendship* (Harvard University Press, reprinted from the Harvard Library Bulletin, Vol 6 No 4)

Nummi, Gerald E. & White, Janet A. *I'm Going to See What Has Happened* (Nummi/White, Ohio, 1996)

Ocean Liners of the Past, Olympic & Titanic, reprint from *The Shipbuilder*, 1911 (Patrick Stephens Limited, 1970)

Pellow, James with Kendle, Dorothy *A Lifetime on the Titanic: The Biography of Edith Haisman* (Island Books, an imprint of Ravenswood Publications Limited, 1995)

Priestley, J. B. *The Edwardians* (William Heinemann/Harper & Row, 1970)

Ryerse, Phyllis 'Rich Men and Poor Men: The Ryerson Family on Board the *Titanic*' (*The Titanic Commutator* 14, Summer 1990)

Spedden, Daisy Corning Stone *Polar the Titanic Bear* (Little Brown, 1994)

Tyler, Sidney F. *A Rainbow of Time and Space* (Aztex Corporation, 1981)

United States Congress, Senate, Committee on Commerce *Loss of the Steamship Titanic, Report of a Formal Investigation ...*, 62nd Congress, 2nd Session, 20 August 1912. Document No 933 (Government Printing Office, 1912)

Voyage, A Quarterly Journal (Titanic International Inc, Freehold, New Jersey)

Wade, Wyn Craig, *The Titanic: End of A Dream* (Rawson, Wade Publishers Inc, 1979)

Wels, Susan *Titanic: Legacy Of The World's Greatest Ocean Liner* (Tehabi Books & Time Life, 1997)

Whitacre, Christine *Molly Brown: Denver's Unsinkable Lady* (Historic Denver Inc, 1984)

Winocour, Jack (ed) *The Story of the Titanic as Told by its Survivors* (Dover Publications, 1960)

INDEX